INTERGENERATIONAL CONTACT ZONES

In *Intergenerational Contact Zones*, Kaplan, Thang, Sánchez, and Hoffman introduce novel ways of thinking, planning, and designing intergenerationally enriched environments. Filled with vivid examples of how ICZs breathe new life into communities and social practices, this important volume focuses on practical descriptions of ways in which practitioners and researchers could translate and infuse the notion of ICZ into their work.

The ICZ concept embraces generation and regeneration of community life, parks, and recreational locations, educational environments, residential settings and family life, and national and international contexts for societal development. With its focus on creating effective and meaningful intergenerational settings, it offers a rich how-to toolkit to help professionals and user groups as they begin to consider ways to develop, activate, and nurture intergenerational spaces.

Intergenerational Contact Zones will be essential reading for academics and researchers interested in human development, aging, and society, as well as practitioners, educators, and policy makers interested in intergenerational gathering places from an international perspective.

Dr. Matthew Kaplan is Professor of Intergenerational Programs and Aging in the Department of Agricultural Economics, Sociology, and Education at Pennsylvania State University. He is an affiliate member of the Penn State Center for Healthy Aging and core faculty member of the Comparative and International Education (CIED) Dual-Title Graduate Degree Program.

Dr. Leng Leng Thang is Associate Professor and Head of Department of Japanese Studies, Faculty of Arts and Social Sciences, National University of Singapore. She is also co-director of the Next Age Institute.

Dr. Mariano Sánchez is Associate Professor of Sociology and inaugural head of the Macrosad Chair in Intergenerational Studies at the University of Granada in Spain. Professor Sánchez is as well International Affiliate at the Center for Healthy Aging (Pennsylvania State University), and director of the Intergenerational Spaces Lab.

Dr. Jaco Hoffman, DPhil (Oxon), is socio-gerontologist and leader of the Optentia Research Focus programme: Ageing and Generational Dynamics in Africa (AGenDA) at North-West University, South Africa as well as James Martin Senior Research Fellow in the Oxford Institute of Population Ageing at the University of Oxford, UK.

INTERGENERATIONAL CONTACT ZONES

Place-based Strategies for Promoting Social Inclusion and Belonging

Edited by Matthew Kaplan, Leng Leng Thang, Mariano Sánchez and Jaco Hoffman

Routledge
Taylor & Francis Group

NEW YORK AND LONDON

First published 2020
by Routledge
52 Vanderbilt Avenue, New York, NY 10017

and by Routledge
2 Park Square, Milton Park, Abingdon, Oxon, OX14 4RN

Routledge is an imprint of the Taylor & Francis Group, an informa business

Library of Congress Cataloging-in-Publication Data
A catalog record for this title has been requested

ISBN: 978-0-367-18902-0 (hbk)
ISBN: 978-0-367-18903-7 (pbk)
ISBN: 978-0-429-19909-7 (ebk)

Typeset in Bembo
by Swales & Willis, Exeter, Devon, UK

CV 08.02.2023 1212

CONTENTS

FIGURES

TABLES

CONTRIBUTORS

Rick Artrip – Penn State College of Medicine, Hershey, PA (USA), rartrip@pennstatehealth.psu.edu

Cláudia Azevedo – Research Fellow, Oxford Institute of Population Ageing, University of Oxford, UK, claudia.azevedo@economics.ox.ac.uk

Rosa Bonachela Pallarés – Head of Macrosad SCA's Department of Quality Methods and Systems, rosa.bonachela@macrosad.com

Louise Chawla – Professor Emerita, Program in Environmental Design, University of Colorado Boulder, louise.chawla@colorado.edu

Shingairai Chigeza – Lecturer and Research Psychologist, Faculty of Humanities, Psychology Department, University of Pretoria (South Africa), shingairai.chigeza@up.ac.za

Nicole Claasen – Senior Lecturer, Africa Unit for Transdisciplinary Health Research (AUTHeR). North-West University (South Africa), claasen.nicole@gmail.com

Jason Danely – Senior Lecturer, Oxford Brookes University (United Kingdom), jdanely@brookes.ac.uk

María Pilar Díaz – Associate Professor-tenure track, University of Granada (Spain), mpdiaz@ugr.es

Daniel R. George – Associate Professor of Humanities, Penn State College of Medicine, Hershey, PA (USA), dgeorge1@pennstatehealth.psu.edu

Phoebe Grudzinskas – Project Manager "Cocktails in Care Homes," Magic Me (UK), Phoebegrudzinskas@magicme.co.uk

Suzanne H. Hammad – Research Assistant Professor, Ibn Khaldon Centre for Humanities and Social Sciences, Qatar University (Qatar), suzanne_hammad@yahoo.com

Nancy Henkin – Senior Fellow, Generations United, nzhenkin@gmail.com

Jaco Hoffman – Associate Professor of Socio-Gerontology, Optentia Research Focus Area, Ageing and Generational Dynamics in Africa (AGenDA) programme, North-West University, South Africa/Senior Research Fellow, Oxford Institute of Population Ageing, University of Oxford, UK, Jaco.Hoffman@nwu.ac.za

Diane H. Jones – Executive Director, PTW Architects and Adjunct Professor BE UNSW Australia, diane.jones@ptw.com.au

Tim Jones – Reader in Urban Mobility, Oxford Brookes University, tjones@brookes.ac.uk

Matthew Kaplan – Professor, Intergenerational Programs and Aging, Department of Agricultural Economics, Sociology, and Education, The Pennsylvania State University (USA), msk15@psu.edu

Masataka Kuraoka – Researcher, Tokyo Metropolitan Institute of Gerontology (Japan), mkuraoka@tmig.or.jp

Alan Lai – Associate Professor, BNU-HKBU United International College, Program Director of Applied Psychology, alanlai@uic.edu.hk

Susan Langford MBE – Director, Magic Me, susanlangford@magicme.co.uk

Robert H. McNulty – President, Partners for Livable Communities and Visiting Fellow, Institute for Population Aging, Oxford University, bmcnulty@livable.org

Joann M. Montepare – Professor of Psychology, Lasell University, Director, RoseMary B. Fuss Center for Research on Aging and Intergenerational Studies, jmontepare@lasell.edu

Yvonne Ng – Artistic Director, Choreographer and Arts Educator, tiger princess dance projects (not-for-profit contemporary dance organization), yve.ing@gmail.com

Patricia O'Neill – Visiting Academic, Contemporary China Studies (SIAS), University of Oxford (UK), Trish1385@gmail.com

Taryn Patterson – Sequoia Living Community Services (USA), tpatterson@-sequoialiving.org

Ann Quinlan – PTW Architects, annquinlan.sydney@gmail.com. Level 11, 88 Phillip Street, Sydney NSW, Australia 2000

Andrés Rodríguez – CEO of Macrosad SCA, andres.rodriguez@macrosad.com

Vera Roos – Professor, Optentia Research Focus Area, North-West University (South Africa), Vera.Roos@nwu.ac.za

Mariano Sánchez – Associate Professor of Sociology, Universidad de Granada, Head of the Macrosad Chair in Intergenerational Studies (Spain), (marianos@ugr.es)

Mark Sciegaj – Professor of Health Policy and Administration, The Pennsylvania State University (USA), mxs838@psu.edu

Sanford S. Smith – Teaching Professor of Forest Resources, Department of Ecosystem Science and Management, The Pennsylvania State University, sss5@psu.edu

Tanja Sobko – Assistant Professor, School of Biological Sciences, The University of Hong Kong (Hong Kong), tsobko@hku.hk

Ben Spencer – Urban Design Researcher, School of the Built Environment, Oxford Brookes University, Oxford (United Kingdom), bspencer@brookes.ac.uk

Philip B. Stafford – Adjunct Professor of Anthropology, Indiana University and Associate of Commons Planning, Inc., Atlanta, Georgia, staffor@indiana.edu

Kah Mun Tham – NSW Board of Architects Registration no. 10107, Australia, kahmun.tham@gmail.com

Leng Leng Thang – Associate Professor and Head at the Department of Japanese Studies, Co-Director of Next Age Institute, National University of Singapore, lengthang@nus.edu.sg

Maegan Tupinio – Penn State College of Medicine. Hershey, PA (USA), mtupinio@pennstatehealth.psu.edu

Catherine Whitehouse – Founder and Chief Educator (retired), The Intergenerational Schools (TIS), Cleveland (USA), cathwh@gmail.com

Peter Whitehouse – Professor of Neurology and current or former Professor of Psychiatry, Neuroscience, Psychology, Cognitive Science, Bioethics, Nursing, History, and Organizational Behavior, Case Western Reserve University, Strategic Advisor in Innovation Baycrest Health Center and Professor of

Medicine and Institute of Life Course and Aging, University of Toronto, President, Intergenerational Schools International, peter.whitehouse@case.edu

Suzanna Windon – Assistant Professor of Youth & Adult Leadership, Department of Agricultural Economics, Sociology, and Education, The Pennsylvania State University, sxk75@psu.edu

Renate M. Winkels – Penn State University, College of Medicine, Department of Public Health Sciences & Wageningen University, Division of Human Nutrition and Health, renate.winkels@wur.nl

Yoshika Yamamoto – Associate Professor, Department of International Tourism, Heian Jogakuin (St. Agnes') University, Japan, yoshika@heian.ac.jp

Eyu Zang – Architectural Designer, M.Arch Graduate, National University of Singapore, eyuzang@gmail.com

Evan C. Zavada – Community, Environment and Development B.S., The Pennsylvania State University (USA), evanzavada@gmail.com

Lisia Zheng – Doctoral student, Department of Anthropology, University of California at Berkeley, and Visiting Scholar, Department of Agricultural, Economics, Sociology, and Education, The Pennsylvania State University (USA), lisiazheng@gmail.com

INTRODUCTION

Matthew Kaplan, Leng Leng Thang, Mariano Sánchez, and Jaco Hoffman

In recent decades, global population ageing and the awareness of age-segregated policies and practices with the undesirable consequences of widening intergenerational gaps between the older and the younger generations have led to a sense of urgency for ways to promote generational connections – towards a society of all generations. On a global scale, there has been an increase in interest, innovation, and dissemination of intergenerational programs and practices. These interventions aim

> to bring people together in purposeful, mutually beneficial activities which promote greater understanding and respect between generations and contribute to building more cohesive communities … [They are] inclusive, building on the positive resources that the young and old have to offer each other and those around them.
>
> *(Beth Johnson Foundation, 2011, p. 4)*

The growing intergenerational studies literature has shown that intergenerational programs can have a substantial impact on participants' knowledge and skills, level of civic involvement, health, arts and recreation pursuits, social relationships, sense of self-fulfillment, and sense of cultural pride and identity (Brabazon & Disch, 1997; Hatton-Yeo & Ohsako, 2000; Kaplan, Henkin, & Kusano, 2002; Kernan & Cortellesi, 2019; Kuehne, 1999; MacCallum et al., 2006; Martin, Springate, & Atkinson, 2010; Morrow-Howell, Hong, McCrary, & Blinne, 2009; Newman, Ward, Smith, Wilson, & McCrea, 1997). Progress has also been made in establishing standards and guidelines for effective practice in the intergenerational field (Larkin & Rosebrook, 2002; Newman & Olson, 1996; Sánchez, Díaz, Sáez, & Pinazo, 2014). Identified competencies needed for professionals working in intergenerational programs include the ability to:

- Work with individuals at many points along the age spectrum.
- Plan age-integrated activities that are developmentally and functionally appropriate for participants.
- Coordinate programs with other community agencies.
- Design effective, sustainable intergenerational programs.
- Be effective at promoting contacts, social relationships, interactions, and bonds between people from different generations.

However, what seems to be lagging is attention to the environment (built, natural, and virtual) and how it has a bearing on program planning, processes, and outcomes. This edited volume aims to draw attention, and contribute to understanding and innovation, to ways in which intergenerational settings that work are created. This goes beyond a focus on formal intergenerational programs. It builds on earlier work focused on the role of physical design and environment in intergenerational engagements. Some examples of recent publications in this domain include Manchester and Facer's (2017) chapter on re-learning cities for intergenerational exchange, Terroir, Arki_lab, and Simpson's (2016) report on intergenerational relations in urban space, Arki_lab (2017) guide to design intergenerational urban spaces, Vanderbeck and Worth's (2015) edited volume on "intergenerational spaces," an article from Buffel et al. (2014) on the "shared places and spaces" campaign in the northern England city of Manchester, a report from the Generations of Hope Development Corporation (GHDC, 2015) highlighting the role of physical design in their "intentional (intergenerational) neighboring" model, Labit and Dubost's (2016) review of distinct intergenerational housing schemes in France and Germany, and Emi Kiyota's Ibasho Café model for creating elder-led community resource and intergenerational connection hubs in areas struck by natural disasters (Kiyota, 2018).

We also note the significance of Generations United's recent publications on intergenerational shared sites: "All In Together: Creating Places Where Young and Old Thrive" (Generations United, 2018) and "The Best of Both Worlds: A Closer Look at Creating Spaces that Connect Young and Old" (Generations United, 2019). These publications, sponsored by The Eisner Foundation, present profiles of model intergenerational shared sites, highlight ways in which they reduce ageism and remove age-segregating barriers, and provide strategies for boosting the number of intergenerational shared sites.

In this volume, we look to build upon this literature by introducing new ways of thinking, planning, and practice regarding the design of intergenerationally enriched environments. Overall, we intend to help our readers to become more sensitized around the spatial dimension present in any intergenerational endeavor.

What is unique in this book is its specific focus on the new concept of *Intergenerational Contact Zones* (ICZ) and its potential for inspiring and guiding from inception through to implementation new ideas for creating and enabling settings for desired intergenerational encounters. More simply put, we explore ways in which the ICZ conceptual framework can serve as a tool to help figure out better, more inclusive and socially smart ways for different generations to live and grow together in ageing societies.

Background: Concept, Context and History

Our working definition of ICZ is the following: *Intergenerational Contact Zones serve as spatial focal points for different generations to meet, interact, build relationships (e.g. trust and friendships), and, if desired, work together to address issues of local concern.* ICZ spaces can be found in all types of community settings, including schools, senior centers, retirement communities, parks, taverns, reading rooms, clubhouses, museums, community gardens, environmental education centers, and multi-service community centers.

With its focus on creating effective and meaningful intergenerational settings, the ICZ concept explored and developed throughout this book represents an endeavor to integrate what is often portrayed as separate spheres of transient intergenerational programs. The focus on ICZ is not intended to simply add another term to the rich and expanding literature on intergenerational practices, but rather to introduce a new multi-dimensional conceptual approach towards the sensitization and understanding, application, reframing, and situating of intergenerational connections in place.

The first use of the term "Intergenerational Contact Zones" can be found in a chapter written by Leng Leng Thang (2015) for a book on *Intergenerational Spaces*, edited by Vanderbeck and Worth. Thang's chapter described her study of a co-(age) located playground in Singapore. Thang's inspiration came from observing Japanese culture, looking particularly at the norm of "keeping in touch" *(fureai)* (Thang, 2001) – and therefore building upon similar work by Pratt (1991) who used the term "contact zones" in the context of sharing cultures, ideas, and values in classroom settings. Essentially, Pratt argued that when people come together from diverse cultural perspectives there is the potential for tension and even confrontation, but also for greater understanding if efforts are made to change the interaction dynamic. The concept of ICZ runs parallel to that of "cultural contact zones," except that in the ICZ instance, the emphasis is placed on bridging diverse generational perspectives and experience.

At the root of how we define ICZ is a basic understanding that the physical environment is more than an amalgamation of physical properties. To explore how people use and perceive any particular space requires attention to the social, psychological, organizational, and cultural dimensions as well as physical properties of that particular space. In other words, "There is no physical setting that is not also a social and cultural setting" (Proshansky, 1976, p. 308). The ICZ framework is a way to look at the psycho-socio-techno-spatial environment and how it enters into intergenerational activity and experience and vice versa.

Table I.1 outlines the parameters (eight dimensions, actually) of our conceptual framework for considering how ICZ spaces develop over time, how

TABLE I.1 The Many Dimensions of Intergenerational Contact Zones

ICZ (Intergenerational Contact Zone) DIMENSIONS	Features and Examples

Physical	• Spatial configuration: Includes the creation of intentional focus points or nodes for IG (intergenerational) interaction (as well as pathways for comfortable exit from such interaction).
	• Spatial features (e.g. artwork, photos, and other artifacts) that serve as catalysts for IG understanding and engagement.
	• Questions to consider:
	  ○ Functionality of space: Accessibility (incorporation of universal design principles)? Safety? Comfort? Convenience?
	  ○ Flexibility of design: Can the design accommodate changes over time in user needs, abilities, interests, concerns, etc.?
	  ○ Is space designed to foster/accommodate unstructured as well as structured IG encounters?

Temporal	• Temporal patterns in how space is used (daily, weekly, yearly patterns of use).
	• Issues to consider:
	  ○ Generational differences in daily schedules and usage can pose as potential IG distancing factors. (For example, students are in school during the day, while many older adults tend to engage in senior centers and other activities in the morning, lunchtime, and early afternoon.)
	  ○ Older and younger users may also have different weekly and yearly schedules as dictated by school, work, or vacation calendars.
	  ○ Transformation of a space over time (consider relevant socio-historical factors).

Psychological
    Perceptual
	• *Space* comes to be perceived as *place* – experienced, remembered, and conceived *place*.
	• Dimensions of *place*:
	  ○ Place identity – where personal meaning and memory comes to be associated with places.
	  ○ Intergenerational place – perceptual shift from *my* space/place to *our* space/place.

TABLE I.1 (Cont.)

ICZ (Intergenerational Contact Zone) DIMENSIONS	Features and Examples
	Shared places can be negotiated and designed to encompass multiple layers of shared meaning and experience.
Cognitive	• Cognitive understanding of age diversity and place-based possibilities for IG engagement.
Psychosocial	• Emotional appreciation of age diversity and place-based possibilities for IG engagement. • Patterns of social inclusion/exclusion with regard to generational position.
Sociocultural	• Ability to use the environment to pursue desired social contact, relationships, and affiliation within and between generations. • Ability to use the environment to practice and maintain activities consistent with cultural traditions and local heritage. • Sources of potential intergenerational tension might include exclusionary pressures and when *places* become *contested* (e.g. changing socio-economic make-up of a neighborhood might pit new, younger residents against long-time, older residents).
Political	• Who is "in charge"? – Social and institutional power structures for making decisions about how a space is developed and sustained/modified over time. • Pathways for participation – Do participants have choice regarding activities?
Institutional	• Policies, regulations, legal issues, etc. • Institutional norms around ages and access (e.g. age requirements for entrance or for seeing certain films/shows).

Virtual	• Online meeting places that provide opportunities for sharing information and experiences.
	• Cyber ICZ that link to physical ICZ can:
	   ◦ Increase the popularity of physical ICZ.
	   ◦ Enable and facilitate the use of physical ICZ.

Ethical	• An empowerment orientation: ◦ Provide people with opportunities for contributing meaningful input into the design, development, and evaluation of ICZ.

(*Continued*)

TABLE I.1 (Cont.)

ICZ (Intergenerational Contact Zone) DIMENSIONS	Features and Examples
	○ Provide people with choice with regard to how they utilize ICZ spaces and engage others in these settings. (In a park, for example, some people may prefer their interaction to be "passive," like sitting and watching children play.) ○ Interaction should not be "forced." Communication should be a fluid process, where the dynamics evolve as participants negotiate their respective needs, interests, and perceptions of the setting and of one another. • An intergenerational justice orientation – Access and usage should be attentive to issues of generational equity and fairness.

they function, and how they are perceived by the inhabitants of these spaces. We developed this "dimensions of ICZ" chart following participation in a meeting convened by the Oxford Institute of Population Ageing, University of Oxford, in 2015. At this unique gathering, a multidisciplinary group of 13 scholars and practitioners engaged in groundwork discussions and collaborative inquiry aimed at exploring existing approaches and charting new strategies for creating and/or enhancing intergenerational spaces (Kaplan & Hoffman, 2015). The Oxford University meeting marked the beginning of our efforts to crystalize our understanding of the overall ICZ concept and its potential value for understanding, creating, and sparking intergenerational engagement in a wide range of settings, including those that exist in the virtual as well as physical environments.

As noted in Table I.1, the conceptual framework involves denoting eight interconnected dimensions of ICZ spaces: the physical, temporal, psychological (perceptual, cognitive, and psychosocial), sociocultural, political, institutional, virtual, and ethical. All eight dimensions are highlighted to varying degrees throughout this book.

Part of the complexity linked to the ICZ conceptual framework furthermore stems from its ability to serve several functions, including as: *conceptual tool* (for studying complex, multi-generational community settings), *programming tool* (for broadening the range of intergenerational activity possibilities), and *design tool* (for generating innovative ideas for developing intergenerational meeting spaces).

In the context of designing ICZ spaces, we believe it is appropriate to frame this pursuit as an aspirational "social good," with a targeted emphasis on outcomes such as the promotion of joint learning, invention, civic engagement, social support, and cultural continuity.

We anticipate that professionals from different fields of practice will have different ways of "using" the ICZ concept. It might be helpful to frame some of these ways.

- For the environmental design professional, for example, entertainment of the ICZ concept might stimulate innovative thinking about designing spaces that are conducive to the type of intergenerational encounters appropriate to the overall setting in question, whether the emphasis is on joint learning, discovery, invention, caregiving, or some other mode of engagement.
- For the intergenerational studies professional, focusing in on ICZ spaces might be a way to reflect on approaches to modify the physical environment to better align with program objectives, activities, and organizational policies.
- The community development oriented professional might tune into the potential of viable intergenerational meeting spaces/places for reducing social isolation and creating new modes of community activity. This is consistent with the research conducted by Partners for Livable Communities on public perceptions of "community livability," where emphasis is placed on the importance of civic gathering places, where people can meet comfortably, and where there is a welcoming environment for newcomers (McNulty & Koff, 2014).

On Space and Place

Before we introduce the structure of this edited volume and the content covered in the following 25 chapters, we provide some context and theoretical underpinnings with regard to how we, the editors of this book, understand space and place.

First, when we talk about ICZ spaces, we are simultaneously alluding to space and place. However, while space in environmental terms has specific physical dimensions, we are primarily concerned with the conversion of a space into a place. In contrast with space, place constitutes a psychological component; a space may remain a space, but it may also become a place as defined by one's emotional feeling and a sense of belonging there. In other words, a "space" becomes a "place" once it has meaning for someone (Thang & Kaplan, 2013). Similarly, Semken and Freeman (2008) describe place as a space "imbued with meaning by human experience" (p. 1042). Hence, places are meaningful spaces, more than just a backdrop or a container for the action.

To further clarify the distinction between space and place, we draw on Harrison and Dourish's (1996) assertion that "place" is largely a subset of "space": "A place is generally a space with something added – social meaning, convention, cultural understandings about role, function and nature and so on. The sense of place transforms the space" (p. 3).

In framing how space is manifested in social contexts, Amedeo, Golledge, and Stimson (2009, p. 7) draw upon Peponis and Wineman's (2002) description of "built space" and its strong ties to social meaning:

> Built space is to be understood as a relational pattern, a pattern of distinctions, separations, interfaces, and connections, a pattern that integrates, segregates, or differentiates its parts in relation to each other. To ask whether space has a "social logic" is to ask how such pattern becomes entailed in everyday behavior, in the structuring of social relationships, and in the way in which society and culture become intelligible through their spatial form.
>
> *(p. 271)*

When considering notions of space and place in the context of intergenerational settings, "meaning making" is a social time-bound phenomenon; concepts of place perception and place identity move from "my meaning" to "shared meaning." There are numerous intersections between the individually and generationally held meanings that inhabitants of a space possess; norms and expectations for the intergenerational engagement in a specific setting are negotiated and in large part socially defined.

Although there is some variation in how chapter contributors use the words "space" and "place," what is consistent is their keen interest and spirited and elucidating investigations into ways in which environments could be designed to accommodate intended intergenerational encounters, whether related to learning, recreation, responsive community planning, social inclusion, caregiving, family bonding, or some other set of objectives.

Overview

This volume explores the foundations and applications of ICZ from an international, interdisciplinary perspective.

- International appeal: The authors represent different regions encompassing the Global North and South. In its totality, this is a collection of globally sourced ideas and examples, innovative concepts and original actual applications for creating and enhancing intergenerational spaces in indoor and outdoor community as well as virtual settings. Across national borders, there is increasing emphasis on the promotion of intergenerational solidarity through programming. For one example, a new Substantive Committee on Intergenerational Solidarity has been constituted, with full standing, at the UN.

- Interdisciplinary context: The authors have roots in a wide range of disciplines within and between the social sciences and design fields, including gerontology, geography, architecture, urban and regional planning, development studies, human development and life-course studies, sociology, social work, education, psychology, and anthropology. Many of the authors are prolific contributors to the literature in specialty areas such as: global ageing, environmental gerontology, cross-cultural gerontology, environmental psychology, childhood and life-course studies, intergenerational studies, participatory community development, and the design of age-friendly and childhood-friendly communities, and several are thought leaders in the realm of "intergenerational design" (i.e. planning/creating physical environments that are conducive to intergenerational exchange).

The book's contributors represent a range of scholars, practitioners, educators, and policy makers, proving that the ICZ framework can actually be a useful instrument for a diversity of agents in the intergenerational field.

Most distinctively, chapters in this volume are filled with poignant examples of how ICZ spaces may breathe new life into communities and social practices. There are ICZ spaces within which and through which: new modes of recreation, new family bonding experiences, new horizons for appreciating the natural environment, new ways to explore local culture and history, new opportunities to teach, learn, and work, and new social groupings and networks are generated.

The chapters further illustrate ways in which the ICZ conceptual framework can inspire new ideas for programming and designing spaces that are conducive to meaningful intergenerational encounters, and have the potential for reducing social isolation, generating new modes of community activity, and enhancing perceptions of belonging, "community livability," and societal sustainability.

Whether through design or serendipity, planned or spontaneous modes of interaction, the chapter authors confirm that ICZ spaces can function as hubs for a wide variety of pursuits that have an overt or latent intergenerational dimension – from play to caregiving and from learning to working – and help people form and sustain social networks and relationships that buffer against the specter of ageism, social fragmentation, exclusion, isolation, and loneliness.

All chapters include at least some information or reference to: site/environmental design considerations, underlying motivation for each project, engaged stakeholders, lessons learned, practical tips, and, to help set the scene, geographical and cultural context. The volume also provides examples of ad hoc boxes likely to suit different types of chapters (e.g. "practical design tips," "dealing with unanticipated challenges," and "policy issues in creating ICZ spaces").

A number of authors in this volume describe distinct conceptual frameworks and operational approaches for creating or modifying existing intergenerational settings. At the same time, many of these chapters are breaking new ground in translating and finding new ways in which the ICZ conceptual framework can inform their intergenerational study and practice pursuits.

Overall, throughout the publication the emphasis will be not as much on presenting theory and concepts as on practical descriptions and developments around ICZ. It has been our purpose to nurture practitioners' and researchers' capacity to translate and infuse the sensitizing notion of ICZ into their work. Hence, the many and diverse examples provided.

Here are some of the socio-spatial focal points highlighted in the chapters:

- Museums, libraries and other arts and cultural institutions that host and animate intergenerational gatherings (McNulty – Chapter 1).
- Communal cooking sites in rural areas of South Africa as intergenerational transmitters of indigenous knowledge about traditional foods (Chigeza, Claasen, & Roos – Chapter 2).
- Toronto libraries that house generation-connecting, community-building dance programs (Ng – Chapter 3).
- A repurposed barn in Central Pennsylvania uses as a site for bringing together a diverse group of community leaders in support of intergenerational action and programming (Kaplan, Windon, & Zavada – Chapter 4).
- City spaces in the UK designed to accommodate family cycling excursions (Spencer & Jones – Chapter 5).
- Bus stops that could be enlivened intergenerationally through the imagination and creativity of children (Danely – Chapter 6).
- Urban parks in China with alluring intergenerational spaces (O'Neill – Chapter 7).
- Urban parks in Portugal with intergenerational engagement-oriented policies and environmental design features (Azevedo – Chapter 8).
- Urban rooftops and early environmental education programming in Hong Kong designed to engage grandparents and grandchildren as "companions in wonder" (Sobko & Chawla – Chapter 9).
- Forest education and hands-on experience through historical interpretation programs (Smith & Kaplan – Chapter 10).
- A hospital-based community garden that pairs adolescent and young adult cancer survivors with older, experienced gardeners to improve diet and physical activity (Winkels, Artrip, Tupinio, & George – Chapter 11).
- A 20-year-old, award-winning *intergenerational school* model in Cleveland, Ohio; lessons learned for animating intergenerational learning and bonding (C. Whitehouse, P. Whitehouse, & Sánchez – Chapter 12).
- College classrooms transformed into vibrant intergenerational teaching and learning zones (Montepare & Sciegaj – Chapter 13).

- English language centers in Hong Kong schools with older adult volunteers at the root of efforts to reprogram and redesign these centers as distinctive intergenerational language learning settings (Lai – Chapter 14).
- Cohousing communities that inspire, support, and sustain intergenerational living patterns and practices (Zheng – Chapter 15).
- Care homes in the UK enlivened by cocktail parties (Grudzinskas & Langford – Chapter 16).
- Senior housing facilities that foster intergenerational connectivity in American communities (Henkin & Patterson – Chapter 17).
- The Japanese teapot, a symbol of the resurgence of Japanese traditional tea culture, as provider of an intergenerational interaction focal point in many Japanese living rooms and schools (Yamamoto & Thang – Chapter 18).
- Intergenerational digital game platforms that leverage and bridge generational capabilities and provide family bonding time (Zang – Chapter 19).
- A multilayered cyclical support system piloted in Tokyo communities; a strategy to promote healthy living practices, provide long-term care, and address other quality of life issues from an intergenerational perspective (Kuraoka – Chapter 20).
- Beaches, swimming pools, and other recreational water settings in Australia designed to accommodate intergenerational gatherings (Tham, Jones, & Quinlan – Chapter 21).
- The olive tree in the contested Palestinian landscape – as socio-economic and political entity and symbol around which communities and generations engage and resist (Hammad – Chapter 22).
- Participatory tools and techniques for visualizing, producing, and assessing new and transformed intergenerational spaces (Sánchez & Stafford – Chapter 23).
- Quality domains, guidelines, and indicators of ICZ for creating effective intergenerational programs (Sánchez, Díaz, Rodríguez, & Bonachela – Chapter 24).
- Participatory mapping strategies for elevating the voices of youth and older adults in public discourse around the design of public spaces (Stafford – Chapter 25).

In sum, the book consists of a series of short chapters showcasing the various possibilities with ICZ. It also includes a how-to toolkit – or methods section – to help various professionals and user groups as they begin to consider ways to develop, activate, and nurture engaging intergenerational spaces. Therefore, the book is framed as a "toolkit" *and* as a scholarly, creative piece aimed at establishing a stronger conceptual basis for creating and transforming compelling intergenerational spaces and places.

References

Amedeo, D., Golledge, R. G., & Stimson, R. J. (2009). *Person-environment-behavior research: Investigating activities and experiences in spaces and environments*. New York, NY: The Guilford Press.

Arki_lab. (2017). *How to design intergenerational urban spaces*. Copenhagen, Denmark: Author.

Beth Johnson Foundation (2011). *A guide to intergenerational practice*. Stoke-on-Trent, UK: Author. Retrieved from: www.emil-network.eu/a-guide-to-intergenerational-prac tice-beth-johnson-foundation.

Brabazon, K., & Disch, R. (1997). *Intergenerational approaches in aging*. Binghamton, NY: The Haworth Press.

Buffel, T., De Backer, F., Peeters, J., Phillipson, C., Reina, V. R., Kindekens, A., De Donder, L., & Lombaerts, K. (2014). Promoting sustainable communities through intergenerational practice. *Procedia – Social and Behavioral Sciences, 116*, 1785–1791.

Generations United (2018). *All in together: Creating places where young and old thrive*. Washington, DC: Author. Retrieved from https://www.gu.org/resources/all-in-together-cre ating-places-where-young-and-old-thrive/

Generations United (2019). *The best of both worlds: A closer look at creating spaces that connect young and old*. Washington, DC: Author. Retrieved from www.gu.org/app/uploads/ 2019/06/Intergenerational-Report-BestofBothWorlds.pdf.

GHDC (2015). *Physical design facilitates relationships – Core component #4 (of the GHDC "Intentional Neighboring" model)*. Champaign, IL: Generations of Hope Development Corp. Retrieved from http://ghdc.generationsofhope.org/principle/physical-design-facilitates-relationships/.

Harrison, S., & Dourish, P. (1996). "Re-place-ing space: The role of place and space in collaborative systems." In G. M. Olson, J. S. Olson, & M. S. Ackerman (Eds.), *Proceedings of the Conference on Computer Supported Cooperative Work (CSCW '96)* (pp. 67–76). New York, NY. Retrieved from www.dourish.com/publications/1996/cscw96-place.pdf.

Hatton-Yeo, A., & Ohsako, T. (Eds.). (2000). *Intergenerational programmes: Public policy and research implications: An international perspective*. Hamburg, Germany: UNESCO Institute for Education.

Kaplan, M., Henkin, N., & Kusano, A. (Eds.). (2002). *Linking lifetimes: A global view of intergenerational exchange*. Lanham, MD: University Press of America.

Kaplan, M., & Hoffman, J. (2015). *Intergenerational Contact Zones: What and why* [Blog post]. Retrieved from www.ageing.ox.ac.uk/blog/2015-intergenerational-contact-zones-blog.

Kernan, M., & Cortellesi, G. (Eds.). (2019). *Intergenerational learning in practice. Together old and young*. London, UK: Routledge.

Kiyota, E. (2018). "Co-creating environments: empowering elders and strengthening communities through design," What Makes a Good Life in Late Life? Citizenship and Justice in Aging Societies, special report, Hastings Center Report 48, no. 5, S46–S49. doi: 10.1002/hast.913.

Kuehne, V. S. (1999). *Intergenerational programs: Understanding what we have created*. Binghamton, NY: The Haworth Press.

Labit, A., & Dubost, N. (2016). Housing and ageing in France and Germany: The inter-generational solution. *Housing. Care and Support, 19*(2), 45–54. doi:10.1108/HCS-08-2016-0007.

Larkin, E., & Rosebrook, V. (2002). Standards for intergenerational practice: A proposal. *Early Childhood Teacher Education, 23*, 137–142.

MacCallum, J., Palmer, D., Wright, P., Cumming-Potvin, W., Northcote, J., Brooker, M., & Tero, C. (2006). *Community building through intergenerational exchange. Report from the (Australian) National Youth Affairs Research Scheme (NYARS).* Retrieved from www.facs.gov.au/internet/facsinternet.nsf/aboutfacs/programs/youth-communi ty_building.htm.

Manchester, H., & Facer, K. (2017). (Re)-Learning the city for intergenerational exchange. In H. Sacré & S. De Visscher (Eds.), *Learning the city: Cultural approaches to civic learning in urban spaces* (pp. 83–98). Basel: Springer Nature Switzerland AG. doi:10.1007/978-3-319-46230-1.

Martin, K., Springate, I., & Atkinson, M. (2010). *Intergenerational practice: Outcomes and effectiveness.* Slough, UK: National Foundation for Educational Research. Retrieved from www.nfer.ac.uk.

McNulty, R., & Koff, R. (2014). *Cultural heritage tourism.* Washington, DC: Partners for Livable Communities. Retrieved from http://livable.org/storage/documents/reports/ CBC/culturalheritagetourism.pdf.

Morrow-Howell, N., Hong, S.-I., McCrary, S., & Blinne, W. (2009). *Experience Corps: Health outcomes of participation (CSD Research Brief 09-09).* St. Louis, MO: Washington University, Center for Social Development.

Newman, S., & Olson, S. (1996). Competency development: Professionalizing the intergenerational field. *The Southwest Journal on Aging, 12*(1/2), 91–94.

Newman, S., Ward, C. R., Smith, T. B., Wilson, J., & McCrea, J. M. (1997). *Intergenerational programs: Past, Present and Future.* Bristol, PA: Taylor & Francis.

Peponis, J., & Wineman, J. (2002). Spatial structure of environment and behavior. In R. B. Bechtel, R. B. & Churchman, A. (Eds.), *Handbook of Environmental Psychology* (pp. 271–287). New York, NY: Wiley.

Pratt, M. L. (1991). Arts of the contact zone. *Profession*, 91, 33–40.

Proshansky, H. M. (1976). Environmental psychology and the real world. *American Psychologist, 31*(4), April, 303–310.

Sánchez, M., Díaz, P., Sáez, J., & Pinazo, S. (2014). The professional profile of intergenerational program managers: General and specific characteristics. *Educational Gerontology, 40*(6), 427–441. doi:10.1080/03601277.2013.844037.

Semken, S., & Freeman, C. B. (2008). Sense of place in the practice and assessment of place–based science teaching. *Science Education, 92*(6), 1042–1057.

Terroir, Arki_lab, & Simpson, D. (2016). *Age integration in the city and the suburbs.* Copenhagen, Denmark: The Danish Ministry of Immigration, Integration and Housing.

Thang, L. L. (2001). *Generations in touch: Linking the old and young in a Tokyo neighborhood.* Ithaca: Cornell University Press.

Thang, L. L. (2015). Creating an intergenerational contact zone: Encounters in public spaces within Singapore's public housing neighborhoods. In R. Vanderbeck & N. Worth (Eds.), *Intergenerational spaces* (pp. 17–32). London, UK: Routledge.

Thang, L. L., & Kaplan, M. (2013). Intergenerational pathways for building relational spaces and places. In G. D. Rowles & M. Bernard (Eds.), *Environmental gerontology: Making meaningful places in old age* (pp. 225–251). NYC: Spring Publishing Company.

Vanderbeck, R., & Worth, N. (Eds.). (2015). *Intergenerational spaces.* London, UK: Routledge.

PART I

Generation/Regeneration of Community Life

1

CULTURE AS ANIMATOR OF INTERGENERATIONAL GATHERING PLACES

Robert H. McNulty

The value of arts and cultural institutions for intergenerational gathering places depends not only on their specific design, but also on how they "animate" diverse gatherings of young and old to associate and mingle. Through this programming, they become "civic glue" and reward any location.

Engaging Older Adults

Americans are enjoying longer and healthier lives. By 2030, all baby boomers will be over the age of 65 and make up 21 percent of the U.S. population, compared with 15 percent in 2018. In 2035, America will meet another milestone when the population aged 65 and over is projected to be 78 million, and for the first time in U.S. history older adults will outnumber children under age 18 (U.S. Department of Commerce Economics and Statistics Administration, 2018).

The vast majority of Americans want to remain in their communities as they age. Contrary to popular belief, only a small minority actually move to warmer climates upon retirement. In 2010, only 3.1 percent (1.3 million) of those age 65 and over lived in skilled-nursing facilities (U.S. Department of Commerce Economics and Statistics Administration, 2011). Instead, most Americans choose to age in place, within the same communities where they have long lived. Every community, from fast-growing suburbs to more stable rural areas, will have to adapt to a maturing population.

Although most residents want to age in place, they confront many barriers to staying active and engaged in their communities. The following are some of the most common barriers:

1. A lack of affordable and appropriate housing options.
2. Few opportunities for walking, bicycling or other forms of physical activity, making it more difficult to remain healthy and engaged.
3. Inadequate mobility options.
4. Limited information about available health and supportive services in their community.
5. Concerns about the safety and security of the community.
6. Limited opportunities for civic participation, including meaningful prospects for volunteer service and employment.

These challenges to aging in place are community-wide concerns that affect residents of all ages and abilities. On a positive note, communities of all shapes and sizes – big cities and counties, medium-size cities, small towns, rural townships, rural counties, suburban bedroom communities, and edge cities – are implementing creative solutions to meet the challenges of a maturing America.

Culture, Place, and Intergenerational Exchanges

What Partners for Livable Communities believes, and what recent studies are showing, is that effectively highlighting the culture and heritage of a place cultivates attachment to that place, and thus makes people want to settle in that area and lay down their roots. Heritage assets can include a wide variety of community amenities including, parks, squares, plazas, and historically preserved neighborhoods. It is in these places that the renewal of American cities is taking place today, and culture and heritage are at the heart of this renewal. More and more, residents want to preserve the community gathering places that existed in the past, places that provide the nodes of community exchange and that thus hold the most value to their cities.

BOX 1.1

Arts and cultural institutions are often the nexus for exchanges between patrons of all ages. This type of intergenerational animation is an indicator of both a community's quality of life as well as its economic competitiveness. Culture embraces a broad range of activities and programs that allow individuals to creatively express their identity and history.

As the baby boom generation ages, the demand for arts and cultural activities will grow. Participation in arts and culture programs has proven health benefits for older adults. However, most communities are unprepared for the coming demand. Providing a range of arts and culture programs attuned to older adults' interests and abilities requires partnerships with youth programs to foster intergenerational learning, as well as with universities, senior centers, libraries, and other groups and institutions. Providing these opportunities can also build a powerful advocacy voice in the community for more funding to libraries, parks, and schools.

Local governments can encourage and help fund programs that use arts and cultural activities to bring together different generations and cultural groups. For example, many programs use theater as a tool to educate the community about cultural and generational differences. Some programs, such as that of San Francisco's Planning for Elders in the Central City, use theater as an educational and advocacy tool on issues such as health care and housing. By encouraging partnerships between repertory theaters, artists, and community organizations and agencies serving older adults, local governments can create new opportunities to fund and increase the relevance of arts and cultural programs in the community.

What Matters Most

A 2010 major U.S. study undertaken by the John S. and James L. Knight Foundation, *Why People Love Where They Live and Why it Matters: A National Perspective*, surveys what sorts of resources provide total attachment of people to a community and make them want to put down roots, build a life, and work together to make it better (Knight Foundation, 2010).

Knight and Gallup (Knight Foundation, 2010) found three elements that were most important: 1) an area's physical beauty, the preservation of its historic open spaces and buildings; 2) opportunities for socialization; and 3) a community's openness to all people including "new" comers.

According to *Why People Love Where They Live and Why it Matters*, what attaches residents to their communities doesn't change much from place to place. While one might expect the drivers of attachment would be different in Miami from those in Macon, GA, in fact the main drivers of attachment differ little across communities. Whether you live in San Jose, CA, or State College, PA, the things that connect you to your community are generally the same. When examining each factor in the study and its relationship to attachment, the same items rise to the top, year after year:

1. *Aesthetics* – The physical beauty of the community including the availability of parks and green spaces.
2. *Social offerings* – Places for people to meet each other and the feeling that people in the community care about each other.

3. *Openness* – How welcoming the community is to different types of people, including families with young children, minorities and talented college graduates.

Institutions as Fulcrums for Change

Traditional institutions already embedded in many communities – such as libraries, faith congregations, heritage organizations, universities, community colleges, museums, zoos, aquariums, botanic gardens, and arts and humanities agencies – can take on new roles of social service and economic development to address emerging challenges. As such, they become new resources for a caring community.

1. *Libraries* can become anchor tenants in downtown revitalization programs.
2. *Parks and recreation departments* can be health and welfare delivery centers.
3. *Historical societies* can help launch goal-setting agendas with their communities.
4. *Universities* in partnership with towns can become research and policy centers that help solve urban problems.
5. *Museums* can be neutral meeting grounds to discuss explosive issues such as racism.

Best Practices

The Queens Museum: Breaking Barriers, Redefining Access to the Arts

[www.queensmuseum.org]

The Queens Museum, housed in the iconic World's Fair building of 1939, is set in the nation's most diverse neighborhood that is home to more than 200 spoken languages: Queens, New York. The Museum's mission, "to present the highest quality visual arts and educational programming for people in the New York metropolitan area, and particularly for the residents of Queens, a uniquely diverse ethnic, cultural and international community," rings true to its invaluable presence in the community. Since 2005, the Museum has rededicated and expanded its outreach education endeavors by establishing a museum department titled The Queens Museum of Art in the Community. Today, the Queens Museum is the marriage of form and function. Expansive, light-filled space houses ambitious exhibitions, forward-thinking educational initiatives, and community-minded programming that engages myriad constituencies – residents, tourists, children, artists, individuals with special needs, families, seniors, and recent immigrants.

The Queens Museum works tirelessly to engage the community outside its four walls. Not only does the Museum have a full-time community organizer on staff working actively in the immediate Corona neighborhood of Queens, a position currently unmatched by any other art museum in the country, but also it provides numerous, ongoing partnerships to community organizations specifically within the immigrant and older adult communities. Catering to the diverse immigrant populations of Queens, the Museum hosts Passport Fridays, sponsored events showcasing a different country every week from South Korea to Colombia to India.

The Queens Museum with the Queens Public Library, one of the largest urban library systems in the world containing 66 branches, created the New New Yorkers (NNY) program – education classes to meet the needs of immigrant adults. The program hosts ESOL classes that teach English as a second language, and provides myriad multilingual research tools, citizenship materials, and arts publications.

The Museum operates as one of its feature community engagement programs: El Corazón de Corona or The Heart of Corona Initiative, a project that "aims to address the health of residents and to activate and beautify Corona's public space." The Initiative boasts several cross-sector projects created in collaboration with local health, business, and elected leaders: Beautification and Clean-Up (see Figure 1.1), *A Healthy Taste of Corona* cookbook, and numerous public arts projects as well as popular street festivals such as the recent 107th Corona Block Party, My Street My Home.

The Corona neighborhood is an historic hub of ethnic diversity, home to such legends as Ella Fitzgerald, Louis Armstrong, and Malcolm X. In the last three decades, Corona has experienced major demographic shifts aligned with national trends; the neighborhood has become home to a steady increase of immigrant populations. As a premier institution located in the heart of Corona, the Queens Museum engages as a primary stakeholder in the community to serve as a vehicle for community revitalization. With high-quality public engagement programs, the Museum promotes such unique initiatives as: The Immigrants & Parks Collaborative, immigrant-led civic engagement programs in public parks; and The Corona Studio, which curates new works of community-engaged public art to traditionally underserved audiences.

Beyond providing ample community engagement and recreational events, the Museum strives to meet many of the social challenges facing neighborhood residents through the umbrella art therapy program, Art Access which serves community members with special needs. An award-winning program recognized by the Institute of Museum and Library Services for exemplary leadership and community partnership, Art Access was launched in 1983 with a mission to "promote exploration through the arts and to highlight the creativity that exists in all people" (Partners for Livable Communities, 2011). Originally, the program was created to provide art education for the visually

FIGURE 1.1 Volunteers from the Corazón de Corona project take a break during the beautification and clean-up of public space near the Museum. Courtesy of Queens Museum

impaired; today, Art Access has widely expanded its mission and capacity to serve over 5,000 New York City school children enrolled in special education programs each year. The program primarily staffs therapists trained in creative art therapies who are able to adapt their expertise to meet community needs.

Acclaimed programming within Art Access includes: The Autism Initiative, Gallery Gatherings, in-house programming for families hosting children in the foster care system, the Multi-Sensory Tour Kit, Sign Language Tours, and more. This extensive, diverse programming proves the Queens Museum's priority in maintaining an accessible institution beyond the parameters of what most consider eliminating barriers to access: The Museum goes above and beyond opening its doors to simply pave the path for all patrons to first get to the doorstep.

The Queens Museum, through incredible outreach programming designed for the older adult and immigrant populations, as well as those with diverse special needs, proves itself as an institution which extends far beyond its four walls to not only conduct programming in community venues but to also bring back residents to the Museum for engaged learning. The Museum today acts as a good leader and role model for all institutions attempting to break down barriers to access and to reach out to all community residents.

Key Lessons

1. The Queens Museum breaks down traditional ideas of a museum and its relations to the surrounding community, and rather presents the institution as community-based, structuring a majority of its programming based on community needs and outside of its four walls.
2. The Museum uses a community organizer to expand beyond the institution to engage the community in places and with methods meaningful to the residents.
3. Access to the arts is considered an inherent right for all residents, especially for those experiencing barriers to access in their daily lives. The Museum provides programming for all specialized populations: immigrants, older adults, and those with disabilities.

Dance Exchange: An Intergenerational Dance Company

Takoma Park, Maryland [www.danceexchange.org]

Based outside of Washington, D.C., Dance Exchange is an intergenerational company of artists that creates dance and engages people in making art. The nonprofit serves as an incubator for creative research, bringing ideas to action through collaborations that range from experts in the field of dance to unexpected movers and makers. Through these exchanges the company stretches the boundaries between the studio, stage, and other environments to make dances that are rooted in the particularity of people and place.

The mission of the Dance Exchange, formerly known as the Liz Lerman Dance Exchange, is to create dances that arise from asking: Who gets to dance? Where is the dance happening? What is it about? Why does it matter? The company recognizes the body and movement as essential resources to understand and investigate across disciplines. Through local, national, international, and online projects the Dance Exchange gathers and creates community to contribute to a healthy and more sustainable environment.

In 1975, its founder Liz Lerman began teaching senior adults at the Roosevelt for Senior Citizens, a city-run residential facility in inner-city Washington, D.C. Shortly after, she created "Woman of the Clear Vision," a dance about her mother's death with a cast of professional dancers and Roosevelt residents. In 1976, the Liz Lerman Dance Exchange was incorporated and she opened a school for professional and avocational dancers in downtown D.C. Since then, the Dance Exchange has produced more than 100 innovative dance/theatre works, presented thousands of performances and conducted innumerable community encounters. With these activities, the company has reached communities of every size, from Los Angeles to Eastport, Maine, and from Yamaguchi, Japan, to Gdansk, Poland.

FIGURE 1.2 Dance Exchange artists and Dallas community members in *Bricks & Bones*, co-directed by Cassie Meador and Paloma McGregor. Photo by Classi Nance

According to Lerman:

> Sometimes art achieves what therapy, medicine or the best care of health professionals cannot. Sometimes art even achieves something that's beyond the best intentions of the artist. These moments can feel like little miracles when they happen, but they are usually instances of art functioning as it normally does: inspiring motivation, engaging parts of people's bodies or brains that they haven't been using, or allowing them to transcend their environments for a little while.
>
> *(Newman-Bluestein & Hill, 2010, p. 24)*

Dance Exchange breaks boundaries between stage and audience, theater and community, movement and language, tradition and the unexplored. Now under the artistic direction of Cassie Meador, Dance Exchange stretches the range of contemporary dance through explosive dancing, personal stories, humor, and a company of performers whose ages span six decades. The work consists of concerts, interactive performances, community residencies, and professional training in community-based dance. Dance Exchange employs a collaborative approach to dance making and administration. Recent and current projects include explorations of coal mining, genetic research, human rights, particle physics, ecology, land use, and rest in a hyper-driven society.

During the 44 years that Dance Exchange has been making dances with people of all ages in a range of community settings, it has regularly seen participants surprise themselves and others by coming alive in unexpected ways. This sense of connection – or reconnection – to life is the essence of wellness. Drawing on this rich history, Dance Exchange champions the integration of the arts into meaningful aging and health care. In 2010, in partnership with the MetLife Foundation, Dance Exchange launched its Healthy Living Initiative, emphasizing Arts in Healthcare and Creative Aging; in addition, Dance Exchange supported the creation and performance of new intergenerational dance works through the Health Living Commissions. Dance Exchange's Creative Aging Program, beginning in 2019, brings a multifaceted approach to aging in place and supporting a community of care and resilience across the aging spectrum.

Arts in Health Care

1. Artistic work with people in health care settings: The Dance Exchange's multidisciplinary approach to art combines movement, verbal expression, and creative collaboration. Methods have been used with a variety of people, including those with Huntington's disease, brain injury, dementia, addiction, chronic mental illness, and mobility issues.
2. Training for artists, health professionals, and caregivers: Experiential activities, model teaching, and new frameworks help participants explore the ways in which dance and art making can enhance the effects of therapeutic work and re-energize relationships with patients, family members, and the self.

Creative Aging

3. Weekly Older Adult Class series: Using Dance Exchange tools and practices that foster adaptability for various bodies alongside artistic rigor, these weekly in-studio classes at Dance Exchange offer support for creative and healthy aging in place for both residents of the facilities we partner with and others aging in place in the Takoma Park region.
4. Biweekly Workshops for Older Adults: Partnering with local senior housing communities, these on-site workshops bring movement and storytelling to older adult communities to encourage physical activity and health, individual and community expression, and community building.
5. Monthly Intergenerational Convenings: These gatherings bring together seniors from multiple facilities, weekly class participants, students from local universities, artists training at Dance Exchange, experts from related fields, and members of the public to build an intergenerational community of

FIGURE 1.3 Dance Exchange artists Matthew Cumbie and Thomas Dwyer in *New Hampshire Ave: This is a Place To ...*, directed by Executive Artistic Director Cassie Meador. Photo by Ben Carver (bencarver.art)

FIGURE 1.4 Dance Exchange artists Dorothy Levy and Kevin Ormsby in *New Hampshire Ave: This is a Place To ...*, directed by Executive Artistic Director Cassie Meador. Photo by Ben Carver (bencarver.art)

support and creativity. These gatherings also catalyze conversations to support workforce development in the arts, inspire program replication in nearby regions, and spark cross-sector partnerships.

Creative Placemaking

The role that arts and cultural centers can play in preserving local character and in reinforcing a sense of place across generations has been advanced substantially by the agenda of *creative placemaking*.

There are two forces within the creative placemaking movement. Project for Public Spaces of New York City, initially founded by the leadership of William H. Whyte who wrote the book *The Social Life of Urban Spaces*, is led by Fred Kent and has advanced placemaking as a conversation between potential users, i.e., citizens, on what they would like to see as a safe and important gathering place that could advance their enjoyment of such a setting, be it a square, vacant lot, park, or neighborhood gathering place. A new movement in recent years called Art Place, organized by a consortium of foundations led by the Ford Foundation in association with the National Endowment for the Arts, believes that artists can play a critical role of serving as catalyst for such creative placemaking.

Both Project for Public Spaces and Art Place focus upon the relationship of local people being engaged, from young to old, workers and retirees, from low income to high income, as decision makers on the first steps of creating vibrant community gathering places. Both movements agree that anchor institutions, particularly cultural institutions, play a critical role in offering resources. Both movements agree that the role of the architect, planner, or landscape architect in creating such intergenerational gathering places is secondary to the role of engaging the local population in decision-making and priorities of first steps for creating valuable gathering places.

The many arts and cultural initiatives noted throughout this chapter, including the Queens Museum, Dance Exchange, and the many "creative placemaking" endeavors taking root in countless communities, serve to "animate" intergenerational gathering places, thereby enhancing community livability and quality of life for all ages.

References

Knight Foundation. (2010). *Knight soul of the community 2010: Why people love where they live and why it matters: A national perspective*. Miami, FL: John S. and James L. Knight Foundation in partnership with Gallup.

Newman-Bluestein, D., & Hill, H. (2010). Movement as the medium for connection, empathy, playfulness. *Journal of Dementia Care, 18*(5), 24–27.

Partners for Livable Communities. (2011). *Culture connects all: Rethinking audiences in times of demographic change*. Washington, DC: Author.

U.S. Department of Commerce Economics and Statistics Administration. (2011). *The older population: 2010 census briefs.* (U.S. Census Bureau Publication No. C2010BR-09). Washington, DC: Government Printing Office.

U.S. Department of Commerce Economics and Statistics Administration. (2018). *Demographic turning points for the United States: Population projections for 2020 to 2060.* (U.S. Census Bureau Publication No. P25-1144). Washington, DC: Government Printing Office.

2

OUR COMMUNITY, OUR TRADITIONAL FOOD

Around the Fire as an Intergenerational Contact Zone

Shingairai Chigeza, Nicole Claasen, and Vera Roos

Introduction

In this chapter, an intergenerational traditional food preparation event around open fires, and women from two rural South African communities having a meal together will serve to illustrate how the generational transferable properties of traditional customs have the potential to generate an Intergenerational Contact Zone (ICZ). Outdoor communal spaces around open fires are significant for many indigenous, rural African communities (including the Setswana-speaking Vaalharts communities in South Africa), as communal gathering places for life events such as weddings and funerals (Claasen & Chigeza, 2019); for intergenerational knowledge transmission of traditional food preparation and beer making (Chigeza, Roos, Claasen, & Molokoe, in press; Roos, 2016a); and for groups of women talking and sharing ideas while preparing food (Mbiti, 1991; Waites, 2009). This research project and programmatic intervention was motivated by observing that this type of ICZ is threatened with extinction due to the focus shifting from indigenous diets towards more globalized (western) diets (Claasen & Chigeza, 2019; Frison, Smith, Cherfas, Eyzaguirre, & Johns, 2005; Vorster, Kruger, & Margetts, 2011), to rural-urban migration, looser family and cultural connections (Hjarvard, 2014; Phaswana-Mafuya et al., 2011) and to strained relations among generations generally (Aboderin & Hoffman, 2015; Whyte, Alber, & Van der Geest, 2008) and between Setswana-speaking older persons and younger people specifically (Roos, 2016a).

Contextualizing the ICZ in South Africa

The Vaalharts region constitutes the largest irrigation scheme in South Africa, with an area of 29,181 hectares situated between the Vaal and the Harts rivers in the Northern Cape Province (see Figure 2.1). The area is regarded as a "food basket" and produces a variety of foods, including staple crops, vegetables, fruit, nuts, dairy and meat (Van Vuuren, 2010). The area is populated mainly by Batswana who live in formal or informal settlements within the farming area and who, despite the high agricultural output, are mostly poor. In 2013, approximately 38% of the black population in South Africa lived below the lower-bound poverty line, below 443.00 ZAR per month (about $32) (Statistics South Africa, 2014). There are high levels of unemployment (41%) among most of the inhabitants of the country (IHS Global Insight, 2015). As in many other rural and low-resourced communities in South Africa, multi-generational households are common, representing 32.2% of all households, with three or more generations living together, in these communities (Stats SA, 2016).

The development and implementation of this intergenerational programmatic intervention is the culmination of a longstanding relationship between the Vaalspan communities and researchers from the Africa Unit for Transdisciplinary Health Research (AUTHeR) of the North-West University. National research funding (NRF) and AUTHeR has enabled research since 2012 on topics related to food security, sustainable diets and local food systems in different communities in the Vaalharts area (Claasen et al., 2015). In this particular

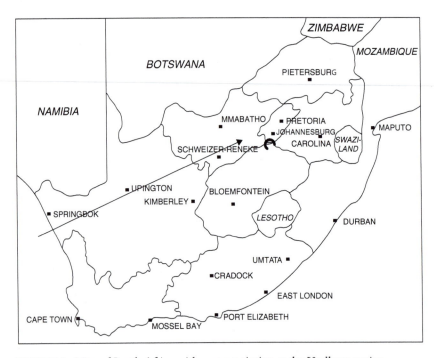

FIGURE 2.1 Map of South Africa with arrow pointing at the Vaalharts region

project, a community-based approach was used to involve representatives of provincial and district government departments, ward councilors, private sector members, individual community members and nonprofit organizations to explore opportunities related to a traditional cooking and intergenerational meal event in the Vaalspan and Sekhing communities.

Engaged Stakeholders

Unrelated Batswana women from the two communities, aged from 14 years and older, and representing three generational groups, were purposively selected. For practical purposes the different generational groups will be referred to as: G1 (50+ years), G2 (21–49 years) and G3 (14–20 years). Altogether 129 women, including 47 G1s (mean age 60 years), 43 G2s (mean age 32 years) and 39 G3s (mean age 17 years) were assigned to nine intergenerational groups of nine to 14 members each. An interdisciplinary research team comprising nutritionists, gerontologists and fieldworkers fluent in Setswana, one of the 11 official languages in South Africa, planned the project, made the logistical arrangements and facilitated its implementation.

Representatives of local government, tribal authorities and the District Department of Agriculture made recommendations regarding the nature of the traditional food activity and granted permission to use open spaces that were easily accessible to participants, safe for making fires, but sufficiently enclosed to prevent bystanders from interfering in the interactions between members of the participating multigenerational groups. The venues were equipped with a kitchen, a dining area, bathrooms and a fire extinguisher. Local artists were invited to perform traditional dances and songs on food preparation day.

Creating an ICZ by Traditional Food Preparation and Having a Meal Together

The event took place over three days, with the following objectives: to 1) establish multigenerational groups engaged in intergenerational activities around the menu planning process; 2) obtain food; and 3) prepare the food, have a meal together and review the different dishes prepared.

Establish groups and plan menus (day 1): Women interested in participating in the traditional food cooking event attended a planning meeting. Each woman was allocated a number and randomly assigned to various groups to ensure that all three generations were represented. Once these intergenerational groups had been formed, each woman was asked to propose traditional dishes they would like to prepare: one starch, one vegetable, one meat dish and one surprise dish (e.g. a non-alcoholic drink, dessert or another complementary dish). Once agreed, the choice of dishes was presented to all the participating groups in turn. Groups that chose the same dishes collectively discussed the suggestions to eliminate duplicated dishes and considered alternative options to ensure inclusion of a wide variety of traditional food.

Obtain food (day 2): Groups compiled a list of ingredients and indicated the quantity of ingredients needed for ten to 12 people. Two members of each group bought the ingredients in grocery stores using money from the research project's budget, while other participants collected ingredients from their households, gardens or from the fields.

Prepare and cook food, eat together and review dishes (day 3): A suitable Saturday was identified to enable working women as well as school children to participate. Women (the majority) dressed in traditional attire, arrived with their pots and cooking utensils. Each group created its own workspace with tables outside around the open fires to prepare ingredients for cooking. Firewood was delivered from a local dealer to the respective venues. The G3s started the fire, while the G2s prepared the ingredients for cooking and the G1s gave instructions for preparing the dishes. Figure 2.2 illustrates how the women cooked the dishes on open fires.

It took approximately five hours from setting the fires to dishing up. Each group set a table in the dining area and explained to all attendees what they had prepared and which ingredients they had used. Figure 2.3 shows one of the groups presenting their dishes.

The women served 36 different dishes and beverages, including *dombi* (dumplings), *mabele* (sorghum porridge), *botata* (sweet potato mash), *lekgodu* (gem squash dessert), and *mageu* (fermented maize meal drink). After the women had the meal together, they rated each dish on a scoring sheet administered by a researcher in a separate room. Dishes were evaluated in terms of taste, and decorative and authentic traditional presentation. After scores were

FIGURE 2.2 As an ICZ, fire and food bring together women from three generations

FIGURE 2.3 From left: Women from three generations present traditional dishes

calculated for each group, each member of the group with the highest score received a small three-legged cast iron pot as a token of appreciation for their efforts. All participating women received a cookbook with recipes for the dishes prepared that day. Six days after the event, participating women gathered into their respective generational groups as G1s, G2s and G3s and reflected on participating in the intergenerational event (see Chigeza, Roos, Claasen, & Molokoe, in press; Claasen & Chigeza, 2019 for a comprehensive discussion of findings).

Lessons Learned

The perspectives of the researchers and participating women will be used to highlight lessons learned from preparing traditional food in spaces around open fires and having a meal together as women from different generations. Creating this kind of ICZ calls for meticulous project management skills and transdisciplinary collaboration to study real-life issues such as strained intergenerational interactions and sustainable nutrition in rural communities. Effective ICZ spaces also depend on ethically informed community engagement principles such as prolonged involvement to build trusting relationships with community stakeholders and by including local and expert advisors familiar with indigenous practices and rituals to guide culturally appropriate actions and methods of engagement (Theron, 2013).

In reflecting on the intergenerational food preparation event and eating together, all the women expressed negative perceptions and emotions, ranging from anxiety, emotional discomfort and resentfulness in anticipation of their interaction with other generational members. Literature confirms that perceptions about the generational other are formed over time and it is well known that perceptions inform behavior (Hoffman, 2016; Smith-Acuña, 2011). After participating in the event, however, the women mostly reported positive perceptions and emotions in relation to the generational other. Positive subjective experiences are related to interacting effectively with others, despite their ages (Roos, 2016b; Vorster, Roos, & Beukes, 2013). Participant G2#1 said: "I have realized that as a person you learn to relate with other people", and G3#10 confirmed that familiarity was not a requirement for intergenerational interactions: "I learned that it does not matter whether you know the person or not, you can relate with someone you have not met before."

The planning of the intergenerational food activity set the scene for the intergenerational interactions. An intergenerational space was created with all women equal in social status and with a shared goal to stimulate cooperative intergroup interaction. These conditions, among others, are conducive to effective relational interaction, following contact strategies (Harrell, 2018). This ICZ was also structured to re-enact a cultural event around food and in a space where everyone could play a part. The authenticity of the ICZ was enhanced by choosing traditional food for the intergenerational interaction and having a meal together; by women dressing up in traditional clothes and responding to traditional music by singing along and dancing. In combination, these components in this particular sociocultural and interpersonal context activated the collective identity of the Batswana women. It is significant that particularly the youngest generation (G3s) expressed a sense of belonging after participating in the event. G3#5 commented: "Looking at all the dishes we have prepared, I was proud to belong to Batswana culture." Values underpinning the collective unity and the uncompromised upward and downward interactions between all generational members were noticed by an older woman, G1#7, who said: "This traditional food preparation activity has united us – both the young and old. We felt the spirit of Ubuntu[1]."

This ICZ had become what Thang & Kaplan (2013) describe as "space changing to place" when meaning is attached to it.

Finally, in a rural, resource-deprived environment, indigenous plant foods can supplement food shortage and also have health benefits. This ICZ stimulated the memories of particular G1s and G2s about their ancestors' diets, which consisted mainly of traditional food. This highlights the importance of the intergenerational transmission of indigenous food knowledge. G2#11 said: "There were not many illnesses back then. It's because our parents ate traditional food every day". G1#8 confirmed this: "Our ancestors were so healthy and strong from eating their food, traditional food gives us strength and build our bodies to be strong and healthy." Several studies have similarly pointed out the health benefits of traditional foods in terms of their high micronutrient content and dietary diversification, their affordability, as well as their ease of cultivation and income-earning potential (Cloete & Idsardi, 2013; Shackleton et al., 2010; Van der Hoeven et al., 2013).

It would be naive to regard the creation of one ICZ as potentially powerful enough to change intergenerational dynamics in the long term or influence and sustain improved eating habits. However, neither would it be appropriate to minimize the sentiment expressed by participants who alluded to the generations-connecting and culturally affirming significance of what they experienced "around the fire".

In terms of intergenerational relationships, dialogues in safe interpersonal contexts around topics that are activated in a particular developmental, interpersonal, historical or sociocultural context should be used to build deeper levels of connection between people from different generations. ICZ can be maximized when "the intervention goes beyond goal-orientated cooperation to include enhancing trust and warmth" (Harrell, 2018, p. 257). The positive experiences resulting from this and other ICZ, however, can mediate effective intergenerational interactions because they stimulate new possibilities for interaction (Frederickson, 2013; Mruk, 2018). A raised awareness of the benefits of using traditional food could be the first step to changing eating and food consumption behavior (Claasen et al., 2015).

Practical Considerations

Some practical suggestions are proposed from an interactional interpersonal perspective and from an ethically orientated community engagement perspective. From an interactional interpersonal perspective: 1) Understand that broader environments (e.g. cultural, historical, political) inform the interpersonal context and how intergenerational relational interactions may potentially play out. 2) Identify what is familiar to participants to prevent systemic resistance in planning and creating ICZ. The more familiar the event, the less chance there is for social systems to reject the intervention. 3) Participants in a multigenerational group engage with their own preconceived ideas in relation to other generations in an ICZ.

Ethical community engagement is guided by principles that differ from individualized health and clinical intervention contexts. It emphasizes that: 1) Communities are functioning social units with a lifespan that extends beyond the often momentary involvement of researchers and programmers; their autonomy and independence should be recognized and respected. 2) A bottom-up approach should be adopted and community stakeholders and an advisory board should be involved to decide if, how and what interventions are necessary and appropriate to the cultural context. 3) Indigenous knowledge and traditional practices are the community's to use. 4) Social structures inform and guide intergenerational relations – what may be acceptable in one context may not be relevant in the next.

On a practical level: 1) To enable the transformation of space into place, ensure that the ICZ includes cultural elements that are authentic and culturally meaningful for participants. 2) Put measures in place to ensure participants' physical and psychological safety. 3) Capture memories of the event with the intention of reviving positive emotions. In this project, photos of the participating women and recipes of the traditional food they prepared were compiled into a cookbook and presented to them (Claasen, 2017). Capturing photos of the event may to a small extent contribute to the sustainability of the project.

Conclusion

The different life-worlds and experiences of the respective generations and the subsequent strained intergenerational interactions have led to a decrease in cultural connections and knowledge transfer among generations in many African communities. In this research, the creation of an ICZ through the preparation of traditional food around open fires enabled knowledge transfer, heritage keeping, positive perceptions of and interactions with the generational other. For an ICZ to be effective, a bottom-up approach is recommended in engaging community stakeholders as well as local and expert advisors in developing interventions that fit the context culturally. It is also essential to include social components that allow equal participation and break down intergroup boundaries.

Note

1 "Ubuntu" is a Nguni word referring to a collective human solidarity and a collective morality '… of co-operation, compassion, communalism … respect … with emphasis on dignity in social relationships and practices. A quality that includes the essential human virtues; compassion and humanity (Mokgoro, 1998).

References

Aboderin, I., & Hoffman, J. (2015). Families, intergenerational bonds, and aging in Sub-Saharan Africa. *Canadian Journal on Aging/LaRevue Canadienne Duviellissement*, *34*(3), 282–289. doi:10.1017/50714980815000239.

Chigeza, S., Roos, V., Claasen, N., & Molokoe, K. (in press). Mechanisms in dynamic interplay with cultural and interpersonal contexts in a multigenerational food initiative involving rural South African women. *Journal on Intergenerational Relationships*.

Claasen, N. (Ed.). (2017). *A Taste of Vaalharts: Traditional Tswana Cooking. Tatso ya Vaalharts. Dijo Tsa Setso tsa Setswana*. Potchefstroom: Africa Unit for Transdisciplinary Health Research (AUTHeR), North-West University. Retrieved from http://bit.ly/2onjL6U.

Claasen, N., & Chigeza, S. (2019). Traditional food knowledge in a globalised world: Mediation and mediatization perceived by Tswana women. In J. Durrschmidt, &

Y. Kautt (Eds.), *Globalized Eating Cultures, Mediatization and Mediation* (pp. 129–155). Basingstoke: Palgrave. doi:10.1007/978-3-19-93656-7_7.

Claasen, N., Covic, N. M., Idsardi, E. F., Sandham, L. A., Gildenhuys, A., & Lemke, S. (2015). Applying a transdisciplinary mixed methods research design to explore sustainable diets in rural South Africa. *International Journal of Qualitative Methods, 14*(2), 69–91. doi:10.1177/160940691501400207.

Cloete, P. C., & Idsardi, E. F. (2013). Consumption of indigenous and traditional food crops: Perceptions and realities from South Africa. *Agroecology and Sustainable Food Systems, 37*(8), 902–914. doi:10.1080/2168356 5.2013.805179.

Frederickson, B. L. (2013). Positive emotions broaden and build. In P. Devine & A. Plant (Eds.). *Advances in Experimental Social Psychology* (pp. 1–53). Burlington, MA: Academic.

Frison, E., Smith, I. F., Cherfas, J., Eyzaguirre, P., & Johns, T. (2005). Using biodiversity for food, dietary diversity, better nutrition and health. *South African Journal for Clinical Nutrition, 18*, 112–114.

Harrell, S. P. (2018). "Being human together": Positive relationships in the context of diversity, culture, and collective well-being. In M. A. Warren & S. I. Donaldson (Eds.), *Toward a Positive Psychology of Relationships. New Directions in Theory and Research* (pp. 247–284). Santa Barbara, CA: Praeger.

Hjarvard, S. (2014). Mediatization and cultural and social change: An institutional perspective. In K. Lundby (Ed.), *Mediatization of Communication. Handbooks of Communication Science* (pp. 199–226). Berlin: De Gruyter Mouton.

Hoffman, J. (2016). Negotiating care of older people in South Africa: Between the ideal and the pragmatics. In J. Hoffman & K. Pype (Eds.), *Ageing in Sub-Saharan Africa: Spaces and Practices of Care* (pp. 1–19). Bristol: Policy Press. doi:101332/policypress/9781447325253.003.0008.

IHS Global Insight. (2015). *ReX Regional Explorer.* South Africa: Centurion.

Mbiti, J. S. (1991). *Introduction to African Religion* (2nd ed.). Oxford: Heinemann.

Mokgoro, Y. (1998). Ubuntu and the law in South Africa. *Buffalo Human Rights Law Review, 4*(17), 15–24.

Mruk, C. J. (2018). Positive psychology, relational self-esteem, and increasing well-being. In M. A. Warren & S. I. Donaldson (Eds.), *Toward a Positive Psychology of Relationships. New Directions in Theory and Research* (pp. 35–54). Santa Barbara, CA: Praeger.

Phaswana-Mafuya, N., Peltzer, K., Schneider, M., Makiwane, M., Zuma, K., Ramlagan, S., ... Phaweni, K. (2011). *Study on Global Ageing and Adult Health (SAGE), South Africa 2007–2008.* Geneva: World Health Organization.

Roos, V. (2016a). The Mmogo-method and the intergenerational group reflecting technique to explore intergenerational interactions and textual data analysis. In V. Roos (Ed.), *Understanding Relational and Group Experiences through the Mmogo-Method®* (pp. 89–118). Cham, Switzerland: Springer.

Roos, V. (2016b). Theorizing from the Mmogo-method: Self-interactional group theory (SIGT) to explain relational interactions. In V. Roos (Ed.), *Understanding Relational and Group Experiences through the Mmogo-Method®* (pp. 141–170). Cham, Switzerland: Springer.

Shackleton, C., Paumgarten, F., Mthembu, T., Ernst, L., Pasquini, M., & Pichop, G. (2010). Production of and trade in African indigenous vegetables in the urban and peri-urban areas of Durban, South Africa. *Development Southern Africa, 27*(3), 291–308. doi:10.1080/0376835X.2010.498937.

Smith-Acuña, S. (2011). *Systems Theory in Action. Applications to Individual, Couples, and Family Therapy*. Hoboken, NJ: John Wiley & Sons, Inc.

Statistics South Africa. (2014). Mid-year population estimates. Statistics South Africa/ Statistical release, P0302. Retrieved from www.statssa.gov.za.

Statistics South Africa. (2016). Community Survey 2016. Statistics South Africa/Statistical release, P0301. Retrieved from www.statssa.gov.za.

Thang, L. L., & Kaplan, M. (2013). Intergenerational pathways for building relational spaces and places. In G. D. Rowles & M. Bernard (Eds.), *Environmental Gerontology: Making Meaningful Places in Old Age* (pp. 225–251). New York: Springer.

Theron, L. C. (2013). Community-researcher liaisons: The pathways to resilience project advisory panel. *South African Journal of Education, 33*(4), 1–19.

Van der Hoeven, M., Osei, J., Greeff, M., Kruger, A., Faber, M., & Smuts, C. M. (2013). Indigenous and traditional plants: South African parents' knowledge, perceptions and uses and their children's sensory acceptance. *Journal of Ethnobiology and Ethnomedicine, 9*(1), 78. doi:10.1186/1746-4269-9-78.

Van Vuuren, L. (2010). Vaalharts – A garden in the desert: Water history. *Water Wheel, 9*(1), 20–24.

Vorster, C., Roos, V., & Beukes, M. (2013). A psycho-diagnostic tool for psychotherapy: Interactional pattern analysis. *Journal of Psychology in Africa, 23*(3), 163–169.

Vorster, H. H., Kruger, A., & Margetts, B. M. (2011). The nutrition transition in Africa: Can it be steered into a more positive direction? *Nutrients, 3*, 429–441. doi:10.3390/nu3040429.

Waites, C. (2009). Building on strengths: Intergenerational practice with African American families. *Social Work, 54*(3), 278–287.

Whyte, S. R., Alber, E., & Van der Geest, S. (2008). Generational connections and conflicts in Africa: An introduction. In E. Alber, S. Van der Geest, & S. R. Whyte (Eds.), *Generations in Africa: Connections and Conflicts* (pp. 1–23). Berlin: LIT Verlag.

3

FINDING FERTILE GROUND IN LIBRARIES FOR INTERGENERATIONAL DANCE

Yvonne Ng

Introduction

Libraries root a community. They are the repositories of past and current knowledge, and incubators for young explorers and creators. Libraries are also bastions from which intergenerational programming can thrive; fostering new relationships between seemingly separate and sometimes marginalized groups. With the establishment of these new relationships, we see a strengthening of the breadth and depth of a community.

Drawing from a dance-based program for youth (ages nine to 12) that has been running for ten years in community library settings in Toronto, Canada, this chapter highlights the generation-connecting, community-building potential when combined with the intentional addition of an intergenerational component. It discusses how this programming has evolved, some of the lessons learned, the limitations and insights gained along the way.

Why Libraries?

Each of the 102 library branches in Toronto functions as a community hub that extends beyond the traditional concept of libraries as mere places for storing books. As a potential venue of delivering intergenerational programming, a library has the benefit of neutrality. Schools are for kids and retirement homes are for senior citizens; but libraries are shared spaces where neither group is an interloper.

The Toronto Public Library system preserves and promotes free, equitable and universal access to a broad range of knowledge, experiences, information and ideas in a welcoming and supportive environment (Toronto Public Library, n.d.).

The official statement does however not mention that libraries also serve as:

- sources of "civic glue"[1];
- foundational community settings for connecting people and building a shared sense of community; and also
- gathering spaces; something much more than the clinical descriptor of "free and equitable."

The description "free and equitable" does not fully capture the importance of libraries. Freedom in the North American context is generally equated with personal liberty while libraries provide more than that. Libraries are imbued with a sense of restraint and decorum that levels the field for all its users.

Libraries in Canada are furthermore commonly regarded as sheltered spaces for the more vulnerable members of society (younger and older people): physically safe with controlled access and facilities generally in good repair. They are also operationally safe as the staff are caring, trained in managing difficult situations when they occur and are supported by a robust infrastructure of management, clear policies and with adequate insurance and access to the emergency response personnel of the city. This means that in planning an intergenerational program, libraries are ideal because of their established legitimacy in the community. Ad-hoc groups can offer programming under the umbrella of a library and parents or guardians of the participants are far more likely to accept and agree to their participation because of the perception that participants will be safe and treated in a respectful manner.

Toronto is a diverse city but with less economic diversity than many cities in North America. Immigrants make up 51% of Torontonians and for approximately 90% of that population, English is not their mother tongue (Statistics Canada, 2016). For our program, the diversity, be it ethnic or socio-economic, is only a minor predictor of participant uptake and our success. Our experience regarding the programming is that a lower median family income and/or a greater number of immigrants translates into higher participation rates. A predictor of success is the engagement of the branch staff and the community.

At times, the diversities of Toronto require some specifics in the delivery of the program. For example, at one of the seniors' residences participating in the program, residents were more comfortable in their native Italian than in English. Some adjustments were made to our program, like for example, using music the participants were familiar with. Those who developed and managed the program had to be flexible in adapting the program to the available resources and to the needs, interests, and physical capabilities of participants.

In our current programming, library branches provide:

- Free space
- Marketing support
- Registration services

- In some cases:

  ○ craft supplies
  ○ snacks
  ○ AV equipment

However, library branches lack homogeneity. The most obvious is that each branch has a different physical layout and is differently equipped. Therefore, the programming cannot be duplicated without reviewing the unique circumstances. For instance, if there is an auditorium, a show for friends and family is a possibility. If there is secure overnight storage for equipment, this decreases our artistic teams' set up, strike and travel time. As important as the physical space is the character of the library branch and neighborhood. This is a combination of the demographics of the catchment area and the level of engagement of the branch staff. The most successful programming has been where the facility has ease of access (primarily for the older adults) combined with the commitment of the branch staff to proactively engage with the younger participants to register for the program.

Why Dance in a Library?

Dance as a Vehicle for Finding One's Flow

One of the goals of this programming is to provide an opportunity that would allow the participants (both young and old) to enter a state of "flow" as conceptualized by Mihaly Csikszentmihalyi (2008) in his book, *Creativity: Flow and the Psychology of Discovery and Invention*. In much of Csikszentmihalyi's writing, he describes individuals attaining a "state of flow" as those who have a high degree of mastery in their area of competence, such as in computer programming or athletics. However, later in his narrative, he introduces the accessibility of a "state of flow" for the masses.

"Flow" can occur in any circumstance or location and to anyone regardless of their skill level or socio-economic situation and Csikszentmihalyi explains that absorption in the world as opposed to self-absorption is the key to happiness. In the deployment of the researcher's programming, the development of technical skills at a high level is not being sought after; rather, the objective is to achieve "flow" through an absorption into the socially oriented and collectively generated goal.

An example of entering a "state of flow" occurred in one of the workshops with a participant who is a natural mover and intuitively understands movement. She, however, constantly had a difficult time letting go of her performance being either "right" or "wrong". The facilitators guided her to the beauty that flowed from the uninhibited movement of the kids and encouraged her to have trust in the ability of the group to absorb any "mistakes" that she may make while dancing and these "mistakes" were welcomed additions to the beautiful complexity of the group.

Dance as an Indiscriminate Vehicle for Interaction

There is a strong parallel to the contemporary complaint that childhood has disappeared, overwhelmed by scheduled playdates. I would argue that this has become extended to older adults, driven by the same well-meaning impulses. In our workshops, a great deal of care is taken to ensure that the student and older adult participants can enjoy the playful feeling of dancing together without being constrained by too much structure. The library-based "flocking" workshop described below provides an example of how our dance activities create a playful, socially oriented and collectively generated atmosphere for intergenerational engagement through dance (see Figure 3.1).

Flocking: Split the group up into two groups of four and one group of five. I had them moving through the room and eventually got them to transit into stillness and then continue, creating "across the floor patterns" and movements. Overall this was great, although one participant is counting out loud as well as transferring leadership vocally. They were all a bit unsure of who was leader and who wasn't, but it was for many their first time; I can't blame them ... too much. Really was beautiful to see them going across the floor and passing each other creating these roving packs of dancers. I got them to finish in the center holding a shape. I was a bit worried the kids would do too much moving for the older adults, but they all seemed all right and quite sprightly; sprightlier than expected. I think the older adults were just into it. (Field note entry from the facilitator of this two-hour workshop conducted at Richview Library on November 3, 2016).

The high energy and warm sense of acceptance and social support that is generated by the exuberant experience of collaborative dance helps to reduce the social and performance anxieties that some participants have. Carefully designed intergenerational dance has many benefits, topping the list is that it is a joyful experience. It is in this state of joy that everything that we hope and wish for happens, and in doing so, also creates a heightened collective sense of community. In a state of joy, differences are shed, and solidarity is developed, and trust is created. There is still an acknowledgement and respect for the otherness in terms of physical capabilities of each of the participants and yet the group coalesces around the unity of creative expression.

FIGURE 3.1 An intergenerational dance activity called "flocking." Photo: Courtesy of Tiger Princess Dance projects, taken by Irvin Chow

Kids as Catalysts – Intergenerational Dynamics

The clearest examples of the catalytic effect of youth on older adults occurred in the instances where they all met for the first time. The youth, with their boundless energy and exuberance, allowed the older adults to be lured into play. *Name Game with Searchlight*, one of the activities used at the start of the program as a vehicle for people to get to know each other, is an excellent example of the catalytic effect (Figure 3.2).

> *Name Game with Searchlight:* The Facilitator stands in the middle of the group and with an extended arm and pointed finger as if the "lighthouse" or "searchlight." Every time the light shines on a participant, the person must say their name and create a gesture which is held (statue pose). The Facilitator turns relatively slowly to get everyone to create their statue. The game allows the participants the freedom to move in ways that are entirely of their own making. It is good to run through a few cycles of the game as the shyer participants are encouraged by the others in the group; typically, in an intergenerational setting, the older adults will quickly match the exuberance and general silliness of the youth.

FIGURE 3.2 Playing the "name game with searchlight." Photo: Courtesy of Tiger Princess Dance projects, taken by Irvin Chow

In one of our workshops, this simple icebreaker turned into a competition between an older adult and a youth; they spontaneously began competing with one another to see who could contort their face the most. The youth were astounded when their silliness was matched and then exceeded by these "grumpy, smelly" (words used to describe old people in the pre-engagement surveys the youth filled out) older adults. In almost every workshop we deliver, there is a golden moment when one of the younger participants grasps the fact that these senior citizens they are dancing with were once vital young kids such as themselves. Rarer, is the sequential leap of understanding that in 70 or 80 years, they themselves will be senior citizens.

Dance is Effective in Impeding Age-related Deterioration

There are several aspects of dance that make this programming an ideal prophylactic against the physical, social and cognitive deterioration associated with ageing and/or a more isolated and sedentary life style framed by social media and video games.

Dancing requires proprioception which is one's overall sense of body position, movement and acceleration. Proprioception is a key component in balance and is vitally important in older persons and importantly, proprioception can be strengthened. The study by Marmeleira et al. (2009) of 18 men and women between 55 and 80 years of age argues that proprioception can be learned/re-learned with a program of creative dance that focuses on proprioception. The researchers used Creative Dance as a vehicle and tested proprioception using a computerized dynamometer. There were various steps taken to minimize external stimuli with the participants in the study such as earphones with white noise, a blindfold, shorts to eliminate skin sensation and the placement of the lower foot and ankle in an inflatable splint. In the exercise, the subject's leg was moved into target positions of knee flexion and then back to neutral. The subject was then asked to reproduce the target position and the degree of error recorded. Following the 12-week long program of 36 90-minute dance sessions, the subjects and the control group were re-tested and significant improvement was seen in the group that had participated in the dance classes. However, the control group deteriorated in line with normal age-related deterioration.

Dance is usually thought of in terms of the physical activity, however, there is another side to dance that is equally, if not more valuable. Cognitive plasticity is the ability to receive multiple inputs and respond in an adaptive way. A person walking in a crowd is constantly making decisions that are translated into changes in gait, direction and speed. Quite literally the introduction of additional stimuli or processes, such as chewing gum, makes the task more difficult. The good news is that studies on dual-task processing skills in older adults showed that training led to improvements in the ability to perform multiple tasks concurrently, to use a colloquialism, "you can teach an old dog new tricks" To see how this concept might apply to dance, see Berson (2010).

The Big Ball Exercise: *This is a fun way for participants to get to know each other and to begin moving together in a safe way. It is suitable for participants of mixed abilities. Using a stability ball, one participant says his or her name and then calls out the person's name to whom the ball is being rolled towards. This exercise is further expanded with the introduction of a secondary object (a soft toy) which is passed around the circle before progressing to throwing it to participants (whose name has been called) at random. The secondary element challenges the participants to raise their arms above shoulder height, initiating horizontal and transverse movement. In addition to the* *increased kinesthetic challenge, the dual-task processing builds cognitive plasti-city. In the enjoyment of this "game," the participant is distracted from any worries of pain, immobility restrictions or being "correct," and in doing so, rediscovers and, in many cases, expands their kinesphere.*

Key Aspects to Keep in Mind when Planning Intergenerational Dance and Other Community Arts Activities

Preparation (and marketing) is Critical/Crucial

Good ideas and honorable intent are not enough. Basic to the preparation is to build partnerships with the relevant libraries, getting to know the respective locations, know their constituencies and how to reach/contact them as well as assessing what other programming has worked and what not.

Useful are registration and completion of Physical Activity Readiness Questionnaires at a meet & greet event. This is another opportunity to become acquainted and to familiarize yourselves with the youth, their parents and more importantly the senior citizens and their physical ability.

Snacks and Break Time

One of the most effective components of our programming is snack breaks. It is basic and might take some of the limited time, however, consider its value:

- Sharing of food is intergenerational. There may be differences (dentures vs. braces or coffee vs. juice) but eating is a common and profoundly social activity that everyone shares and it provides a touchstone for conversations. Sharing of food is an activity that implies trust and the bonds of community.
- Eating provides energy and ameliorates hyper-activity brought on by low blood sugar.

Furthermore, breaks give the mind time to process. Dance places a significant cognitive load on the brain and as with any cognitive activity, the brain needs time to integrate learning into its current paradigm. In addition, we have to be mindful that the participants are individuals, each with their own level of comfort with what is often a highly stimulating (socially, sonically, physically) environment. Many benefit greatly from a pause to regain equilibrium.

Mind Your Metrics

Any programming needs funding and most funders require reporting regarding their contribution. The challenge of this programming is that it is hard to draw out concrete metrics on the value provided. The benefits that this programming offers are revealed in the shared laughter between a shy ten-year-old and a lonely 70-year-old. An observation during this program is the possibility that friendships can arise between these two alien species (the young and the old) that inhabit our libraries. Relationships that continue subsequent to the programming is proof of this and it informs the rest of the community that this is possible. Knowing this in the planning stage is critical in managing relationships with funders.

When a Space Becomes a Place?

From our experience in running programs for the last decade, a space only becomes a place when the sum of the following elements is aligned:

- A physical space trusted by the community that has a basic physical and administrative infrastructure where community activators can work efficiently and economically.
- Individuals or organizations with resources and a degree of competence to sustain the start-up phase and the inevitable ebb and flow of delivering programming.

In the evaluation of the use of a public space, simple quantitative information can be deceiving. If different groups use a space in parallel, proximate to each other, but with minimal interaction, that space is not one place, but many. Each siloed group has their own space that resides in the same geography. A community space necessitates the integration of distinct groups of people which will only happen through considered and ongoing programming such as with the Toronto Public Library.

Considering the generation-connecting, community-building properties of dance programs, they have the potential to help transform public library *spaces* into meaningful *places*. Add in a carefully crafted intergenerational component, rooted in the cross-generational appeal of dance and activities that promote the shared experience and joy of collaborative dance, and we see how public libraries can also function as unique and compelling *Intergenerational Contact (and dance) Zones*.

Note

1 "Civic glue" is the phrase that Robert McNulty uses to describe the capacity of arts and cultural institutions, including libraries, to bring together different generations and cultural groups in ways that strengthen community (see Chapter 1 in this book).

References

Berson, J. (2010). Old dogs, new tricks: Intergenerational dance. In V. B. Lipscomb & L. Marshall (Eds.), *Staging age* (pp. 165–189). New York: Palgrave Macmillan.

Csikszentmihalyi, M. (2008). *Creativity: Flow and the psychology of discovery and invention.* New York: HarperCollins Publishers.

Marmeleira, J. F., Pereira, C., Cruz-Ferreira, A., Fretes, V., Pisco, R., & Fernandes, O. (2009). Creative dance can enhance proprioception in older adults. *The Journal of Sports Medicine and Physical Fitness, 49*(4), 480–485.

Statistics Canada. (2016). *Census of population.* Toronto, ON: Social Policy, Analysis & Research. Retrieved from www.toronto.ca/ext/sdfa/Neighbourhood%20Profiles/pdf/2016/pdf1/alltoronto.pdf.

Toronto Public Library. (n.d.). *Vision, mission & values.* Retrieved from www.torontopubliclibrary.ca/about-the-library/mission-vision-values/.

4

TRANSFORMING A BARN INTO AN "INTERGENERATIONAL PLANNING ZONE"

Matthew Kaplan, Suzanna Windon, and Evan C. Zavada

> The fact that this Intergenerational Ideas Summit was held in a beautiful old German overshoot barn was not lost on me. Having grown up in and around these barns as a child, I have always seen them fondly as intergenerational places. Barns such as this were built over 150 years ago, and to me they are like living monuments to the generations of the families that built, repaired, rebuilt, and loved them. They were built by hand – aided by human and animal muscle power. The craftmanship, designs, dreams, and sweat of beloved ancestors was fashioned into the very wood in the building. You can see, touch, feel, and even smell it. This wood was probably cut and sawn from trees in the farm's woodlot (now long gone). Each room and specific place in such barns speak of memories and markers in a family's history. Some of these memories might seem insignificant, but they all can be significant touchstones between the family members that shared or lived them and faithfully carried them forward.

The author of these comments was a participant in the first "Intergenerational Ideas for Enriching Quality of Life in Centre County Retreat" in Centre County, Pennsylvania. This was his response to the question of how he felt about holding the Retreat in a large barn on the grounds of a local environmental center.

In alluding to the many layers of meaning that he associated with barns – rooted in his personal, family, cultural, and community experience – he provided some insight into how a site, seemingly as nondescript as an empty barn, can stimulate intergenerational thinking and collaborative program planning.

Upon further conversation with other Retreat participants, and a review of post-event evaluation survey results[1], we gained additional understanding of how a barn setting, under certain circumstances, can invigorate, inspire, and enable a group of local educators, human service professionals, planners, and volunteers, many of whom work with a generation-specific lens, to engage in a collective intergenerational program planning process.

In the remainder of this chapter, we explore some of the properties and potentialities of barns that may enable them to function as effective *intergenerational (program) planning zones.*

Background Context

The idea of organizing a county-wide retreat on intergenerational programming emerged at one of the monthly meetings of the State College, PA chapter of the Intergenerational Leadership Institute (ILI), a certificate training program developed by Pennsylvania State University for older adults (55+) seeking new lifelong learning and civic engagement experiences as well as opportunities to take on leadership roles in developing new intergenerational programs.[2] Members of three cohorts of ILI participants (who joined the intergenerational short course component of the program in 2016, 2017, and 2018) played central roles in the planning and much of the facilitation for this event. They were assisted by colleagues from ILI partnering organizations such as the Osher Lifelong Learning Institute (OLLI) at Penn State and the Centre County Office of Aging.

The Retreat was conceived as a daylong intervention aimed at "jump starting" a county-wide planning process that would generate ideas for intergenerational programs that could address priority needs or otherwise improve local quality of life. This information would not only be helpful in terms of informing the program development efforts of future cohorts of ILI participants, but also in providing local organizations with a platform for interorganizational networking and collaborative planning to bolster and broaden their intergenerational program plans.

Several hundred invitations were sent out to administrators, staff, and volunteers affiliated with community organizations, groups, and agencies in Centre County – primarily through email, presentations, word of mouth, and, occasionally, hard copy letters sent through the mail; 50 responded favorably, and 48 attended. The expectations set for their role in the Retreat were that they would be active participants in the process of: generating a large list of potential project ideas (through a brainstorming process), narrowing the list down to those of highest priority, and selecting three to five project ideas for further development.

After some deliberation, the Retreat planning committee narrowed the search of potential meeting sites to two distinct settings on the grounds of the Millbrook Marsh Nature Center, an environmental education center located less than two miles from the Penn State University campus and within eight miles of Centre County's five most populated communities. One space was a traditional classroom/meeting facility within the "education building" and the other, the ultimate choice for the meeting site, was a large, 1850's forebay bank barn.[3]

Why Have an Intergenerational Networking, Brainstorming, and Planning Event in a Barn?

Historically, American barns have been associated primarily with agricultural production, providing spaces for livestock, hay, and various other agricultural goods and services. However, with technological advancements, changing economic circumstances, and evolving farming practices leading to a decline in the prevalence and agricultural functionality of barns, many barns have been repurposed to serve other functions, including as local historical museums, visitor centers, community theaters, artist studios, restaurants, stores, and as spaces for trainings and workshops (Endersby, Greenwood, Larkin, & Rocheleau, 2003; Noble & Wilhelm, 1995).

The remainder of this section notes some barn-related features that made it a compelling choice as the setting for the first intergenerational programming Retreat event held in Central Pennsylvania:

To Pique Interest in the Retreat

We conceived of the Retreat as a unique event, so we wanted to find an out-of-the-ordinary setting and space to hold the meeting. A large red barn (see Figure 4.1) seemed to fit the bill; it generated much interest and curiosity among local professionals considering attending.

To Highlight the Distinctiveness of the Rural Location

The Retreat planning committee wanted to hold the event at a site which reflected the rural flavor and cultural heritage of Central Pennsylvania. Old barns like the one at Millbrook Marsh are symbols of Pennsylvania's agrarian history and picturesque landscapes. Efforts to preserve and restore such barns, as spearheaded by organizations such as the Historic Barn & Farm Foundation of Pennsylvania and the National Barn Alliance, illustrate the high level of respect afforded to these historical icons of Pennsylvania's farms.

FIGURE 4.1 The Millbrook Marsh Nature Center Barn. Photo credit: Millbrook Nature Center. Centre County Parks and Recreation

To Infuse Awareness of the Time Dimension in Human Life

The selection of an old barn, which is very much connected to local history, was also an attempt to sensitize participants around time-bound processes. Since intergenerational programs do need a clear sensitivity about the temporal component of human life, the thinking was that an old barn may make it easier for attendees to broach conversations about differences and similarities in generational experience and consider possibilities for collaboration and interaction.

To Provide a Flexible, Modifiable Space for Achieving Multiple Goals

A large empty barn provides a fair amount of environmental flexibility for arranging chairs, desks, and tables in diverse design configurations to accommodate the intended *participatory process and multiple goals* for the event (Figure 4.2).

After viewing the exhibits, with additional time allotted for refreshments and informal conversation and networking, Retreat participants broke into five thematic groups according to their professional pursuits and personal interests:

(1) Health & Wellness.
(2) Community Development & the Social Environment.
(3) Community Development & the Physical (built & natural) Environment.

FIGURE 4.2 The inner walls of the barn were lined with exhibits that highlighted intergenerational programs conceived and implemented by ILI participants and colleagues from collaborating organizations

(4) Education and Lifelong Learning.
(5) Arts, Culture & Recreation.

In these groups, participants discussed local needs, reviewed existing programs and resources, and began *framing intergenerational intervention strategies for addressing unmet needs* in each content area (Figure 4.3).

Participants then reconvened in a large group, listened to brief presentations from participants of the five thematic groups, and began a process of prioritizing intergenerational program ideas for further development and consideration for implementation following the Retreat. The goal was to *generate three to five actionable plans for developing new (or augmented) intergenerational programs* (Figures 4.4 and 4.5).

The wide open, modifiable use of space within the barn was conducive to creating micro-spaces for one-to-one, small group, and large group interactions, both of a formal and informal nature, and for positioning these spaces to accommodate rapid transitions between Retreat segments.

To Ensure that Participants from Diverse Groups and Organizations Would Feel Welcome

The selection of a barn on the grounds of an environmental center and nature preserve was considered "neutral ground," not belonging to any single sector, whether government agency, university, non-profit organization, or commercial interest.

One participant commented, "I think that [the meeting] place was appropriate for this type of activity, since it is kind of neutral place between PSU and the

FIGURE 4.3 Small group breakout session

FIGURE 4.4 Reconvening in a large group to review intergenerational program ideas generated by each of the five breakout groups

community of Centre County. It was located where people's needs are, within community."

Barn as Symbol of Intergenerational Continuity and Community Building

Barn as Symbol of Intergenerational Continuity

Barns are not only historical landmarks on the agrarian landscape, they also serve as mental landmarks from a generational perspective. They

FIGURE 4.5 Large group discussion and decision-making process to prioritize intergenerational program ideas for further development

communicate with us about family history, and broader social and economic changes that have influenced the way of life in rural communities. What the organizers did not fully anticipate was the depth in the personal meanings that Retreat participants associated with barns. Several participants shared personal, family, and community memories that formed and were sustained through barn-related activity taking place during and after their childhoods.

"As the daughter of a painter who regularly explored the Finger Lakes region of New York State for barns he could render on canvas, and the granddaughter of an antique collector from the Hudson River Valley, barns have special meaning to me. I come from a family that values old, hand-built things that last. When I learned the ILI Retreat was going to be held in a barn I was intrigued and felt positive and relaxed about the day at hand."

"As a participant who has thrived in outdoor environments since I was a little girl, I was pleased to hear the event was going to be held in the historic barn."

"It was a great place for the idea generation related to intergenerational aspects [of community]."

Barn as Metaphor for Community-building

At the opening segment of the Retreat, participants were asked the following question: "What can 'intergenerational practitioners' – like us – do to create the type of positive intergenerational dynamics that we see occurring naturally in some settings?" They were then asked to consider the *barn raising* tradition in the Amish community. This reference to barn raising was meant to provide a poignant example of what a collaborative approach to community building could accomplish. It also helped to convey the point that intergenerational practice is about more than just *programs*. It's also about *values and the way we choose to live*.

Certainly, many people have positive experiences and associations related to barns, however, there needs to be caution against understating some of the challenges associated with farm life. In many rural areas across the country, including Pennsylvania, operations on small and medium-sized family owned farms are continuing to decline (Dandes, 2019, April 22). Tight profit margins, price instability, and weather uncertainty are putting farm bankruptcies on the rise (Colombo, 2018, November 29), along with the associated distress to families affected by these conditions. Amid dimming prospects for American family farms, for some, the barn may be symbolic of economic anxiety and the struggles of keeping the family together.

Post-Retreat Outcomes

The Retreat served to uncover new possibilities for expanding the footprint of intergenerational work in Centre County, PA. All around, we witnessed high-energy networking, and the beginnings of new interpersonal and interorganizational relationships centered around the common goal of supporting intergenerational initiatives in the county.

Leveraging New Connections Made at the Retreat

> It was incredibly valuable to me to network with the individuals representing other organizations or initiatives. I am now following up on many ideas we discussed for how we can better work together now.
>
> *[Retreat participant]*

Eighteen of the 23 respondents strongly agreed with the statement on the evaluation survey, "At the Retreat, I connected with people from other organizations who could significantly enhance my ability to make a positive impact on the community."

On average, Retreat participants reported making eight new contacts with individuals they met at the Retreat and with whom they followed up after the Retreat.

When asked, "What modes of action have you taken (or plan to take) as a function of what you learned from the Retreat?" participants noted the following plans and actions for following up with new contacts:

"I plan on reaching out to other community organizations when I plan intergenerational activities."

"We have sent out notes to colleagues to meet about a programming idea we came up with at the event."

"(Will) share information and data that we have collected to help other groups."

"I plan to use more collaborative methods in my work as an educator."

Post-Retreat Actions to Extend Local Intergenerational Programming Efforts

To extend the discussions and collaborative planning efforts initiated at the Retreat, members of the planning committee sent Retreat participants a six-page summary of new and enhanced intergenerational program ideas generated at the Retreat. This document continues to serve as a rough blueprint for several modes of future intergenerational program development in the county.

Furthermore, to provide Retreat participants with another venue for collaborative work on new intergenerational program plans, they were invited to join the Intergenerational Leadership Institute's monthly "application sessions," which were renamed as "Intergenerational Think Tank" meetings. In the first of these meetings, Retreat highlights and lessons learned were shared via an outreach education video created by members of the Retreat planning team (Kaplan & Zavada, 2018).

Conclusion

In this chapter, we have highlighted a number of ways in which we believe the selection of a historical barn in Central Pennsylvania as the site for this daylong retreat contributed to the realization of several goals set for the event, including, exposing participants to a wide range of existing intergenerational programs and plans, identifying issues of common concern, framing intergenerational strategies for addressing unmet needs, and prioritizing a handful of project ideas for further development.

We have noted several ways in which the Millbrook Marsh Barn was emblematic of intergenerational thinking and ideals. The barn was widely understood as a place of rich historic and community meaning, and for some, historic barns have special personal meanings. Several participants alluded to how this 150-year old barn evoked poignant memories and associations with intergenerational connections in family and community contexts. We contend that such rich personal and communal meanings associated with the Retreat's barn setting helped to set the tone and create an atmosphere of openness and inclusivity throughout the collaborative planning process.

Another effectual factor that contributed to the success of the Retreat was the emphasis on ensuring participation from volunteers, educators, planners, and human service professionals working in organizations serving generationally diverse populations (e.g., the local area agency on aging, Youth Bureau, school district offices, community centers, retirement communities, environmental centers, and university outreach education centers). This helped infuse a widespread sense of "generational awareness" into the planning process, and this was particularly important in the prioritization of local needs to be addressed via intergenerational interventions, and in the framing of activities and processes for developing new programs.

Acknowledgements

This work is supported by the USDA National Institute of Food and Agriculture and Hatch Appropriations under Project #PEN04668 and Accession #1017530. Special thanks to Sanford Smith, Anne Burgevin, and Mariano Sánchez for their helpful comments on previous drafts.

Notes

1 Of the 48 individuals who participated in the Retreat, 28 responded to the online evaluation survey. After removing incomplete surveys, the final data set consisted of responses from 23 participants. The response rate was 48%.
2 For more information about the ILI, see: https://aese.psu.edu/extension/intergenera tional/program-areas/intergenerational-leadership-institute.
3 A Pennsylvania barn is a type of banked barn built in the US from about 1790 to 1900. The style's most distinguishing feature is the presence of an overshoot or forebay, an area where one or more walls overshoot its foundation. As noted, in the Centre Region Parks and Recreation website, the Millbrook March barn was a functioning barn in the 1800s but today it exists as a "retreat for birds in migration, plants, and people ... The old barn and silo remain and give the nature center some Central Pennsylvania authenticity."

References

Colombo, J. (2018, November 29). Here's why more American farms are going bankrupt. Forbes. Retrieved from www.forbes.com/sites/jessecolombo/2018/11/29/heres-why-more-american-farms-are-going-bankrupt/#7b48427065a7.
Dandes, R. (2019, April 22). Pennsylvania loses 6,156 farms over 5-year stretch. The Daily Item. Retrieved from www.dailyitem.com/news/pennsylvania-loses-farms-over-year-stretch/article_90d87036-64eb-11e9-8377-7f803f0fec61.html.

Endersby, E., Greenwood, A., Larkin, D., & Rocheleau, P. (2003). *Barn: Preservation & adaptation: The evolution of a vernacular icon.* New York: Universe Publishing.

Kaplan, M., & Zavada, E. (2018, November 18). *Intergenerational ideas for enriching quality of life in centre county* Retreat [Video file]. Retrieved from www.youtube.com/watch?v=qNBCMth0cb8&t=1s.

Noble, A. G., & Wilhelm, H. G. (1995). *Barns of the midwest.* Athens, OH: Ohio University Press.

5

CITY CYCLING SPACES FOR WELCOMING AND ENGAGING ALL AGES

Tim Jones and Ben Spencer

This chapter reviews ways in which cycling spaces can be designed to provide family oriented, community-building social and physical activity as well as an additional mode of transportation.

Introduction

There is a general consensus that cycling should be promoted as healthy and sustainable mobility. The major trend over the last half-century across many countries, however, has been towards a decline in cycling for everyday local transport.

We describe how the concept of *Intergenerational Cycling Zones* could help engage younger and older generations to work together to develop more civilized, harmonious and inclusive cycling environments *that enable cyclists of all ages and abilities to use bicycles with ease and to interact with each other positively.* Finally, we discuss potential facets of *Intergenerational Cycling Zones* and the challenges to their acceptance within the UK context.

Background

The majority of the UK population seldom engages with cycling in any form – around two-thirds of the population use cycles less than once a year or never (UK Department for Transport, 2018). Cycling for transport in the UK, with the exception of some cities including Cambridge, Oxford and York, is unusual. What over half a century ago was a major mode of urban mobility has today become a very minor one. Cycling now accounts for only 2% of all trips and 1% of all distance travelled in the UK (UK Department for

Transport, 2018). Cycling is also becoming less significant for people in achieving recommended levels of physical activity[1]. Between 1995 and 2010 the average time spent cycling declined from 6 hours to 5 hours per person per annum (UK Department for Transport, 2011a).

The share of journeys made by bicycle in the UK is low but particularly low for older age groups. There is also gender disparity with older men twice as likely to cycle as older women (UK Department for Transport, 2018). Only 1% of all journeys made by people aged 65 and above in the UK are by bicycle compared to 9% in Germany, 15% in Denmark and 23% in the Netherlands (Pucher & Buehler, 2012). Older people's cycle journeys are typically shorter and more localized than younger adults' and are more likely to be for personal business or social purposes as opposed to commuting (UK Department for Transport, 2011b).

The main reason that puts people off cycling in the UK, and particularly older people, is the perception that cycling on roads dominated by large numbers of fast-moving motorized vehicles is dangerous (Pooley et al., 2013). Older 'empty nester' householders generally have more leisure time and potential to rediscover cycling but they are inhibited from doing so because of concerns about traffic danger and also personal fitness levels and ability. Indeed, nearly half of older people feel it is difficult for them physically to cycle and only one in five are confident cycling on the roads (UK Department for Transport, 2011c). There is potential to engage older people in cycling if these concerns were addressed as 42% say they would cycle more if there were more dedicated cycle paths (UK Department for Transport, 2011c).

The Marginalization of Cycling in the UK

UK mobility culture has been shaped by mass car ownership which in turn has shaped how the transport system has evolved under a paradigm that has fueled faster and longer distance travel (Banister, 2008). Car use is now the norm and is convenient and considerably safer than half a century ago whereas cycling has become less convenient, less comfortable, less safe and therefore less desirable. This is because to cycle in UK cities more often than not involves negotiating space shared with cars and larger motor vehicles. The fact that many people do not even contemplate cycling is unsurprising given that the transport system has focused historically around ensuring safe passage and smooth flow of motor traffic.

Cycling for general mobility in the UK is now restricted to a minority of mostly committed cyclists or those who have little choice but to cycle for economic reasons. The remainder of the population eschews cycling or at best engages in occasional cycling for leisure in green and quiet spaces away from motor traffic on a weekend. This is despite a strong desire by older cyclists to share, encourage and enjoy cycling with younger generations (Jones et al.,

2016). This serves to consolidate the belief that to drive in the city is 'normal' and to cycle is somehow 'abnormal', even for short journeys where cycling would be the most sensible option. Cycling therefore continues to become marginalized and cyclists on city streets are regarded as a 'nuisance'.

Those who continue to cycle in most UK cities today are typically young, male, white, 'hardened' cyclists. They are the product of a predominantly car-based system that marginalizes cycling and creates an expectation that the performance of cycling requires riding quickly and assertively adorned in special protective gear. This type of 'vehicular cycling' underpinned by the notion that, 'cyclists fare best when they act and are treated as drivers of vehicles' (see Forester, 1994), often looks more like sport cycling than an ordinary method of moving around the city – see YouTube 'Effective Cycling excerpt' for example (Chan, 2013). The perpetual acclimatization to current hostile (vehicular) cycling conditions has shaped UK cycling identity and practice so much so that in the process of 'being a cyclist' committed cyclists often struggle to understand why more people do not cycle. Paradoxically, narratives on the advantages of cycling are often accompanied by tales of experiences of accidents and 'near-misses' (Aldred & Crosweller, 2015); this inadvertently perpetuates the identity of a 'cycling elite' (Steinbach, Green, Datta, & Edwards, 2011) and indeed in some cases as miscreants behaving as 'kamikazes' (Hanson, 2015).

The picture then is of one where the emphasis is on promoting cycling safety through riders taking responsibility for their own protection (cf. helmet wearing) within a predominantly car-based transport system. The lack of progress in creating a comprehensive cycling system similar to those experienced in other northern European cities stymies any hope of intergenerational cycling. A more diverse landscape for cycling which embraces all ages and abilities is clearly needed. We now turn to some strategies for moving in this direction.

Towards UK Intergenerational Cycling Zones

Established 'cycling cities' such Amsterdam (NL) and Copenhagen (DK) have a long heritage of planned interventions for cycling at both city and national level that provide conditions for intergenerational cycling. Other cities across Europe beginning to reallocate space for cycling include Munich (DE), Malmo (SE), Bordeaux (FR) and Seville (ES). So how could intergenerational cycling in the UK be achieved? Fundamentally, to encourage more cycling in urban areas requires adapting current infrastructure to provide people with the choice to be able to cycle in a safe, comfortable and inclusive environment. A number of actions will help to achieve this. The reallocation of road space from motor vehicle use to create space for cycling and walking is a key first step as set out in Cycling UK's Space for Cycling Campaign (Cycling UK, n.d.). This would include local interventions in residential areas such as slower speed zones and Home Zones or *Woonerfs* (re:Streets, n.d.). These balance the needs of residents to use streets as social spaces, with the need for vehicular traffic access such that street space is not dominated by fast moving through-traffic and parked cars. It makes possible the growth of cycling as a family oriented recreational and practical activity in people's neighborhoods and by linking to a wider cycle-friendly network.

Traffic speed reduction and dedicated cycle space is required on busier urban roads, particularly arterial routes into towns and cities. These roads are usually the most direct routes to urban centers but are also themselves frequently the location for many of the services and facilities people wish to access, such as shops, health and education centers and parks. Providing sufficiently wide consistent and continuous dedicated cycle paths also enables safe and social side-by-side cycling along these roads by different generations together. These approaches are being tested in parts of London through the Mini-Holland program. This aims to encourage a more diverse range of people to cycle more safely and more often through provision of better streets and places that encourage positive social interaction – see box 'London's Mini-Holland Program'.

LONDON'S MINI-HOLLAND PROGRAM

Transport for London's (TfL) Mini-Holland program aims to improve streets and public areas along a network of cycle routes as part of the Mayor of London's Healthy Streets agenda (TfL, 2017). In 2013, 18 outer London boroughs were invited to apply for funding from the Mayor of London's 'Mini-Hollands fund'. The boroughs of Enfield, Kingston and Waltham Forest were successful and each was awarded a total of 30 million UK pounds to complete their Mini-Holland program by the end of 2021.

The Waltham Forest Mini-Holland program is perhaps the most advanced and is made up of 13 schemes. It has the bold aim of getting 100% of the population cycling 10% of the time instead of only 10% cycling 100% of the time (Waltham Forest Council, 2017). The program adopts a holistic approach to street management which includes dedicated space to cycle along busier roads that also offers physical protection from motor vehicles; measures to ensure residential streets are more appealing and safer for all; and, enhancements to public space that provide more attractive places for social interaction. Complementary programs include cycle training, cycle road shows, bike maintenance courses, cycle hubs and cycle parking. The borough has also produced a Design Guide providing detailed information on developing 'safer and more expansive infrastructure for people on bikes, children's scooters and pedestrians' (Waltham Forest Council, nd, p. 4).

The potential benefits of the anticipated uptake of cycling (and walking) among residents of different ages, abilities and background are manifold. These include improved health and fitness of residents, improved air quality associated with a reduction in motor traffic, and a boost to the local economy due to increased 'footfall' for existing businesses owing to improvements to the public realm. Early evidence shortly after schemes were implemented appears to demonstrate positive trends towards more cycling and walking and associated improvements in public health. For example, Aldred, Croft, & Goodman (2019) demonstrate that Waltham Forest Mini-Holland program has had a positive impact on cycling and walking activity and perceptions of the local cycling environment. Meanwhile, Dajnak, Walton, Gregor, Smith, & Beevers (2018) have predicted that five-year-olds born in 2013 in Waltham Forest would each live on average for an extra six weeks as a result of the Waltham Forest Mini-Holland program, and furthermore, the borough's 265,000 residents would gain a total of 41,000 years of extra life if air quality continues to improve because of the fall in traffic in residential areas. Further research will undoubtedly need to investigate the extent to which such spaces are also providing family oriented, community-building, social and physical activity, but so far, the signs are positive (Figures 5.1 and 5.2).

FIGURE 5.1 Cyclists pass through a closure in Grove Road, Walthamstow (Mark Kerrison/Alamy Stock Photo)

FIGURE 5.2 Orford Road in Walthamstow is closed to all traffic other than cyclists and local buses between 10 am and 10 pm (Mark Kerrison/Alamy Stock Photo)

Through widespread implementation of Mini-Holland type measures across the UK people of all ages can be encouraged to cycle together and experience positive intergenerational social interaction. There is also need to promulgate the notion of a 'generationally intelligent city' (Biggs & Carr, 2015, p. 108). This concept moves beyond the 'working age city' and recognizes that, 'each generational group will have life projects, arising from the point they have reached in their life course, which give rise to distinctive requirements of urban space' (p. 108). There are implications here for advocates of cycling and committed cyclists who cherish the ability to travel at speed around UK city streets. This fast 'vehicular' cycling in cities is often at the cost of more sedate cycling for all age groups and capabilities. A generationally intelligent use of space will ensure that planning and design does not cater for one type at the expense of the other although compromises will need to be made among 'speedier' cyclists that may require a rethink on the performance of cycling and expectation of travel time.

There is a need to avoid falling into the same trap that purveyors of autopia fell into in the 1960s where the desire for speed and unfettered automobility was often at the expense of quality and civilized urban space. Expectations of cycle speed will need to be addressed that recognize that cycling is not simply about getting from A to B as fast as possible, but also about the reliability of the journey time and the positive social and sensory experience along the way that can make cycling a more desirable activity. Participants in a study of older people's cycling in the UK reported the negative impacts of the behavior of some younger cyclists (Jones et al., 2016). This included the perception that they cycle too fast in city streets and pass too close to other riders. Participants explained their own attempts to cycle in a civilized way by leaving sufficient journey time and interacting with other road users in a courteous and considerate manner.

Enhancing the quality of experience of riding through the city will be important in garnering appreciation of the need to think beyond simple speed. This could be achieved through concerted campaigns promoting a vision of civilized (and not competitive) 'smoother cycling' for young and older alike. It will require a move away from a single 'cycling identity' towards multiple and diverse identities of bicycle users (Handler, 2014). The creation of safe, comfortable spaces for cycling would not require high levels of cycling capability and vigilance. A more forgiving and relaxed environment would enable greater appreciation of the wider surroundings whether historic architecture or the social 'street ballet'. The provision of smooth, consistent surfaces is of course fundamental in allowing riders to be able to look up and appreciate their local surroundings rather than being fixated on road conditions below their wheels. Finally, in order to enhance the aesthetic experience of cycling in urban areas, the urban design profession needs to apply the same attention to cycling as it currently does to walking and ensure that this is not left to the purely functionalist tendency within traffic engineering (Forsyth & Krizek, 2011).

Conclusion

We have outlined how Intergenerational Cycling Zones could be created in the UK that enable more civilized, harmonious and inclusive cycling by all ages. This would create towns and cities that 'are more than simply rat-runs between centers of work, consumption and closed door domesticity' (Biggs & Carr, 2015, p. 109). It implies an abandonment of the current focus on training and improving the capability of riders to survive a system developed for the motor-vehicle. Instead we argue for fundamental change to the system to provide greater spatial justice for all ages and types of cyclist. This has the potential to break down ageist social norms about who can and should cycle, reduce social isolation, and ensure the safety of vulnerable members of the community. Intergenerational Cycling Zones would not only improve connections to activities within neighborhoods and across towns and cities but also make the experience of cycling enjoyable and sociable, therefore providing greater opportunity for active living and positive social contact for all.

Note

1 Public Health England advises that adults aged between 16 and 65 should be at least moderately active for 150 minutes per week (Public Health England, 2014).

References

Aldred, R., Croft, J., & Goodman, A. (2019). Impacts of an active travel intervention with a cycling focus in a suburban context: One-year findings from an evaluation of London's in-progress Mini-Hollands programme. *Transportation Research Part A: Policy and Practice, 123,* 147–169. doi:10.1016/j.tra.2018.05.018.

Aldred, R., & Crosweller, S. (2015). Investigating the rates and impacts of near misses and related incidents among UK cyclists. *Journal of Transport & Health, 2–3*(3), 379–393.

Banister, D. (2008). The sustainable mobility paradigm. *Transport Policy, 15,* 73–80. doi:10.1016/j.tranpol.2007.10.005.

Biggs, S., & Carr, A. (2015). Age- and child-friendly cities and the promise of intergenerational space. *Journal of Social Work Practice, 29*(1), 99–112. doi:10.1080/02650533.2014.993942.

Chan, C. (2013, September 25). *Effective cycling excerpt* [Video file]. Retrieved from www.youtube.com/watch?v=5leVR-xnk6g.

Cycling UK. (n.d.). *Space for cycling campaign.* Retrieved from www.cyclinguk.org/campaign/space-for-cycling.

Dajnak, D., Walton, H., Gregor, S., Smith, J. D., & Beevers, S. (2018) *Air quality: Concentrations, exposure and attitudes in Waltham Forest.* Environmental Research Group, School of Analytical, Environmental and Forensic Sciences, King's College London. Retrieved from https://walthamforest.gov.uk/sites/default/files/WalthamForest_Kings%20Report_310718.pdf.

Forester, J. (1994). *Bicycle transportation: A handbook for cycling transportation engineers.* Cambridge, MA: MIT Press.

Forsyth, A., & Krizek, K. (2011). Urban design: Is there a distinctive view from the bicycle? *Journal of Urban Design, 16,* 531–549.

Handler, S. (2014). *A research & evaluation framework for age-friendly cities.* Stoke-on-Trent: UK Urban Ageing Consortium. Retrieved from www.ageing-better.org.uk/publications/research-evaluation-framework-age-friendly-cities.

Hanson, M. (2015, November 9). *Still here: Reflections on later life – Cycling. I want to be nice to cyclists – But I'm sick of kamikazes.* The Guardian. Retrieved from www.theguardian.com/lifeandstyle/2015/nov/09/cyclists-urban-bikes-kamikaze-safety-pedestrians.

Jones, T., Chatterjee, K., Spinney, J., Street, E., Van Reekum, C., Spencer, B., … Beale, N. (2016). *Cycle BOOM. Design for lifelong health and wellbeing. Summary of key findings and recommendations.* Oxford, UK: Oxford Brookes University.

Pooley, C., Jones, T., Tight, M., Horton, D., Scheldeman, G., Mullen, C., … Strano, E. (2013). *Promoting walking and cycling: New perspectives on sustainable travel.* Bristol, UK: Policy Press.

Public Health England. (2014). *Everybody active everyday: An evidenced based approach to physical activity.* London: PHE.

Pucher, J., & Buehler, R. (2012). *City cycling.* Cambridge, MA: MIT Press.

re:Streets. (n.d.). *Home zone case studies.* Retrieved from www.restreets.org/case-studies/home-zones.

Steinbach, R., Green, J., Datta, J., & Edwards, P. (2011). Cycling and the city: A case study of how gendered, ethnic and class identities can shape healthy transport choices. *Social Science & Medicine, 72,* 1123–1130. doi:10.1016/j.socscimed.2011.01.033.

Transport for London (TfL). (2017). *Healthy streets for London. Prioritising walking, cycling and public transport to create a healthy city.* Retrieved from http://content.tfl.gov.uk/healthy-streets-for-london.pdf.

UK Department for Transport. (2011a). *National travel survey 2010*. London: DfT.

UK Department for Transport. (2011b). *National travel survey 2008–2010*. London: DfT.

UK Department for Transport. (2011c). *Climate change and transport choices: Segmentation study final report*. London: DfT.

UK Department for Transport. (2018). *Transport statistics Great Britain*. London: DfT.

Waltham Forest Council. (2017). *About Mini Holland*. Retrieved from https://www.enjoy walthamforest.co.uk/about-mini-holland/.

Waltham Forest Council. (n.d.). *Waltham Forest Mini-Holland design guide*. Retrieved from www.enjoywalthamforest.co.uk/wp-content/uploads/2015/01/Waltham-Forest-Mini-Holland-Design-Guide.pdf.

6

PLAYFUL PERSPECTIVES AND EVERYDAY SPACES

Imagining a Bus Stop as an Intergenerational Contact Zone

Jason Danely

This chapter looks at the Intergenerational Contact Zone (ICZ) framework as a way to not only transform spaces, but also to enhance the human processes of (re)creating those spaces. These processes include chances to get caught up in enchanting visions, to experiment with risky ideas, and even to make mistakes that help us reflect and recalibrate (Akama, Pink, & Sumartojo, 2018).

Collaboration and inclusion in ICZ design provides a chance to try to see the world from the point of view of a person of a different age, but not only to gain a kind of knowledge about that person's limitations (as in the case of wearing an "age simulation suit", e.g. Kullman, 2016), but also about their capabilities; not according to fixed assumptions about what generations are, but also about how generations *could* be. ICZ can teach us that taking perspective also means playing with perspective.

What do the built environments we move through feel like to a seven-year-old child or an 87-year-old adult? What happens when these perspectives are brought together into a shared cognitive and communicative ecosystem (Hydén, 2014) like an ICZ? I suggest that ethnographic approaches may offer some insights for cultivating this multi-perspective approach.

As a cultural anthropologist specializing in ageing societies and the care of older people, I was immediately drawn to ICZ and the idea of translating notions of well-being, relationality, play, and community into real designs for living. Critics of the "ageing-in-place" model of later life point out that simply staying put does not automatically mean that one retains a healthy sense of community, as people and environments are not bounded and static (Andrews, Evans, & Wiles, 2013, for example). Connecting generations is potentially much more complex (Hopkins & Pain, 2007), but the benefits to health and well-being are clear (Portacolone, 2015). Who wants to age-in-place all alone?

The sense of belonging and mattering that make a place feel like a community is central to the notion of "dwelling," or being-at-home-in-the-world (Ingold, 2000) such that one is capable of caring for and being cared for by others (Zigon, 2014). Yet what happens to a community's ability to dwell when different generations embody and inhabit places differently and exert uneven influence on the work of building those places and the kinds of actions they afford? ICZ approaches suggest a solution through building new designs for living, rethinking fundamental concepts like welfare, well-being, and community in ways that open up new possibilities for dwelling.

American cultural anthropologist Ruth Benedict famously remarked, "The purpose of anthropology is to make the world safe for human differences." Anthropologists take as a fundamental starting point the idea that while each individual composes their own unique world of feelings, memories, and ideas, there are nonetheless ways in which we share in each other's worlds, the same way members of a speech community share a common tongue but do not (usually) speak wholly in unison. Other gestures, like the giving and receiving of gifts, feasting, and dancing are all ways humans have developed to cultivate sustainable connections between culturally distinct communities who might otherwise ignore each other, or even come into direct conflict.

ICZ must also supply a set of norms and conventions that utilize and enhance shared experiences while minimizing the disruptive effects of cultural barriers. But how does one do this without creating something so constrictive that it is only engaging for a select few, or so boring that it fails to enhance life?

Then It Came to Me: Best to Ask the Experts

Which is why I asked my seven-year-old son, Auden, what he would do.

The day after I attended a workshop on ICZ, I told Auden about a group of people I met who wanted to come up with all the ways for grannies and grandpas and little kids and everyone to do more things together.

It was a glorious spring afternoon, the sunlight dappling the pavement with warm golden pools of light. People were brushing past each other running errands, rarely making eye contact as they went on their way. Auden and I walked past a small bus shelter. I pointed to the shelter; an older woman sat with some shopping at her feet, a teenager was leaning on the Plexiglass, thumbing her phone, some bored-looking children waited slumped against their father. Here were several generations brought into proximity by their common mode of transportation, biding their time as they waited for the weekend bus.

"What about a bus stop?" I asked. "How could we redesign a bus shelter to be an Intergenerational Contact Zone?"

Auden loved the idea. "I know what I would do," he said, building my curiosity like a good salesman. "I would make a chess set that could come out of the side, so you could just pull it out."

"Oh, so then you could just start a game with whomever is there, right?"

"You don't have to play, you could just watch too. That would be cool."

I encouraged Auden to think about it more, and he decided that since pieces would get lost, you could have an electronic chess set. His imagination was fired up, and he was starting to get excited about all sorts of features he would add, like holograms and audio announcements of the moves. His vision was full of unencumbered enchantment, possibility rather than practicality, each thought leaping to the next in expansive strides. The idea that an everyday bus shelter could be fun was making him think differently about the place where he lived. I suggested the he draw the idea up (Figure 6.1):

Even in this plain pencil sketch, the scene is lively and people are engaged. For people who use buses to make a regular commute, familiar faces appear every day, each attending to the grim task of waiting without interacting. But this scene was bursting with activity and more importantly, imagination, which seeped out beyond the game itself and into the spaces and relationships all around it. The crude figures were almost dancing with joy; a child who has just made a good move shouts "yes!" as his bearded opponent raises his arms

FIGURE 6.1 Auden's (age 7) proposal for converting a bus stop into an Intergenerational Contact Zone

in defeat. Was this their first game together or one they play every week? Were they neighbors or did they just meet? The drawing captured a moment that invited possibilities not present before.

Auden and I talked about the picture he drew and the kinds of alternate possibilities he thought it afforded. Older people and children could teach each other about new technology and ancient strategy, onlookers might become players as a bus arrives and disrupts a game, children might be more motivated to get out of the house quickly just to use the special bus shelter. Some players might even appear when they do not have a bus to catch. There were chances for encounters both subtle and dramatic. The idea that all of this could happen at the most mundane of public spaces, places that were not explicitly marked for play, didn't seem odd at all from the point of view of a seven-year-old. Now what if some seven-year-olds and some 70-year-olds collaborated with designers and social scientists?

Chess seemed an odd choice to me when Auden came up with the idea (he was not in a chess club or anything), but it seemed like the sort of game adults and children could both enjoy. The game itself involves playing with perspective, envisioning possible futures, seeing lines of movement and counter-movement on a field of imagination. In big cities in the US, I had always seen chess players of different ages and ethnicities enjoying games in public parks. Growing up on the outskirts of Detroit, these scenes always caught my eye when I visited downtown; they stuck with me because they challenged my assumptions about inner-city blight and danger. Chess wasn't something that only belonged to highly educated white adults, but it crossed borders, claimed public spaces and created relationships. Unfortunately, recent years have seen the disappearance of these scenes in the US, with increased policing of the places where children play. Even in parks with built-in chess tables, men have been arrested for occupying a park unaccompanied by children. While some have risen to defend the accused, concerned parents have called for the elimination of chess from parks. While these legal challenges to intergenerational contact reinforce a notion of public moral responsibility for safeguarding the vulnerable, the discussion must not end there; we must also consider how the separation and restriction of generational play-worlds affects the ability for communities to *dwell*, to explore multiple generational identities and positions as a fundamental basis for building empathy and mutual concern (Pain, 2005).

But bringing games into otherwise game-free spaces was only a small part of what I learned from talking to a seven-year-old. For him, imagining an ICZ was all-encompassing project – it was not about simply completing some discrete task, like improving measurable health outcomes – it was about the playfulness of imagining a cultural world where anyone could join in. The insight of the chess bus shelter was that any ICZ could have an element of play that calls us out of our everyday age-segregated worlds and invites us to establish new relationships, unfolding in unexpected ways but without any genuine risk. This is an insight found in the new field of *gerontoludics*, which explores the importance of play in old age. Gerontoludics brings together a growing body of literature that breaks down stereotypes of older people (yes, older people do play video games) and calls our attention to new design principles, like "playfulness over usefulness" (de Schutter & Vanden Abeele, 2015). This is a wonderful lesson to apply to an intergenerational/life-course rich environment.

Search through books on intergenerational place-making and "fun" is rarely mentioned except as a part of "fun-ction" or "fun-ding." Is it too much to aspire to make places not only "age-friendly" but also "age-*fun*"? But having fun comes natural to experts in play, both young and old. What these inter-locutors remind us is the fun of becoming unstuck from socially determined categories of age, place, and well-being. By transforming a utilitarian bus shel-ter into a setting of play, by subverting the default attitude of "killing time" with an activity that is both engrossing and spontaneous, different generations not only tolerate each other's differences, but also thrive because of them.

> The insight of the chess bus shelter may be that ICZ is about play.

References

Akama, Y., Pink, S., & Sumartojo, S. (2018). *Uncertainty and possibility: New approaches to future making in design anthropology*. London: Bloomsbury Academic.

Andrews, G. J., Evans, J., & Wiles, J. L. (2013). Re-spacing and re-placing gerontology: Relationality and affect. *Ageing & Society, 33*, 1339–1373.

de Schutter, B., & Vanden Abeele, V. (2015). Towards a gerontoludic manifesto. *Anthropology & Aging, 36*(2), 112–120. doi:10.5195/aa.2015.104.

Hopkins, P. E., & Pain, R. (2007). Geographies of age: Thinking relationally. *Area, 39*(3), 287–294.

Hydén, L. C. (2014). Cutting brussels sprouts: Collaboration involving persons with dementia. *Journal of Aging Studies, 29*, 115–123. doi:10.1016/j.jaging.2014.02.004.

Ingold, T. (2000). *The perception of the environment: Essays on livelihood, dwelling and skill*. London: Routledge.

Kullman, K. (2016). Prototyping bodies: A post-phenomenology of wearable simulations. *Design Studies, 47*, 73–90. doi:10.1016/j.destud.2016.08.004.

Pain, R. (2005). *Intergenerational relations and practice in the development of sustainable communities*. Durham, UK: International Centre for Regional Regeneration and Development Studies (ICRRDS) Durham University. Retrieved from https://lemosandcrane.co.uk/resources/ICRRDS%20intergenerationalrelations.pdf.

Portacolone, E. (2015). Older Americans living alone: The influence of resources and interge-nerational integration on inequality. *Journal of Contemporary Ethnography, 44*(3), 280–305.

Zigon, J. (2014). An ethics of dwelling and a politics of world-building: A critical response to ordinary ethics. *Journal of the Royal Anthropological Institute, 20*(4), 746–764.

PART II
Parks and Recreation

7

CONNECTING GENERATIONS IN CHINESE URBAN PARKS

Patricia O'Neill

For years I have worked, lived in or visited virtually all of East Asia, a region whose cultures I have deeply loved from the very beginning. Looking back, I vividly remember my first impressions of the beautiful parks I found scattered throughout massive urban landscapes, particularly in China, and how extraordinarily peaceful, even spiritual, they were and still are. Water, flowers, trees and breathtaking views blend with architectural elements and art to create spaces that feel far removed from what surrounds them. These sanctuaries are like magnets pulling people in from all backgrounds and ages, at all times of day and night, in all seasons and for a multiplicity of purposes.

Chinese urban parks, in my view, are perfect Intergenerational Contact Zones (ICZ). Here I discuss two of my favorite parks and one new park to show how these venues develop over time in different environments and how they can be recreated. The first is West Lake, Hangzhou, a majestic setting inspiring contemplation. The second is Green Lake, Kunming, a small bustling park in the city center. The third is Lake Dian, south of Kunming, where a new resort is reinterpreting the traditional Chinese park.

West Lake

West Lake is over 2,000 years old. Originally part of a forest and river leading to the sea, it was a source of irrigation for local farmers. By the Tang Dynasty (618–907) it had joined the Grand Canal from Beijing to Hangzhou. Thereafter, it became part of a transportation hub and a center for tourism and worship. Through many centuries and incarnations, it has remained essentially the same.

The lake covers roughly 6.5 square kilometers. It sits at one end of the sprawling metropolis of Hangzhou, in which 21 million people reside. Its east end abuts a business and shopping district, and beyond that the city. Its other three sides are surrounded by rolling hills with lush vegetation. Pagodas, pavilions and temples rise imposingly from the hills and the lake, each bearing the imprint of the dynasty it emerged from.

A modern road rings the lake, with businesses, hotels and residential districts bordering it. However, it is all set back and does not intrude. Trees, especially weeping willows and peach that bloom profusely in the spring act as a stunning natural barrier. The lake is divided by three causeways featuring traditional arched bridges. Pathways cover both the causeways and the areas they connect so it is possible to walk or bike around the lake, which many people do. Benches and lawns line the pathways, allowing people to stop and rest, talk, eat and enjoy the spectacular views. Three artificial islands, gardens, trees and lotus ponds add to the ambience. Teashops and coffee houses dot the shores. Some offer both indoor and outdoor spaces and may be located in historical buildings, exuding charm. Nearby, there are historical sites and museums for visiting. There are ferries that traverse the lake, mimicking the classical style of ancient Chinese vessels. There are bicycles and boats for hire.

The parks along the lake's perimeter have two principle components: designated open space and pavilions where people can gather. Both contain seating. Benches are built into the sides of the pavilions, and the open spaces incorporate low walls or benches. The pavilions offer shelter from the sun and rain. The open areas are beautifully landscaped and incorporate sculpture. The latter have cultural or historical significance, portraying acclaimed individuals from the past (e.g. Confucius) and people from everyday life like fishermen or scholars. These artistic endeavors are aesthetically pleasing and inviting. People photograph and admire them, and children play on them. From my experience, both the covered and open spaces are continuously filled with people singing, dancing, talking, taking photos, playing musical instruments, mahjong and board games. In short, the spaces invite activity.

Every evening, at one end of the lake there is a 'dancing waters' show with music and lights. There is no cost, and anyone can attend. At the other end there is a (paid) performance entitled 'Impression West Lake', a unique production based on traditional Chinese folklore. The entire performance takes place on a specially designed platform constructed just under the water's surface. Exploring the surrounding hills one can find even more entertainments in the form of tea plantations and villages, cliff carvings and a Buddhist monastery.

Admittedly, West Lake is unique. Its history and natural beauty are renowned. For centuries it has been the subject of painting and poetry, and its gardens have been celebrated throughout Asia. In 2011, UNESCO designated West Lake a World Heritage Site. On its World Heritage List (UNESCO, n.d.), West Lake was described as bearing 'an exceptional testimony to the *cultural tradition of improving landscapes* to create a series of vistas reflecting an *idealized fusion between humans and nature*' (emphasis added). I agree. West Lake is

FIGURE 7.1 Dancing at West Lake

a manifestation of the culture from which it emanates. It harmonizes the natural world and the people who inhabit it. It is a welcoming setting where people of all ages and backgrounds can gather.

Green Lake

In some ways, Green Lake is the antithesis of West Lake. West Lake is ancient, even by Chinese standards. It is large, encircled by hills and famed for its spectacular natural beauty. Although it sits on the edge of a large city, it feels isolated and untouched by the cacophony of the world around it. In contrast, Green Lake is a tiny dot in the middle of Kunming, a city of over 6.5 million people. It adjoins a ring road so that the surrounding buildings and omnipresent traffic are never out of sight. Above it on one side is a low hill, from which Yunnan University's pastoral campus peers down. On another side, modern high-rise apartments stand out above the trees. Elsewhere, there are hotels, shops and restaurants and the Kunming Academy, a former army facility that is now a tourist attraction. The lake is small, only 37 acres, with the park adding 15 more. Both the lake and the park are assimilated into the noisy metropolis, absorbing its energy. Green Lake is alive, vibrant and busy. Yet remarkedly, it feels tucked away. It is a beautiful and tranquil microcosm, not in the contemplative way of West Lake, but in a homely, comfortable way. If West Lake is the aristocrat of lakes, with its stunning vistas and peaceful ambience, Green Lake is the warm fuzzy.

Prior to the middle of the fourteenth century, Green Lake (then called Caihaizi) was a bay on Dianchi Lake, a huge body of water that is now on the outskirts of Kunming. As the waters receded, Green Lake became a freestanding lagoon fed by nine natural springs. It also became a water reservoir for the city. During the Ming Dynasty (1368–1644), the lake became a popular venue for local politicians who constructed pavilions around it. By the seventeenth century it had become a park. Then, in the nineteenth and early twentieth centuries, two causeways were built, one of which is said to be modelled after West Lake's Su Causeway. These divided the lake into five sections and four smaller basins.

In subsequent years, the five sections, joined by traditional Chinese bridges, have become beautiful and purposeful. Weeping willows line the pathways and bridges. The park boasts a temple and two pavilions. One pavilion is for fish viewing. The other is used for exhibitions and mutual interest groups who regularly gather, especially to sing and play musical instruments. There is a basin with lotus flowers, and throughout the park trees have been strategically planted to form mini forests. Located in different areas are cherry trees, cedar and camphor, bamboo and subtropical plants. Interspersed among the trees are activities: a playground, children's amusement park and an opera pavilion where anyone can bring their boombox and sing. There is a pond from which the springs originate and a memorial to the composer of the Chinese national anthem. There are shops and stalls selling food and souvenirs, and aquatic devices for rent, including boats. Since 1985, seagulls have migrated from Siberia to inhabit Green Lake every winter. Vendors sell food to park-goers who feed them. It is a popular activity.

Within the park are intentionally designed open spaces, where people of all ages come to exercise and dance. Like West Lake, this takes many forms, including ballroom dancing, folk dancing, tai chi and calisthenics. However, there is more of it. The activities last all day and into the night, and there are generally two or three groups in the park at any given time. Because the park is small, the groups are more visible and integrated into the environment. Stories are told of how friendships are made, especially among retirees who meet at dance or exercise class. Green Lake is unique in another aspect. Yunnan Province, where Kunming is located, is home to at least ten ethnic minorities. They can be seen in the park wearing their traditional costumes, practicing their time-honored dances. It is a way to maintain their culture, and anyone can join in the dancing.

All of Green Lake is intensely used. It is a quintessential Intergenerational Contact Zone (ICZ). I even experienced my own intergenerational contact there. One afternoon, as I watched Chinese opera, a woman sat down next to me and put her arm around me so her friend could take our photo. Similarly, I have sat and watched the dancing for hours, talking to people and feeling perfectly at home. There is a true community feeling to Green Lake, in an easy unstuffy

FIGURE 7.2 A singing group meeting in a pavilion at Green Lake

way. I suspect this is facilitated by its location and small size in addition to its relaxing environment. It is not only the activities that draw people there. It is a central location where workers can drop by to enjoy their lunch or friends can stroll over the bridges, chatting. Some take tea or a meal in the lovely outdoor restaurants around the periphery. Something wonderful happens when passing under the lanterns overhanging Green Lake's entrance.

Lake Dian (Dianchi Lake)

As mentioned, Green Lake was once part of Lake Dian. The latter is huge, about 300 square kilometers. Even so, it is almost incomprehensible to think of it as stretching all the way to Kunming, a 30-minute drive. The lake is fed by more than 20 rivers, and it is surrounded by hills, including the famous Western Hills of Yunnan Province. Numerous parks are spread along its vast coastline, and

FIGURE 7.3 Tibetans dancing at Green Lake

there is an ethnic village built as a tourist attraction. The lake is situated in a subtropical climate surrounded by a flower growing region. Its location and climate make it an idyllic destination. As a further draw, it has a long history dating to the third century BC, when it was known as the Dian Kingdom.

At one corner of the lake is its newest edition: Ancient Dian Town. It is a purpose-built resort consisting of a wetlands park, marina, hot springs, amusement park, hotels and restaurants, a museum, community center and both residential and senior housing. The infrastructure is built in the architectural style of the ancient Dian Kingdom.

The wetlands, marina and amusement park essentially form one large park adjacent to the lake, and they are the core of the project. The wetlands were once swampland. At considerable cost they were meticulously reconfigured to integrate ponds, native grasses, trees and flowers punctuated by traditional bridges, walkways and pavilions. The marina has boats for hire, and there is

FIGURE 7.4 A view of the new wetlands park at Lake Dian

a central hall where food and tourist information are available. The amusement park had not opened when I was last there in late 2017, and no doubt other features will be added. Thus, it is too soon to predict the success of this modern twist on a Chinese park. The important thing to note that it has followed the classical pattern, as discussed below.

Chinese Urban Parks as ICZ

One particularly outstanding quality of urban Chinese parks is that they do not allow the cities that surround them to intrude into their environment or puncture their tranquility. West Lake is peaceful and meditative. Green Lake is lively but crossing its threshold the city is held at bay. The wetlands feel removed and serene. Their location on the lakeshore separates them from the town, yet they are close enough to walk or cycle to.

Chinese parks share important features. They have beautiful places to walk, with flowers, trees, water and bridges. There are pagodas, pavilions and temples with both secular and spiritual significance, and there is public art. The parks are easy to navigate, especially where there are causeways. There are covered spaces to gather that are architecturally attractive and open spaces to encourage dancing and exercising. There are activities like boating and places to eat. There are dedicated spaces like playgrounds and gardens. There is something for everyone, even if it is just watching. Most of all – and this cannot be emphasized enough – the parks are culturally relevant. They integrate timeless elegance with history through their architecture and landscapes. There is a unifying aspect to this that transcends generations.

What We Can Learn About ICZ from Chinese Urban Parks

West Lake and Green Lake developed in two ways: organically and deliberately. Both the lakes and their surrounding parks reflect the Chinese peoples' love of nature and both have been traditional gathering places throughout their long histories. As UNESCO observed of West Lake, it is a 'testimony to the cultural tradition of improving landscapes …'. These kinds of spaces are an integral and meaningful part of the Chinese culture. Because of that, they will always draw people.

Having said that, none of the lakes and parks discussed above would have endured as ICZ without government intervention. The Grand Canal, the oldest man-made waterway in the world, was instrumental to the early development of West Lake. All three lakes and parks, on a grand scale, have relied and continue to rely on the government for their infrastructure and maintenance. West Lake, for example, has suffered from centuries of floods, droughts and silt deposits, requiring remedial measures such as dams and dikes. It has been regularly dredged since the tenth century. One of its causeways was built from the weeds and dirt dredged from the lake to save it! Centuries ago the government dug wells to feed Green Lake after Lake Dian receded. Dian's wetlands were intentionally researched and designed for environmental correctness, to help abate the lake's ubiquitous pollution problem. On a smaller scale, flowers and trees must be planted, trimmed and nurtured; edifices require upkeep and repairs. Safety must also be ensured through maintenance and policing, and restaurants and shops must be regulated to protect customers. The venues must also be accessible. Roads and public transportation are critical. At Lake Dian, for example, a train line and canal are being built from Kunming to provide greater access, and new roads have already been completed.

There is also a social aspect to this. The spaces must be open to all. At one time both West Lake and Green Lake were retreats for the wealthy. The government transformed them into public venues. Now Lake Dian is deliberately introducing a senior living community, close enough to Kunming for retirees to live near but not with their children. Transportation makes it convenient and easy to access, and there are activities for the entire family to enjoy.

I have chosen to examine the Chinese context. However, these principles could translate into successful ICZ in other locations. I have some suggestions:

1) Create venues around bodies of water with *natural beauty*, then plan and situate spaces within them to take advantage of the views.

2) Create venues that are responsive to the *cultural needs* of the people who are intended to use them.

3) Resources should be made available to maintain, refurbish and enhance the spaces, and to make them accessible and safe. In this regard, the spaces should be open and accessible enough to accommodate equipment like wheelchairs. Paths should be wide, and ramps should replace stairs.

4) Provide 'amenities' that are age neutral. Beautiful lakes and parks with walkways and gardens provide people with a focal point or means to follow their own interests. Not only can they walk, bike, boat, sing, play games, dance and exercise, they can also, for example, bird watch, read, take photographs or videos, enjoy the gardens or just talk. What you don't see at these parks/lakes are sports facilities and other spaces dedicated to a particular age or interest group, or that disrupt the tranquility of the space. That is not to say these are not appropriate uses of ICZ – just somewhere else.

5) Sometimes less is more. The combination of pavilions and open spaces may be enough if they are well thought out and purposeful. Many of the activities taking place at these venues do not require more. The people I see in Chinese parks bring their own equipment. If they share a common interest, people will find ways to identify each other and communicate regardless of their age or background.

6) Resist the temptation to overdevelop. Restaurants, for example, should be small, unobtrusive, blend with the natural environment and kept to a minimum. Importantly, they should not interfere with people's views or quiet enjoyment of the space but enhance it. Likewise, surrounding business and residential areas should be set back enough so they do not intrude.

West Lake and Green Lake have matured over time and are favored by their location. Whether by luck, intention or both, the right balance was achieved. The concept and orientation are worthy of reflection and application elsewhere. Lake Dian may be the blank canvas on which this is proven out.

Reference

UNESCO. (n.d.). West Lake Cultural Landscape of Hangzhou. World Heritage List. New York: UNESCO. Retrieved from https://whc.unesco.org/en/list/1334.

8

URBAN PUBLIC PARKS
Magnets for Social Inclusion and Engagement Across Generations

Cláudia Azevedo

Introduction

Due to the gradual increase of urbanization across the globe, 55% of the world's population now live in urban areas. By 2050 it is expected that more than 68% of the population will live in cities (UN, 2018). These transformations, and the impacts of the processes of globalization, reflect in our relationship with space, time and with others. Castells (2002) argues that the way we organize space is a crucial element for the understanding of contemporary society. In addition, space as such likewise influences our perceptions of time and our relationships within society.

In this particular case I am eager to explore how urban city parks can maximize its potential to generate meaningful possibilities for intergenerational engagement and inclusion. Since city parks are potentially already places for multigenerational usage, with innovative design of the physical landscape we can encourage generations to mingle and socialize, thus, promoting greater intergenerational dialogue and interaction. Normally, city parks are public spaces without any restrictions on access based on individual characteristics. However, if we look carefully at the spaces and activity opportunities in city parks, we may observe some age-based boundaries. For example, children mostly occupy the playgrounds; the sport fields are typically directed to youth and gymnastic equipment and the tea rooms or green spaces with benches tend to attract older people.

The literature broadly recognizes the multiple social benefits of urban public parks such as: its importance for the enhancement of quality of human life, health and well-being (Kabisch & Haase, 2012; O'Brien, Williams, & Stewart, 2010); its potential as meeting places and as places for social interactions

(Swanwick, Dunnett, & Woolley, 2003); and as a therapeutic complement to a society subjected to daily routines and often confined to interior spaces (Chiesura, 2004).

The concept of Intergenerational Contact Zones (Kaplan & Sánchez, 2014; Kaplan, Thang, Sanchez, & Hoffman, 2016; Thang, 2015) brings a new focus to the social benefits associated with urban public parks where the social interactions and cultural meaning-making co-created by the people who inhabit that space help it to become a socially meaningful "place" (Thang & Kaplan, 2013). Intergenerational Contact Zones (ICZ) can be defined as purposeful places that facilitate meetings, interactions and relationships between older adults and younger generations. By designing an ICZ, with the purpose of bringing different generations together – building trust and enhancing relationships, as well as generational inclusion – a more holistic understanding of society can be addressed. The focus of this chapter is on how to move from so-called "intergenerational parks" into parks as ICZ in Portugal. Research on intergenerational parks in Portugal is an innovative area. In this chapter, several examples of intergenerational parks around the country will be described. These descriptions will be drawn upon to serve as a starting point for a subsequent discussion.

Our Three Case Studies

The Infante D. Pedro City Park

Beginning in 2010, the P=LHNS project (Vieira & Guerra, 2012) aimed to redevelop and re-energize the Infante D. Pedro City Park in a way that preserved its biodiversity and social resources to attract and engage a generationally diverse body of park users. Based on the evidence collected, this mixed participatory site redevelopment and evaluation planning process contributed to mutual understanding, improved dialogue and a shared sense of community among citizens of all ages. To this end a collaborative approach was essential in listening to the insights and suggestions of all participants, including those affiliated with local non-profit organizations, the city council, and the local university. It was also a way of giving individual users of the city park a sense of active participation in the project (Keast & Waterhouse, 2006; Pain, 2005; Vieira & Guerra, 2012).

The project's priorities were twofold: (1) to demonstrate and reinforce the intergenerational practices within the city park redevelopment campaign; (2) to gather citizens around a common goal that turned the city park into a place with rich stories, nature, and pro-social, community relationship-building socialization opportunities (Vieira & Guerra, 2012).

The city park was first opened in 1927. In its glory days it was a meeting point and thus, a meaningful place for the entire community (Vieira & Guerra, 2012). Initially, the city park appeared to foster community engagement and promote contact between different generations. A variety of activities

FIGURES 8.1 AND 8.2 Infante D. Pedro Park in Aveiro, Portugal

happened in the space: from sporting events to dating, and meeting friends and family. The P=LHNS project thus aimed to restore the park, drawing on the concerns and insights of the community.

Intergenerational Park of Marvila

In late 2014, the Intergenerational Park of Marvila was built as a result of a partnership with Ateliermob,[1] Warehouse,[2] and University Lusófona. The collaboration of several volunteers and members of the local community

FIGURE 8.3 Intergenerational Park of Marvila in Marvila, Portugal

was vital. Previously, the place was an abandoned site in the middle of an old neighborhood in the center of Marvila. The idea of an intergenerational park emerged from the meetings between local authorities and citizens. The aging community expressed the need of a place to interact with their grandchildren. This park's priorities were thus twofold: (1) to foster intergenerational interactions between grandparents and grandchildren; (2) to redevelop an abandoned site in the center of Marvila.

This space encompasses an open-air amphitheater made of concrete bricks and pinewood on top. At the end of each of the benches there is a ramp that connect the top level of the site to the playground. The playground floor was filled with- pine bark as it is more practical than sand. At the lower end a concrete slab and benches were placed. It is also here where chairs and tables were placed (Ateliermob, & Collective Warehouse, 2015).

Intergenerational Park Quinta Das Lages

The Intergenerational Park Quinta das Lages was built in 2012 as part of the urban renovation of Penafiel. Like in the previous example, this park was conceptualized on an unused and empty space near the local health center. The urban park's central priority was to meet the citizens' expectations of counting on a public space that fostered well-being and leisure for all the generations. In addition, and similar to the

FIGURE 8.4 Intergenerational Park Quinta das Lages, in Penafiel, Portugal

Intergenerational Park of Marvila, both parks were built from scratch to bring different generations together. This park adopted two main objectives: (1) to foster intergenerational interactions by offering a multiplicity of different spaces for that purpose; (2) to redevelop an unused site in the center of Penafiel.

It contains a playground, skates training and fitness areas, a sports ground and an open-air amphitheater. Pedestrian pathways were opened as well as a green area with gardens.

ICZ and Design Implications for Public Parks

To the best of the author's knowledge, in general quality public parks are characterized by: adequate physical access, security measures (lights, wardens, signs, contact points, and self-policing), cleanness, enjoyable landscapes with diverse types of vegetation, green areas, lakes and fountains, wildlife (birds, ducks). It is not difficult to see how these features might transfer readily to those of an ICZ that specifically offers facilities for different age groups (fitness equipment stations, children's playgrounds, tea rooms, amphitheaters, sport and skate grounds). Quality intergenerational parks as ICZ may offer as well a great living experience with opportunities for social interaction with others age groups if they so choose, and can provide real comfort, well-being, and social inclusion in terms of giving support and protection.

It can be argued that an ICZ approach is needed for the interrelated phases of planning, procurement, co-design, construction and delivery of a new generation of public places in Portugal that are able to adapt as we age. The three examples of intergenerational parks described above allow the author to discuss design implications for city parks to become ICZ promoting intergenerational exchange.

The Infante D. Pedro City Park

The refurbishments carried out through the P=LHNS project launched a new site, the so-called Sustainability Park. The three most promising ICZ areas within this refurbished park are: the *Recreational Zone*, the *Walkways* and the *Tea Room*. These three sites are heavily utilized, with people flowing freely in and out of these places. Moreover, these ICZ provide choice in how much and how to interact with others, a characteristic very much appreciated by city park's users.

The *Recreational Zone* is situated near the boundaries of the Sustainability Park, and contains a tennis court, a football field and a skate ground, fitness equipment stations and children's equipment. This is a public space that might bring together four generations (children and younger people, adults and older people). It is a central physical facility for generating multigenerational contact, a prerequisite for intergenerational relationships. Looking to the recreational zone's overall structure, it is clear that the intentional focus was on creating a multigenerational site capable of accommodating a wide range of intergenerational activities. To foster intergenerational interactions and relationships, it might be a novel idea to revisit some of the activities initially developed by the P=LHNS project, such as grandparents' day traditional markets or concerts. The project's report demonstrated a selection of events which achieved good public attendance. This might help to convert the recreational zone into a functional ICZ, as per the tips included in Box 8.1.

BOX 8.1

ICZ as physical design tool to generate intergenerational engagement:

- Accessibility – avoid fences – in this way people can access easily and freely to any of the sport areas.
- Inclusivity – avoid restrictive age signs for any age group.
- Safety – visible pathways and wide visibility of the site in general.
- Proximity – join children's playground and gym equipment for adults in the same area.
- Creativity – multiuse chessboard tables near the recreational area for enjoying food and a giant chessboard.

The *Walkways* along the lake and all around the park have different dimensions (very wide walkways and narrow ones); are mostly flat with some inclines; equipped with streetlights; with numerous benches along the way and at the lake. The walkways are lined with mature trees and a wide range of other flora with the sounds of running water from fountains and birds and ducks. The walkways offer flexible environments to foster intimate encounters, places for meetings by friends or colleagues, spaces for reading and enjoying the landscape as well as jogging.

The *Tea Room* is another place that could be strategically developed to generate more intergenerational contact. After its renewal, the tea room serves as a practice space for the *Beiras'* orchestra and as a storage room for the park's groundskeeping tools. Although it lacks utility, people often said that it was very pleasant listening to music while they walked or played in the park. Transforming the tea room into a more attractive place, with the inclusion of facilities that accommodate a broader range of social activities (including a café with a playground space for caregivers with babies), would be a good strategy for making this section of the park more functional as ICZ.

Intergenerational Park of Marvila

In contrast to the previous example, the Intergenerational Park of Marvila was from the start developed to be an ICZ. Consequently, the park was conceptualized to foster intergenerational exchange following a request from the older residents that demanded a considered place to be with their grandchildren. Moreover, the building of this park was accomplished with support of volunteer architecture students from the University Lusófona resulting in a participatory planning process. Since its development the park has played a significant role in the social life of this ethnic community and has facilitated the growth of community ties.

Despite its small dimensions, this intergenerational park's main feature is its *Amphitheater* with its wooden steps and a beautiful view to the River Tejo. This spot offers the perfect site for fruitful conversations and interactions between people of different generations. Above all, for the development of local communities and social ties – the main goal of this intergenerational park project – people of different generations have to be able to meet to establish relationships. The *Amphitheater* provides opportunities for social interaction, social mixing, and social inclusion of people from different ages and not only for grandparents and grandchildren as previously thought by the local community. This space, situated in Marvila's downtown, offers special conditions for summer evening plays or music concerts.

The *Playground* includes swings and merry-go-rounds. Although, it seems to be used more by children it has no fences and no age limitations. It is an open space, with free access within the intergenerational park. The *Playground* places children in a position to exercise and participate in creative activities. In addition, when parents or grandparents, as it is the case, participate and encourage social interactions during trips to the *Playground*, children benefit from positive adult guidance in social situations.

Intergenerational Park Quinta Das Lages

Like in the previous example the Intergenerational Park Quinta das Lages was designed to be used by all generations. Taking advantage of a natural amphitheater with a magnificent view towards the Cavalum valley, this intergenerational park encompasses a fitness area that can be used by people of all ages, a sports ground and a skate park. Various walkways through an invigorating and diverse green landscape intersect the park. These sites are heavily utilized, with people flowing freely in and out. Similarly to the previous case studies no walls or gates are limiting generational access to the park, a basic main feature to qualify as an ICZ area. The three most active ICZ areas within the Intergenerational Park Quinta das Lages are the *Walkways*, the *Fitness Area*, and the *Promenade*.

The *Walkways* are utilized by people of all ages: runners, older people, mums with strollers, adults and children. These walkways are fully finished-off: there are signals to indicate the way, the lighting is functional and the pavements are walkable. The terrain can accommodate people with reduced mobility including older people and young children. Along the walkways, well cared for vegetation, flower beds and collections of trees are visible. A number of tables and benches, some with plugs and USBs for cell phone charge, can be found along the walkways. People of all ages can interact with each other more naturally. These walkways facilitate a co-existence for children, adults, and older people alike and opportunities for more intense intergenerational interaction if they wish, complemented by various other facilities across the park.

The *Fitness Area* proves to be beneficial since it gives free and public access to exercise facilities and has been identified as an important space to increase physical activity. Often in urban parks exercise equipment is arranged together in one area of the park. However, in this case the *Fitness Area* was arranged in a central area. The exercise equipment may be used by children, adults and older people. It is surrounded by benches and sitting areas as well as connected by walking paths. The playground and the skate ground are nearby, and the entire area has no fences or labelling for age restrictions. The exercise equipment allows large numbers of people to engage in activities that improve musculoskeletal fitness. The equipment stations are free to use and thus accessible to everyone, environmentally friendly as they require no electricity and minimal maintenance, and they can help build a sense of community: the way this urban park displays its equipment stations encourages park users' communication and interactions with strangers.

Finally, the *Promenade* is a balcony that offers a view of both the whole park and the Cavalum valley and acts as the park's main entrance without gates. Because it can be accessed from the street the promenade can be a strategic encounter point. It works like a hub for those who are passing by and those who intentionally want to come to the intergenerational park. Surrounded by benches, it is the perfect spot for formal or informal interactions, such as small conversations, eye contact or just nodding. This part of the intergenerational park can be used almost as if it was a private place.

Conclusion

Looking closely at the three examples of intergenerational parks in Portugal presented above, I note some lessons about ICZ in large city parks.

* Lesson #1: *Be intentional and do not take the success of an ICZ for granted.* Sometimes intentional planning occurs alongside spontaneous and creative initiatives from the community. On one hand, intentional planning is a process subjected to ambivalence, i.e. a range of positive and negative criteria may be at the basis of this changing process. On the other hand, intentionality and meaningfulness are two principles of successful ICZ. The three mentioned examples provided the community with great public spaces, to be utilized by entire community and all generations according to its tagging as "intergenerational parks". These treasured community assets were filled with recreational spaces and activities suitable for families, children and young people as well as older people. Nevertheless, a straightforward correlation between the intergenerational parks' focus and the intensity of the intergenerational relationships actually taking place cannot be made so far, despite initiatives already carried out.

* Lesson #2: *Utilize participatory methods for getting multigenerational community voices and promoting social cohesion.* As Vieira and Guerra (2012) have argued, community residents and local organizations took note of the growing public and private interest and commitment to improving the park, and this contributed to their enthusiasm to participate in the planning process and advocate on behalf of efforts to restore the park as a community-wide gathering place. Similarly, the Intergenerational Park of Marvila organized several meetings between the local authorities and the citizens. Those meetings resulted in the former abandoned site giving birth to the park – a common need.

* Lesson #3: *Keep in place mechanisms for community participation even after the park's planning and (re-)development processes have been completed.* Through community interviews (Vieira & Guerra, 2012) conducted after (re-)developing several areas of the Infante D. Pedro City Park and two additional adjacent parks, it was determined that there were some features of these parks (e.g. poor lighting and limited seating areas) that hindered some

residents from frequenting these spaces. The Intergenerational Park of Marvila keeps fostering community participation through enhanced volunteer work from the School of Architecture nearby. Seeking and heeding this additional community feedback is vital for realizing the vision of local parks as sustainable local intergenerational engagement hubs.

Notes

1 Ateliermob is a Portuguese multidisciplinary platform which develops projects, ideas, and research within architecture, landscape, design, and urbanism.
2 Warehouse is a Portuguese architecture and art collective founded in 2013. Warehouse develops participatory architecture projects in the cultural and social spheres.

References

Ateliermob & Collective Warehouse. (2015). *Project Info – #C018 – PARQUE INTERGERACIONAL DE MARVILA*. Lisboa. Retrieved from http://warehouse.pt/projects/parque-intergeracional-de-marvila-lisboa/.

Castells, M. (2002). *A sociedade em rede*. Lisboa: Fundação Calouste Gulbenkian.

Chiesura, A. (2004). The role of urban parks for the sustainable city. *Landscape and Urban Planning, 68*, 129–138. doi:10.1016/j.landurbplan.2003.08.003.

Kabisch, N., & Haase, D. (2012). Green spaces of European cities revisited for 1990–2006. *Landscape and Urban Planning, 110*(1), 113–122. doi:10.1016/j.landurbplan.2012.10.017.

Kaplan, M., & Sánchez, M. (2014). Intergenerational programmes. In S. Harper & K. Hamblin (Eds.), *International handbook on ageing and public policy* (pp. 367–383). Cheltenham, UK: Edward Elgar.

Kaplan, M., Thang, L. L., Sanchez, M., & Hoffman, J., (Eds.). (2016). *Intergenerational contact zones – A compendium of applications*. University Park, PA: Penn State Extension. Retrieved from https://aese.psu.edu/extension/intergenerational/articles/intergenerational-contact-zones.

Keast, R., & Waterhouse, J. (2006). Participatory evaluation: The missing component in the social change equation?. *Strategic Change, 15*(1), 23–35. doi:10.1002/jsc.744.

O'Brien, L., Williams, K., & Stewart, A. (2010). *Urban health and health inequalities and the role of urban forestry in Britain: A review*. Melbourne: The University of Melbourne and Forest Research.

Pain, R. (2005). *Intergenerational relations and practice in the development of sustainable communities*. Thornaby, UK: Durham University, International Centre for Regional Regeneration and Development Studies. Retrieved from https://lemosandcrane.co.uk/resources/ICRRDS%20intergenerationalrelations.pdf.

Swanwick, C., Dunnett, N., & Woolley, H. (2003). The nature, role and value of green space in towns and cities – An overview. *Built Environment, 29*(2), 94–106. doi:10.2148/benv.29.2.94.54467.

Thang, L. L. (2015). Creating an intergenerational contact zone: Encounters in public spaces within Singapore's public housing neighborhoods. In R. Vanderbeck & N. Worth (Eds.), *Intergenerational spaces* (pp. 17–32). London, UK: Routledge. doi:10.1080/15350770.2016.1229535.

Thang, L. L., & Kaplan, M. (2013). Intergenerational pathways for building relational spaces and places. In G. D. Rowles & M. Bernard (Eds.), *Environmental gerontology: Making meaningful places in old age* (pp. 225–251). New York City: Springer Publishing Company.

UN (United Nations). (2018). *World urbanization prospects: The 2018 revision.* New York: UN Department of Economic and Social Affairs, Population Division. Retrieved from www.un.org/development/desa/publications/2018-revision-of-world-urbanization-prospects.html.

Vieira, S., & Guerra, S. (2012). Revitalizing city parks through intergenerational activities: The Park *Infante Dom Pedro*, city of Aveiro, Portugal. *Revista Temática Kairós Gerontologia, 15*(1), 135–152. Retrieved from https://revistas.pucsp.br/index.php/kairos/article/viewFile/12837/9316.

9

INTERGENERATIONAL GARDENING ON URBAN ROOFTOPS

The Example of the "Play and Grow" Program in Hong Kong

Tanja Sobko and Louise Chawla

Benefits of Rooftop Gardens

A large body of research establishes the value of regular access to nature for all ages (van den Bosch & Bird, 2018). For children, opportunities to play and learn in nature, in contrast to hardscape built settings, have been associated with less physiological stress, more effective coping with stressful life events, better general health and mental health, healthier weight, better balance and coordination, more positive moods, greater working memory, more focused attention, better impulse control, and more creative and cooperative play (see reviews by Chawla, 2015; Kuo, Barnes, & Jordan, 2019; Tillmann, Tobin, Avison, & Gilliland, 2018; Wells, Jimenez, & Mårtensson, 2018). A history of childhood play in nature is related to active care for the natural world later in life and a greater likelihood that people will seek out nature for recreation as adults (Chawla & Derr, 2012; D'Amore & Chawla, in press; Wells & Lekies, 2012). In residential settings in particular, nearby nature is associated with better health and cognitive functioning, psychological well-being, more social interaction and connection, and more physical activity for all ages (van den Berg et al., 2015; Wells & Rollings, 2012). The elderly show specific benefits like reduced risks of mortality and depression, longer life spans, lower stress, more social contacts with friends, less loneliness, and better self-perceived general health when they have nature near their homes (Banay et al., 2019; Takano, Nakamura, & Watanabe, 2002; Wang et al., 2017), and access to gardening and time to rest in a garden (Ottosson & Grahn, 2005; Simons, Simons, McCallum, & Friedlander, 2006; van den Berg, van Winsum-westra, de Vries, & van Dillen, 2010).

Given the many benefits from contact with nature, the urban planner Timothy Beatley (2012, 2016) recommends a Nature Pyramid, or "diet" of regular exposure to nature experiences. (See Figure 9.1.) It rests on a foundation of daily interactions with nature at home and in the local neighborhood through access to green yards, gardens, street trees, local parks, and nature in schools and workplaces. Beatley recommends visits to larger regional parks once a week, more extensive areas like national parks on a monthly basis, and immersion in nature during annual vacations. He notes important ecosystem benefits that nature also provides for cities, such as mitigating heat, capturing storm water runoff, and harboring biodiversity; but his concept of "biophilic cities" emphasizes the value of creating places that promote people's emotional connection to nature, where elements of nature foster well-being and people become motivated to care for the natural world (Beatley, 2016).

Although Beatley (2012, 2016) recommends experiences of nature at different scales, many populations are dependent on nature in their immediate neighborhoods. This is commonly the case for children, the elderly, people with disabilities, and people with limited financial resources, who often lack the independent mobility and means to reach regional parks, much less more distant destinations. Yet in densely populated cities where there is intense

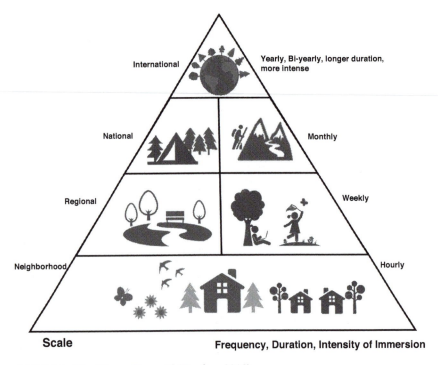

Scale   **Frequency, Duration, Intensity of Immersion**

FIGURE 9.1 The Nature Pyramid (Beatley, 2012)

competition for space, integrating nature into people's daily lives can be a great challenge. Since ancient times, one of the sites where nature has been introduced into cities has been rooftop gardens. Once a feature of palaces for the aristocracy and the great homes of wealthy families, rooftop gardens expanded during the Industrial Revolution as an escape from crowded, hot and dirty streets below (Hanson & Schmidt, 2012). In the early 20th century, rooftop gardens began to bloom on progressive tenement developments, settlement houses, and church centers, to provide access to sunshine, fresh air and beauty for children in day nurseries and kindergartens and peaceful rest for working-class families (Anonymous, 1913). With the invention of air conditioning, the use of rooftop gardens declined; but since the introduction of new technologies in the 1970s, such as lightweight soil and better waterproof barriers, they have rapidly multiplied across the world (Hanson & Schmidt, 2012).

This chapter features the "Play&Grow" early environmental education program in Hong Kong. It reflects the expanding urban garden movement in Hong Kong, which sees roofs, balconies, and other concrete spaces as both a challenge and opportunity to bring nature and healthy eating and activity into the city. The program encourages caregivers, who are often grandparents, to create hubs of nature on the closest available rooftops, where their children and grandchildren come to play, grow, and learn. The gardens serve as Intergenerational Contact Zones (ICZ) as well as places for environmental appreciation and learning. They provide easy access to nature for both young and old, in a city that is often named as a true example of a concrete habitat[1], and they provide time and space for families to experience and enjoy nature together.

When Sobko, Jia, and Brown (2018) interviewed parents of preschool children about family opportunities to connect with nature, parents reported that going outside meant venturing into noisy built streets with heavy traffic. Loss of access to outdoor play in nature is aggravated by the fact that many caregivers emphasize academic extra-curricular pursuits, even for young children. The result is a "chicken or egg" paradox: Are caretakers not motivated to take their children to play outside in concrete settings, or is the absence of children outside leading to a decrease in government motivation to build natural green spaces? Under these conditions, the prevalence of sedentary lifestyles and obesity among Hong Kong children has become a prominent public health concern (Sobko, Tse, & Kaplan, 2016). A growing "Children and Nature" movement is finding solutions of its own, bringing nature to spaces where children are, and reconnecting families to nature.

Not only children, but also adults have much to lose by the diminishing availability of green spaces. For all ages, roofs represent an important option for city greening. In residences, green roofs make nature quickly accessible – just a staircase or elevator ride away. They are remote from the noise, heavy particulate pollution, traffic, and other risks at street level. Nature in the living environment not only brings benefits for physical and mental health (van den

Berg et al., 2015; Wells & Rollings, 2012); but also people with nature near their residence report more social integration and social support (Kweon, Sullivan, & Wiley, 1998). When rooftop greening includes community gardens and children's gardens, it can support intergenerational relationships, environmental learning, and healthy eating (Litt et al., 2011; Mayer-Smith, Bartosh, & Peterat, 2007).

Play&Grow Program

The Play&Grow program, locally developed in Hong Kong, is modeled on other evidence-based preschool interventions to encourage healthy lifestyles for families with young children (Sobko et al., 2016). Other programs have emphasized healthy eating and physical activity; but in recognition of the growing evidence that access to nature promotes well-being, Play&Grow adds a third novel component, connectedness to nature. Everybody has much to gain from new rooftop green spaces that welcome families and provide interactive nature experiences. The program therefore relies on the active participation of parents, grandparents, and other relatives. It began as a pilot study in 2014 with funding from a Hong Kong university. With further support from the Hong Kong Government General Research Fund, it was expanded into a randomized control trial of 240 Hong Kong families with children aged two to five. The program is currently being disseminated to the entire Hong Kong community and supported by the Hong Kong Environment and Conservation Fund. For a period of ten weeks, participating families meet for weekly one-hour sessions that introduce them to information about healthy diets and eating habits, the importance of physical activity, and games that promote discovery and multisensory awareness of nature. Some nature activities include creating gardens and growing plants. (See Table 9.1.) A detailed manual and resource kit guides session planning.

At the time of this writing, 27 community centers across 18 districts have been involved in disseminating the program. The program takes a holistic approach to nature education by integrating families in every part of the experience. Families usually find roofs on the buildings in which they live or others nearby to use as a gardening space. As building roofs are most often underused, the building management welcomes the development of this space. Engaged grandparents usually cover the minimal costs of converting the space (garden construction, such as getting soil, moving materials to the roof, constructing the garden beds and fence). The program is sustained by trained instructors and volunteers under the supervision of the program designers, including the Director and Principal Investigator of the Play&Grow program. The initial research round targeted 100 families. This has grown to over 2000 families who have benefited from behavioral changes and healthier lifestyle habits and involved more and more grandparents.

TABLE 9.1 Details of the P&G Curriculum

Session	Activities during the program
1	*Introduction of environmental education program*: Introduce environmentally friendly ideas, healthy lifestyle and child safety practices. Outdoor nature play aiming to increase exposure to nature: such as active nature games, discovering nature, practicing awareness of sounds, touch, smells, temperature, etc.
2	*Environmental education and healthy eating*: Learn about and appreciate the origin of food. The appropriate amounts of food to consume for different ages of children. Develop parents' understanding regarding basic nutrition principles. Outdoor nature play aiming to increase exposure to nature.
3	*Environmental education and active play*: Learn strategies to promote active outdoor play. Safety issues that caregivers should be aware of when participating in active outdoor activities. Outdoor nature play aiming to increase exposure to nature.
4	*Environmental education and sleeping time*: Explain how sleep can be influenced through increased exposure to nature. Outdoor nature play aiming to increase exposure to nature.
5	*Environment and fussy eating*: Discuss parental day-to-day feeding habits and tricky scenarios, such as fussy eaters and food rejection, and the most appropriate way to introduce new food into children's diets. Outdoor nature play aiming to increase exposure to nature.
6	*Environment and limit setting*: Discuss positive family values, including responsibilities in the family, care for nature, and power struggle. Outdoor nature play aiming to increase exposure to nature.
7	*Environmental awareness and fun with food*: Introduce ways to involve children while cooking. Explain the concept and the significance of parental modelling on sedentary behaviors and physical activity. Outdoor nature play aiming to increase exposure to nature.
8	*Environmental awareness and healthy habits*: Rules and routines while having outdoor activities in nature. Throwing, catching, and bouncing skills. Outdoor nature play aiming to increase exposure to nature.
9	*Nature and me*: Run & Fun: The safe way to perform physical activity in nature. Discuss appropriate parental skills required for creating/identifying a safe outdoor space for activities in a natural environment. Outdoor nature play aiming to increase exposure to nature.
10	*Farewell and graduation*: Summarize the entire program and farewell. Outdoor nature play aiming to increase exposure to nature.

The program's curriculum takes advantage of the available natural environment to integrate participants into the benefits of healthy eating and the joys of play in nature. Increasing access to nature through rooftop gardening and play has been a major component in the program's development and success. During the ten-week curriculum, each session includes 15 minutes devoted to education about a healthy diet, physical activity, or the value of time in nature, along with 30 minutes of indoor and outdoor nature-related activities, such as searching for nature's treasures or playing with objects in nature. In these ICZ, key interactions involve an instructor-led activity, homework, and caregiver-child activities.

Grandparents as Companions in Wonder

The program relies on the initiative and dedication of caregivers, who are often grandparents in participating families. Grandparents have both time and patience to develop garden environments and engage in learning activities with young children. They often project a sense of wonder for the natural environment: they know how to respond to it and express their feelings for it (See Figures 9.2 and 9.3). They notice changes in nature: and by paying close attention to something in nature, they communicate to children that it has

FIGURE 9.2 One of the young participants, Hayden Wong, curiously explores the worms in the compost bin. Figure courtesy of Kelvin Wong and Tammy Lee

FIGURE 9.3 Sophie Ho, one of our young participants and her grandfather, Mr Hon are appreciating the pattern of a dried leaf in the nature. Figure courtesy of Kathy Hon

significant value (D'Amore & Chawla, in press). They talk about nature: and their narratives encourage children to turn their innate sense of empathy for other living things into understanding sympathy (D'Amore & Chawla, in press). From the physical perspective of a very young child (1 meter above the ground), bugs and butterflies are huge, flowers can be smelled without bending down, and even small stones must be picked up with both hands. Grandparents are well qualified to serve as children's "companions in wonder" as they engage with nature together at this scale (Carson, 1956; Dunlap & Kellert, 2012).

Grandparents, at least in Hong Kong, are inventive when it comes to reusing materials. For example, they turned wooden boxes from dried seafood into planters, saved water from washing cooking rice to water the plants, and upcycled red envelopes used for gifts of money for Chinese New Year into seed bookmarks that can be planted because the paper contains seeds. They showed children how to reduce waste and see creative new possibilities in materials. Grandparents also played a substantial role in collaboratively funding the gardens.

Lessons Learned and Evidence of Program Benefits

Over the course of the program, some unanticipated challenges, such as inclement weather and issues with garden security, influenced the practical design and management of the garden spaces as they have expanded across Hong Kong. These challenges and practical design tips are listed in Box 9.1 and Box 9.2, modified from Pryor (2016).

BOX 9.1 DEALING WITH UNANTICIPATED CHALLENGES

1. Security issues (e.g. preventing children from climbing wall fences): Place planters close to walls to prevent children from getting near the edge.
2. Elderly participants with walking difficulties: Place strips of coarse tape on slippery surfaces.
3. Typhoons/strong winds: Install hooks anchored to walls to secure planters.
4. Grandparents' education differs from parents': Make a checklist of aims that everyone agrees to follow in the garden. Additional instructions to the grandparents are often given as well to promote synchronicity in educational goals between grandparents and parents.
5. Holidays: Establish a volunteer calendar to ensure that the garden is always tended.

BOX 9.2 PRACTICAL DESIGN TIPS

1. Obtain the floorplan of the roof from facility management staff.
2. Locate and identify potential areas that can be used as the rooftop garden.
3. Locate areas that cannot be used for the garden due to structural limitations.
4. Identify and assess the structural loadbearing capacity, waterproofing, and drainage of the roof.
5. Consider the environment for growth of crops on the rooftop garden (e.g. wind, sun exposure, shade).
6. Check for access points to necessities (e.g. water and electricity) on the rooftop.
7. Identify potential safety, hygiene, or pest issues (if any).

The overall success of the program is evidenced in the overwhelmingly positive response of the participants. Participants remarked on the "practical nature of the program" and emphasized the value of the program for the "whole family." An assessment of the Play&Grow pilot study demonstrated significant positive changes in participants on a number of outcomes, including healthier food habits and an increase in caregiver physical activity (Sobko et al., 2016).

The Play&Grow program promotes positive interactions between parents, grandparents, and their children.

Opportunities for Replication and Extension

The success of the Play&Grow program suggests that connecting families with young children to nature can be an effective way of working toward other goals as well, including healthy eating and physical activity. It builds upon the large and steadily growing body of evidence of benefits from engagement with nature for all ages (van den Bosch & Bird, 2018). Its curriculum has been tested over time; and with adaptations to reflect different conditions of nature and different cultures of child-rearing and diet in other parts of the world, it is ripe for replication by other organizations that seek to promote healthy family lifestyles. It has shown that it is possible to bring nature into families' lives in even one of the most densely populated, concrete urban areas of the world, by taking advantage of opportunities to create small-scale, affordable gardens high above the street. Research on the importance of access to nature for the well-being of all ages indicates that introducing nature into densely populated cities like Hong Kong is an urgent direction for public health as well as urban planning and policy.

In Hong Kong, there is potential to extend the Play&Grow model to rooftop farms and larger gardens and more mixed intergenerational groups that include older children and adolescents, in addition to young children, parents, and grandparents. Pryor (2016) did a review of Hong Kong roof farms, based on their structural and operational principles (See Table 9.2). Due to the small scale of current Play&Grow gardens, they are not a source of food production: but if the program were extended to rooftop farms, it would open new curriculum possibilities for children's learning about agricultural ecosystems and where food comes from, and add valuable harvests of fresh fruits and vegetables to families' diets. Research shows that children in gardening programs are more likely to eat fresh fruits and vegetables and engage in physical activity (Blair, 2009; Wells, Myers, & Henderson, 2014).

Grandparents are important resources for achieving these goals. Many grew up in rural areas or less dense urban conditions, with experience working in family gardens. They often know traditional practices for sustainable small-scale farming and healthy food preparation. They have much to contribute to current initiatives to restore local agricultural systems. In conceptualizing rooftop green spaces as Intergenerational Contact Zones, we see new possibilities for passing these rich traditions on from one generation to another. Such

TABLE 9.2 Different types of roof gardens that exist in Hong Kong, that can be used as ICZ (Pryor, 2016)

Project type	Building Types	Description
Occupier-led	Residential, cooperatives, and local industries	Interest groups, which are formed by the residents/tenants of the building and estate management staff, construct and manage day-to-day operations of the roof garden.
Owner-led	Cooperatives and local industries	Owners of a building construct the roof garden as part of their business initially, while the residents/tenants of the building and estate management staff construct and manage day-to-day operations of the roof garden.
Institutional community group	Institutional: e.g. schools, student halls, hospitals, and care homes	Institutions' management teams/staff develop and construct the rooftop garden initially, while institutional community groups consisting of the building's occupants, such as students and patients, run the garden.
Commercial enterprise	Rented corporate or industrial	Private commercial organizations (profit-making) construct the garden, and it is operated by their members.
Community social enterprise	Rented or sponsored corporate or industrial	Non-profit communities/social organizations construct the garden, and it is operated by their members.

exchanges also enrich and animate the lives of older adults, as they get the chance to experience, up close, the spirit of wonder that young children bring to ordinary – yet still extraordinary – miracles like the sprouting of a seed.

Note

1 Green space accounts for 70% of greater Hong Kong, but most of it lies on the city's periphery. Seven million people live on less than a third of the city's area of 1104 square kilometers, with little exposure to nature.

References

Anonymous. (1913). Gardens in the air where the children flourish with the flowers. *Craftsman*, July, 253–257.

Banay, R. F., James, P., Hart, J. E., Kubzansky, L. D., Spiegelman, D., Okereke, O. I., ... Laden, F. (2019). Greenness and depression incidence among older women. *Environmental Health Perspectives*, *127*(2). doi:10.1289/EHP1229.

Beatley, T. (2012). *Exploring the nature pyramid*. Retrieved from www.thenatureofcities. com/2012/08/07/exploring-the-nature-pyramid/.

Beatley, T. (2016). *Handbook of biophilic city planning and design*. Washington, DC: Island Press.

Blair, D. (2009). The child in the garden. *Journal of Environmental Education, 40*(2), 15–38. doi:10.3200/JOEE.40.2.15-38.

Carson, R. (1956). *The sense of wonder*. New York: Harper & Row.

Chawla, L. (2015). Benefits of nature contact for children. *Journal of Planning Literature, 30*(4), 433–452. doi:10.1177/0885412215595441.

Chawla, L., & Derr, V. (2012). The development of conservation behaviors in childhood and youth. In S. Clayton (Ed.), *The Oxford handbook of environmental and conservation psychology* (pp. 527–555). Oxford, UK: Oxford University Press.

D'Amore, C., & Chawla, L. (in press). Significant life experiences that connect children with nature: A research review and applications to a family nature club. In A. Cutter-Mackenzie-Knowles, K. Malone, & E. Barratt Hacking (Eds.), *Research handbook on childhood nature*. New York: Springer.

Dunlap, J., & Kellert, S. R. (Eds.). (2012). *Companions in wonder: Children and adults exploring nature together*. Cambridge, MA: The MIT Press.

Hanson, B., & Schmidt, S. (Eds.). (2012). *Green roofs and rooftop gardens*. Brooklyn, NY: Brooklyn Botanic Garden.

Kuo, M., Barnes, M., & Jordan, C. (2019). Do experiences with nature promote learning? Converging evidence of a cause-and-effect relationship. *Frontiers in Psychology, 10*. doi:10.3389/fpsyg.2019.00305.

Kweon, B. S., Sullivan, W. C., & Wiley, A. (1998). Green common spaces and the social integration of inner-city older adults. *Environment and Behavior, 30*, 823–851.

Litt, J. S., Soobader, M., Turbin, M. S., Hale, J., Buchenau, M., & Marshall, J. A. (2011). The influences of social involvement, neighborhood aesthetics and community garden participation on fruit and vegetable consumption. *American Journal of Public Health, 101*, 1466–1473.

Mayer-Smith, J., Bartosh, O., & Peterat, L. (2007). Teaming children and elders to grow food and environmental consciousness. *Applied Environmental Education and Communication, 6*(1), 77–85.

Ottosson, J., & Grahn, P. (2005). A comparison of leisure time spent in a garden with leisure time spent indoors. *Landscape Research, 30*, 23–55.

Pryor, M. (2016). *Edible roof: A guide to productive rooftop gardening*. Hong Kong: MCCM Creations.

Simons, L. A., Simons, J., McCallum, J., & Friedlander, Y. (2006). Lifestyle factors and risk of dementia. *The Medical Journal of Australia, 184*(2), 68–70.

Sobko, T., Jia, Z., & Brown, G. (2018). Measuring connectedness to nature in preschool children in an urban setting and its relation to psychological functioning. *PLOS One, 13*(11), e0207057. doi:10.1371/journal.pone.0207057.

Sobko, T., Tse, M., & Kaplan, M. (2016). A randomized controlled trial for families with preschool children – Promoting healthy eating and active playtime by connecting to nature. *BMC Public Health, 16*, 505. doi:10.1186/s1288-016-3111-0.

Takano, T., Nakamura, K., & Watanabe, M. (2002). Urban residential environments and senior citizens' longevity in megacity areas: The importance of walkable green spaces. *Journal of Epidemiology and Community Health, 56*(12), 913–918.

Tillmann, S., Tobin, D., Avison, W., & Gilliland, J. (2018). Mental health benefits of interactions with nature in children and teenagers: A systematic review. *Journal of Epidemiology and Community Health, 72*(10). doi:10.1136/jech-2018-210436.

van den Berg, A. E., van Winsum-westra, M., de Vries, S., & van Dillen, S. M. E. (2010). Allotment gardening and health: A comparative survey among allotment gardeners and their neighbors without an allotment. *Environmental Health, 9,* 74.

van den Berg, M., Wendel-Vos, W., van Poppel, M., Kemper, H., van Mechelen, W., & Maas, J. (2015). Health benefits of green spaces in the living environment: A systematic review of epidemiological studies. *Urban Forestry and Urban Greening, 14,* 806–816. doi:10.1016/j.ufug.2015.07.008.

van den Bosch, M., & Bird, W. (Eds.). (2018). *Oxford textbook of nature and public health.* Oxford, UK: Oxford University Press.

Wang, D., Lau, K. K., Yu, R., Wong, S. Y. S., Kwok, T. T. Y., & Woo, J. (2017). Neighbouring green space and mortality in community-dwelling elderly Hong Kong Chinese. *BMJ Open, 7*(7), e015794. doi:10.1136/bjmopen0-20160-015794

Wells, N. M., Jimenez, F. E., & Mårtensson, F. (2018). Children and nature. In M. van den Bosch & W. Bird (Eds.), *Oxford textbook of nature and public health* (pp. 167–176). Oxford, UK: Oxford University Press.

Wells, N. M., & Lekies, K. (2012). Children and nature: Following the trail to environmental attitudes and behaviors. In J. L. Dickinson & R. Bonney (Eds.), *Citizen science* (pp. 201–213). Ithaca, NY: Comstock Publishing Associates.

Wells, N. M., Myers, B. M., & Henderson, C. R. (2014). School gardens and physical activity. *Preventive Medicine, 69,* S27–S33.

Wells, N. M., & Rollings, K. A. (2012). The natural environment in residential settings: Influences on human health and function. In S. Clayton (Ed.), *The Oxford handbook of environmental and conservation psychology* (pp. 509–523). Oxford, UK: Oxford University Press.

10

FORESTS AS INTERGENERATIONAL CONTACT ZONES

Teaching About and Experiencing Forests Through Historical Interpretation

Sanford S. Smith and Matthew Kaplan

Introduction

Environmental educators, like all educators, face the challenge of introducing their subject matter in relevant and compelling ways. This chapter highlights a *historical interpretation through planned re-enactments approach* for building youth interest, knowledge, and exploration of forest landscapes and their history. Forest stewards, educators, and volunteers – often older adults – create on-site scenes and vignettes drawn from examples of real historical figures. These figures then interact with young visitors in ways that help them better understand the values, needs, knowledge, and identities of those who influence how forests emerge and are sustained over time.

The historical re-enactment approach to teaching is not new; it is used widely on location at many historic sites around the world. However, the use of this method to teach about forests and forest history has not been widely used. But why not? Forests provide alluring "windows into the past." Forests covered much of the North American continent prior to and during European settlement, played a critical role in building the nation, and were a key focus of the North American conservation movement in the late 19th and early 20th centuries. The things we see in forests today, such as species composition, tree age structure, and biological diversity, are the direct result of events and practices that occurred on each specific site in the past.

Using historical interpretation to portray common folk who once lived and worked in the "woods" can be effective and engaging for a variety of audiences and provides opportunities for intergenerational learning. Stories about past conditions, practices, forest industries, and people's lives can be told in compelling ways. And, it can be used to contrast what once was, with what is today and what might be in

FIGURE 10.1 Learning and touching forest history through an intergenerational historical interpretation through re-enactment program in Central Pennsylvania forests. Photo: Andrew Gapinski

the future. Sensitivity to local and national feelings about historical events or eras is essential when using this method. While this chapter only addresses the use of a re-enactment method to teach and convey cultural practices, understandings and past human life in the context of the forest environment, others stress the importance of practicing ethical and cautious judgement when re-enacting historical situations that might invoke strong emotions about past violence, tragedies, or human abuse of others (Roos, Hoffman, & van der Westhuizen, 2013).

In this re-enactment approach, the engagement of older generations is both literal and implied. Senior volunteers with an interest in history and youth development apply their interests constructively, while historic re-enactments of older adult characters from the past challenge youth to think about how differently people once viewed and used forests. The forest, then, becomes a milieu, or an Intergenerational Contact Zone (ICZ), for gaining insight into the historic context of forests. Through planned and unplanned intergenerational exchanges, youth gain an understanding about forests as places of value, with their own history and important ecological roles and interrelationships with human settlement.

Examples of the Living History/Re-enactments Approach

Some examples of individuals using this method include an elder gentleman who re-enacts a colonial "long hunter" from the French and Indian War era.

He demonstrates forest survival methods and hunting as a way of subsistence, in the days of year-round hunting without wildlife protection laws or environmental regulations. Another, individual re-enacts a "collier" who made charcoal from wood in the forest to be used as fuel in iron furnaces and by blacksmiths in the mid-19th century. He describes his everyday work in the forest and the annual cycle of cutting wood through the winter months and making charcoal from early spring until autumn. His work often cleared the forestland for future farms or second growth forests. A third individual, portraying a pioneer woman, sits on a log stool in the woods and bakes corn bread in a cast iron Dutch oven using natural charcoal for fuel. She shares how early settlers relied on corn for their survival, and how the limited diets in the past were supplemented with edible forest plants, meat from wild animals, and mushrooms. Lastly, a younger individual, who is also a professional folk musician, impersonates a "river rat" who rafted lumber down rivers from remote forest areas during the US Civil War. Between singing historical and original tunes, he demonstrates how primitive hand tools were used to construct huge wooden rafts – some over 200 feet long by 70 feet wide (60 x 21 meters) – and relates how rivers were the only way to transport logs to sawmills from remote forest areas.

Each of these examples teaches about forests' past and how they were used by people, and then generates discussion about present-day environmental conditions. In doing so, the re-enactors help participants understand the values, needs, and identities of those who lived or worked in forests, and gain insights into the modern concepts of forest sustainability, protection, and management. The individual re-enactors' motivations are built upon the conceptualization that the future of forests hinge on the intergenerational transfer of traditional and ecological values and understanding. The re-enactors also cite the benefits of sharing their passion for local heritage, rejuvenating interactions with youth, and opportunities for making connections with other senior history buffs.

Forests as Intergenerational Contact (and Learning) Zones

When considering intergenerational work in forests, it is useful to draw upon some of the dimensions and features of effective ICZ settings (see Table 1.1 in the Introduction Chapter, pages 4-6). In particular, when conceptualizing how forest spaces function as engaging ICZ, there are temporal, sociocultural, psychological, and ethical dimensions of forest experience worth considering. For example, ICZ are places where youth and older generations can reflect together on the impacts of time. In forests, trees and other vegetation grow and develop over varied time lines, and annual seasonal and long-term landscape transformations occur continuously. Additionally, time-related sociohistorical dimensions can also be explored in forest ICZ. Intergenerational learning about past and present traditions, local heritage, human/wildlife interactions, forest industries, wild edibles, wood-working practices, costumes, tools, and many other topics can generate meaningful interactions between generations.

Psychological and ethical dimensions of ICZ play out in forest settings as well. How people perceive and derive meaning from forests often arises from the nature of their interactions with forest settings, whether through work, vacation, or other pursuits. While locations throughout the forest may hold powerful memories of people, special experiences, past hunts, wildlife encounters, injuries, or even adverse weather, forests also provide an important context where meaningful relationships have been forged and sustained. This includes intergenerational bonding in contexts such as the passing on of forest food harvesting or hunting traditions and mentoring related to forest stewardship, woods lore, or wildlife behavior. These are just a few examples where deep bonds of shared meaning and nature connections are forged.

Ethical discussions and challenges can also be explored in intergenerational forest programs. Youth are often exposed to conflicting media messages about forests and wildlife, and adults can help them understand and sort through issues and dilemmas involved. Ethical questions can arise such as: "Is it wrong to harvest trees?"; or, "What responsibilities do people have in controlling exotic forest pests or diseases?"; or even, "Does hunting play a positive or negative role in forest management today?" Older adults who have thought through these issues and have a broad perspective can impart wisdom and insights to youth by sharing background information, current understanding, and experience, as well as their own thoughts on how to address ethical issues.

A specific example of this involves the individual who teaches youth about past forest harvesting for charcoal-making and how forests were completely cleared in this process. When youth learn that the forest they are standing in was clear-cut two or three times and yet still regenerated back naturally into a forest after each cutting, their perspectives about tree cutting and using trees for human purposes are challenged. Typical questions raised by youth at such a program include: "So, forests are not destroyed by clear-cutting?", "What impacts did clear-cutting have on the environment in the past?", or, "Didn't people have any other (alternative) fuels in the past they could use to stay warm or produce needed objects?" Regardless of the issue or ethical dilemma being addressed, forests are ICZ with great complexity and diversity. They allow individuals to consider the choices people made in the past, and must make now and in the future, such as how we should or shouldn't use forests or nature in general.

The Role of Storytelling

While this intergenerational approach for teaching about forests involves many different educational tools, perhaps the most fundamental is that of storytelling.

When older individuals engage in teaching youth about the past, they often have some instant credibility – as youth may assume that the re-enactor, being older, has personal knowledge or experience with the story and in the topics being presented. While personal experience in the past would be a plus, it is seldom the case. Re-enactors must pull from the lives and experience of others to find stories that help them tell and teach about forests. Or, they may create plausible stories that allow them to teach and inform their learners. Fortunately, forests have some special features that enhance storytelling. Forests are places that captivate people, and in turn, stories told in and about the forest can come alive for youth in ways that an indoor storytelling session might never achieve.

Storytelling in forests improves youth attentiveness and listening partly because they are more motivated to listen to a story in a new and exciting environment. Forests allow direct contact with trees, weather, wildlife, tools, plants, insects, mushrooms, and other objects that play major roles in the stories being told. Beyond the natural objects in forest settings, inclusion of man-made objects such as those associated with tree harvesting, food gathering, fur trapping, or lumber making during specific historical periods, can be used to stimulate additional understanding and imagination as to how people lived and coexisted with nature in forest landscapes. Youth can envision and understand stories and lessons better when they handle and experience the objects directly in front of and around them.

BOX 10.1 UNDERTAKING FIRST-PERSON HISTORICAL INTERPRETATION IN FOREST SETTINGS

Undertaking first-person historical interpretation can be an adventurous yet challenging task when attempted for the first time. An excellent book on the topic is *Past into Present* by Stacy F. Roth (Roth, 1998). Here are a few practical tips compiled from individuals who use this intergenerational teaching approach in the context of a forested ICZ:

- Select inviting forested locations that help to tell a story. Investigate the history of forests in your area and the ways people interacted with forests there. It is not required that the specific forest site you choose for inter-generational teaching was the actual location of the historical practices or human activities that you are teaching.
- Do your homework on the type of character you wish to re-enact. Make sure the character you choose connects directly to the forest history you wish to teach about. Research what is known about these types of individuals and learn about specific people who you might try to impersonate.

- Choose or create a character you personally respect and enjoy. You might want to create a "composite" or fictional character to portray historic practices or occupations. Tie characters to their period's social customs, economic conditions, and environmental values.
- Explore using both "first-person" and "third-person" methods of historical role-playing. Presentations done in first-person are often best with youth ages 7–12 years old, or adults. Third-person methods are best for high school students as they tend to be less willing to "play along" and suspend their disbelief.
- Practice portraying your character before you go straight to the forest to perform. Try this in front of a mirror at first, and then in front of family members or friends for feedback. Learn to communicate in different ways, such as varying your tone of voice, making hand gestures, changing your posture, or using expressive facial and eye movements (Lipman, 1999).
- Consider stepping out of your character toward the end of a presentation to relate the past to the present. This works best with adult audiences.
- Avoid slipping into "lecture mode." One way to avoid audience passivity or non-participation is through strategically planned question-and-answer segments. For example, after drawing participants' attention to a spot where barbed wire is growing through the center of a tree, you might ask, "How do you think this wire got here? What might have been the history of this forest?" It also helps to have a "hint" or two in your back pocket in case questions such as the one above draws silence; in that case, you might add, "Hmmm. I wonder if cows could have anything to do with it." (Adapted from Smith, Muth, & Finley, 2015[1]).

Implications for Living and Learning

Environmental education that focuses on local issues and challenges is shown to be more effective and beneficial for individuals and their communities than efforts focused on faraway locations (EPA, 2002). Yet environmental educators, like all educators, face the challenge of introducing the subject matter in a relevant and compelling way – especially against the backdrop of children and youth becoming more absorbed in online activities, shifting family work schedules, and housing trends toward more suburbanization and less non-formal outdoor play areas. The historical re-enactment approach to teaching about forestlands is one way to make such learning more interesting and interactive.

It is also important to keep in mind that the benefits of being exposed to forest history and ecology extend beyond the act of learning. Before people act on protecting, restoring, or conserving the natural environment, they need to feel a connection or closeness to nature. The approach described in this chapter introduces a way to help young people see forests not as a separate domain from their lives, but as an important part of their state's and nation's history, and a part of their lives today. While there are many ways this connection can be fostered, this method of using historical re-enacting by older volunteers to strengthen the ICZ potential of forestland has several advantages. These include:

1) a pool of potential older volunteers who have career backgrounds in forestry and natural resources and a passion for passing on what they know to future generations;
2) an interdisciplinary approach bringing together subjects such as natural science, history, biology, storytelling, and performing arts;
3) an alternative way to initiate nature connections for youth who might otherwise be hesitant to explore the natural world; and
4) an opportunity for older adults to make contributions of time and effort in youth education and enjoy the outdoors at the same time.

As with all intergenerational work, success is dependent on both groups undertaking activities with positive attitudes and an openness to learning about the forest and about one another. And, success can also result in positive environmental impacts.

Whether the children and youth own forestland in the future is not critical, but positive connections with forests as a child can lead to well-informed consumer behaviors, wise forest recreation decisions, and savvy voting on future conservation issues. Who knows, they might even become "future forest stewards"[2] someday.

Notes

1 For additional ideas for constructing questions about the environment that function as intergenerational "discussion stimulators," see Liu (2004) and Liu and Kaplan (2004).
2 A forest steward is a person who owns and cares for a piece of forestland. A "future forest steward" is a youth who, through guidance and encouragement, is exposed to various aspects of forestry and stewardship and, hopefully, begins to envision themselves, someday, functioning as a "forest steward" (Smith et al., 2015).

References

EPA. (2002). Community culture and the environment. A guide to understanding a sense of place. Office of Water. Publication EPA842-B-01-003.

Lipman, D. (1999). *Improving your storytelling: Beyond the basics for all who tell stories in work and play*. Little Rock, AR: August House Inc.

Liu, S. T. (2004). Effectiveness of an intergenerational approach for enhancing knowledge and improving attitudes toward the environment (Unpublished doctoral dissertation). Pennsylvania State University, University Park, PA.

Liu, S. T., & Kaplan, M. (2004). *Let's talk about the environment: A strategy for promoting intergenerational discussion about the environment. Factsheet.* Retrieved from https://aese. psu.edu/extension/intergenerational/program-areas/environmental-education/discus sion-stimulators/lets-talk-about-the-environment.

Roos, V., Hoffman, J., & van der Westhuizen, V. (2013). Ethics and intergenerational programming: A critical reflection on historic environment education in South Africa. *Journal of Intergenerational Relationships, 11*(4), 449–458.

Roth, S. F. (1998). *Past into present, effective techniques for first-person historical interpretation.* Chapel Hill, NC: University of North Carolina Press.

Smith, S., Muth, A. B., & Finley, J. C. (2015). Future forest steward: Learn about and help Penn's woods. University Press, PA: Penn State Extension. Retrieved from https://extension.psu.edu/future-forest-steward.

11

SOWING CONNECTIONS IN A COMMUNITY GARDEN

An Intergenerational Partnership between Young Adult Cancer Survivors and Master Gardeners

Renate M. Winkels, Rick Artrip, Maegan Tupinio, and Daniel R. George

Background

Within the last decade in the United States, the Affordable Care Act (ACA) has sought to encourage non-profit hospitals to establish themselves as "anchor institutions" within communities (Patient Protection and Affordable Care Act, 2019). Not only are such institutions "anchored" in the populations they serve, their mission, invested capital, and customer relationships tether them to their communities (Robert Wood Johnson Foundation Culture of Health Blog, 2017). By requiring non-profit hospitals to conduct formal Community Health Needs Assessments and increase their focus on population health within their service areas, the ACA has encouraged the creation of community projects that reach beyond institutional boundaries (Young, Chou, Alexander, Lee, & Raver, 2013). Hospitals have found particular value in addressing needs through the implementation of nutrition-related health education initiatives that aim to prevent or delay the onset of major chronic disease (George, Rovniak, Dillon, & Snyder, 2017).

At Penn State Milton S. Hershey Medical Center in Hershey, PA, we have responded to the health needs in our community by establishing an on-site farmers' market in 2010 (George, Kraschnewski, & Rovniak, 2011), and a community garden in 2014 (George, Rovniak, Kraschnewski, Hanson, & Sciamanna, 2015). Both are located within walking distance of the main hospital and run from early spring to late fall, with the market serving over 8,500 people annually and the garden offering 225 plots tended by faculty/staff members, patients, and community members. In addition to increasing access to healthy foods, opportunities for physical activity, and greater social connectedness, the farmers' market and community garden on our hospital campus serve to facilitate cross-generational interactions and meaningful engagement outside of a clinical environment.

In 2018, we implemented a pilot initiative in the community garden with an intergenerational focus that involved pairing Adolescent and Young Adult (AYA) cancer survivors from our hospital with older "Master Gardeners" in the community. Master Gardeners are individuals who receive training through Penn State Extension's Master Gardener program which has as its primary mission to educate the public and communities on best practices in sustainable horticulture and environmental stewardship. In return for receiving instruction in horticulture, adult volunteers (many of whom are older adults) assist others who need gardening support and advice. The program has created a skilled cadre of gardeners who, in addition to having a strong interest in horticulture, are highly motivated to do community work.

Given that AYA cancer survivors tend to have poor adherence to lifestyle recommendations of diet, exercise, and weight management (Carneiro, Santos, & Pellegrini, 2018; Nathan et al., 2009) – a tendency that puts them at greater risk of long-term health problems and poor quality of life – we felt that an intergenerational relationship fostered within a community garden setting could be a beneficial post-treatment "intervention" (Carretier et al., 2016). We also believed that benefits would be experienced by the Master Gardeners who served as mentors and were thus able to meaningfully impart their expertise to an at-risk member of a younger generation. Below, we describe aspects of our intervention, summarize lessons learned, and provide practical tips to support efforts at replication.

Methods

Site

The study took place in the Hershey Community Garden, located on the campus of the Penn State Hershey Medical Center in Hershey, Pennsylvania. Central Pennsylvania is a region with an especially rich agricultural heritage, and the medical center sits in the middle of several thousand acres of prime farmland (Pennsylvania Historical & Museum Commission, 2019). In 2014, two acres were devoted to the launch of the community garden, an organization open to all members of the Hershey community including employees, community members, medical students, researchers and others. Initially, the garden featured 125 plots; however, in 2018, nearly 100 more plots were added to accommodate growing community demand, including elevated plots expressly for use by older gardeners with physical limitations. As part of a "Food as Medicine" initiative that seeks to use community garden plots as clinical interventions, two 8 x 15-foot plots were allocated for this feasibility project. Gardening tools, compost, and hoses were available within the community garden for all members. Bedding plants for the feasibility study were donated by the Rodale Institute of Kutztown, PA.

Participants and Mentors

As described elsewhere in greater detail (Winkels et al., 2019), AYA cancer survivors were recruited through the AYA clinic within the Penn State Cancer Institute between March and April 2018. Flyers explaining the study were distributed in the clinic and the head of the clinic approached potential eligible participants. To be eligible, participants had to be between ages 18 and 39, have a history of cancer, have received chemotherapy as part of treatment but completed chemotherapy at least one year prior, have stable disease (i.e. no planned treatment during the coming year), physician approval, live within a reasonable distance of the Hershey Community Garden (<15 miles), and have reliable transportation to and from the garden. Exclusion criteria were: currently tending a vegetable garden, or >1 year of overall gardening experience, non-English speaking, pregnancy, a medical condition that precluded safe pursuit of a garden (i.e. severe orthopedic conditions, pending hip/knee replacement, paralysis, dementia, blindness, unstable angina or uncontrolled arrhythmias, uncontrolled heart failure, or uncontrolled asthma). The study coordinator (RW) discussed the study protocol with participants and obtained written informed consent from participants.

Five AYA survivors consented to participate in the study, though one dropped out of the study before it began. Each of the four participants were matched with four community partners who were either highly experienced gardeners or formal Master Gardeners – all of whom were recruited through either informal contacts or through contacts with Penn State Agricultural Extension offices. Eligible mentors had extensive experience in planning, starting, and maintaining a vegetable garden or were Master Gardener affiliated with Penn State's Agricultural Extension office. Additionally, they possessed interest in mentoring and communicating with participants; were willing and able to visit the Hershey Community Garden on a regular basis; had reliable transportation; were at least 18 years old (age of the mentors in our project was 56 years and older) and English-speaking. Mentors received an informational flyer to explain the expectations of their involvement. Verbal consent was required to participate in the project and the qualitative mid- and end-point interviews.

Intervention

The intergenerational gardening intervention's design was based on the behavioral Social Networks for Activity Promotions (SNAP) model (Rovniak et al., 2013), acknowledging the importance of three ecological levels in long-term behavior change: the Physical Environment (the community garden), Social Network (a network of motivated gardening mentors around each cancer survivor), and Social Network Interaction (tending the garden and meeting on a regular basis with the Master Gardeners and/or other gardeners).

The intervention started in April 2018 with an introductory meeting of participants and mentors in the community garden. Participants and mentors were encouraged to meet again in the garden the following weeks to forge a plan for developing their plots. The intergenerational dyads (n=4) were instructed to meet as regularly in the garden as they wished, though the researchers encouraged all participants to work in the garden at least weekly. By the end of April, gardeners received a donation of cool-weather crops from the Rodale Institute (e.g. kale, cabbage, lettuce), but gardeners were also permitted to buy and plant other vegetables with the guidance of their mentor. In May, the Rodale Institute provided a donation of warm-weather plants (e.g. corn, melons, tomatoes, peppers, eggplant). The study concluded in October 2018.

Data Collection

One-on-one qualitative interviews with participants and mentors took place at the halfway point in June–July 2018 and following the gardening season (November–December 2018). Throughout the gardening season, AYA participants recorded garden plot visits in a log kept in a shed in the garden. We defined the intervention feasible if we succeeded in recruiting at least four cancer survivors; if participants successfully planned, planted, and harvested produce; tended the garden at least once per week during the whole intervention, and met with their gardening mentor at least once per month.

Data Analysis

All interviews were transcribed and saved in the form of Word documents. Qualitative data were analyzed using a content analysis approach to identify emergent themes. This method of coding is appropriate for studies whose intent is to provide knowledge and understanding about a concept or phenomena. Four members of the research team independently reviewed all transcripts to create broad categories that emerged from the data. The research team met in person to reconcile differences in interpretation and identify exemplars of major emergent themes.

Findings

The results with regard to feasibility were reported elsewhere and include a description of the impact on diet and physical activity. Here, we focus on the findings as they relate to the intergenerational aspects of the intervention.

Benefits for AYAs

Importance of Receiving Mentorship & Building Confidence

All participants spoke of how critical it was to have mentorship from an experienced gardener in planning and maintaining a garden. The groups met in person, but also developed communication strategies via technology (e.g. texting, social media like Facebook) to allow for mentors to share real-time practical guidance and moral support to participants. Over the course of the project, all participants felt they gained confidence and self-sufficiency from being beneficiaries of their partner's knowledge and encouragement. As an AYA participant expressed:

> I felt so successful when I was able to harvest and eat things I grew! I think it was a confidence builder, as people who know me tell me I have a "black thumb" and my husband calls me a "plant killer".

Part of gaining confidence was linked to the role of mentors pushing their mentees out of their comfort zone. For instance, one AYA participant said:

> I think it's been really helpful, just very reassuring, very supportive – definitely she challenged me to plant things that I didn't necessarily want to plant, and she was just like "plant it and try one thing with it". If you don't like it then you never have to plant it again. What is the harm? I think that is really cool that she gave me the challenge to plant outside my comfort zone.

In several instances, later in the growing season, participants expressed they had gained enough confidence to become a mentor for others. As one mentor stated regarding his mentee: "She was excited about her accomplishments in the garden and what she was able to produce. She was able to share her garden plot with her daughter, her family, and her friends, and became a mentor in her own right." An AYA participant held an educational session in the garden for a local Girl Scout troop where she provided mentorship on healthy food cultivation.

Benefits for Mentors

Sharing Knowledge & Building Relationships

For the mentors, having an opportunity to share their knowledge on gardening was an important and satisfying part of the project. Mentors frequently spoke about how receptive their younger partners were to their advice, and also expressed how the experience helped them develop new methods and skills to share and explain gardening techniques and impart knowledge (e.g. bug control, harvesting, recipes). In this way, the opportunity seemed to validate the expertise of Master Gardeners. One of the mentors explained that her participation in the project helped to build her own self-confidence:

> I always felt I had nothing to offer. I am not a technical person. I don't use the Latin names of plants; I have to look up bugs and how to naturally remove them; I have been growing Veggies since a child. I learned that I *do* have information I can share.

Mentors frequently spoke about how working specifically with a cancer survivor deepened their empathy, and provided a direct way to apply their knowledge in the service of a younger person's long-term wellbeing. Such an experience was something mentors felt conferred greater benefits to them than even their mentees, and allowed for a deep and caring relationship to form. As one mentor reflected:

> I think anytime you teach someone, you get out of it more than what you put into it. Like for me, what was the most fun in the world, I never planted a garden to nourish someone's soul before. I loved working with her, and finding out what are her favorite colors, what are her favorite things to eat. That felt so satisfying, that satisfied me as a person.

Another mentor reflected about her mentee:

> I kind of felt like her mom for a little while ... her mom was from Texas, and her mom was actually a Native American. We tried to build the garden with some of those influences. Colorful, and sometimes growing the vegetables she was eating when she was growing up. So I feel like she appreciated my help, she would call me and tell: "I have a boyfriend" and things like that.

In all but one case, mentors expressed that they would stay in touch with their partner after the growing season ended; as one mentor said: "I'm sure I'll stay in touch with [name] on Facebook and over email to ask him questions!"

Discussion

Our pilot initiative established the feasibility of a gardening intervention for AYA cancer survivors in a community garden under the mentorship of an experienced gardener. Participants successfully planted, harvested, and consumed vegetables from the garden demonstrating how a hospital-based community garden can serve as an Intergenerational Contact Zone. Qualitative analysis identified a range of reciprocal benefits for AYAs and mentors. Main benefits for AYAs were that, through receiving mentorship, participants built confidence in their ability to start and maintain a garden, and some even became teachers to younger persons themselves. For mentors, the opportunity to share knowledge and to build relationships with a younger generation was greatly valued.

Given the current health care policy landscape in the US, gardens and farmers' markets may be especially valuable for hospitals because they represent non-institutional spaces where health education and promotion can take place. People from different generations – particularly those who have undergone serious medical treatments – may feel more comfortable in an environment that does not explicitly evoke a hospital setting. Moreover, these types of interventions may be especially successful in regions that, like Central PA, possess a strong agricultural heritage.

With regard to future initiatives, there could be a more rigorous focus on the intergenerational component. It was implicit in our project that a mentoring program would involve older gardeners and younger AYA cancer survivors but this could have been made more explicit. Additionally, participants reported that they would have appreciated formal educational content including food preservation, cooking skills, and education on the nutritional benefits of eating fruit and vegetables. These activities may also have created even greater solidarity across all participants (cooking classes, gardening workshops, etc.). Moreover, some participants reported that more interaction and communication about garden results would have been a valuable addition to the project. Social media platforms and email conversations provide opportunities to facilitate this further communication/interaction, for example by sharing and tagging pictures, recipes, or gardening tips and achievements.

There are various ways to expand this model of a mentored gardening intervention within a hospital community garden to other populations. For example, it would be worthwhile to explore the possibility of having older (or younger) community members at risk of or suffering from chronic disease work in the garden together with younger or older family members (potentially grandchildren), under the mentorship of a Master Gardener (Lalli, Tennessen, & Lockhart, 1998). In such a setting a "prescription produce" model, whereby a physician formally "prescribes" a gardening intervention as a means of pursuing better health, may be worthwhile to pursue.

For a hospital or health care organization and for the Master Gardener program these partnerships offer opportunities to join forces and to expand their physical boundaries and service delivery. For the hospital, the intergenerational garden provides a physical bridge between the therapeutic milieu of the hospital and community-based assets that can help transform such bridge settings in health-promoting ways. Such spaces could also potentially serve as a site for further collaborative activities, particularly if family services-oriented organizations could be engaged as third-level partners to deliver programming or resources to families or community members who may use plots. For the Master Gardener program, this initiative can open up an entirely new thread of purposeful community engagement possibilities well beyond Master Gardeners simply sharing their gardening-related skills and assistance.

A hospital-based community garden can also form the natural epicenter of additional social engagement activities tied to the natural environment and health, which could have an intergenerational component. These activities could, for example, include: storytelling on folklore and seasonal/regional traditions, "environmental autobiographical" interviewing that explores oral histories pertaining to the natural world, developing an edible and interactive forest garden (George, Whitehouse, & Whitehouse, 2011), and an intergenerational biodiversity contest to enhance learning about plants and promote values of conservation and respect for traditional ecological knowledge (Chand & Shukla, 2003). A garden can serve as a living laboratory for developing and testing environmental design features for more effectively engaging individuals with certain physical and mental disabilities; for instance, creating garden plots with raised garden beds for those participants who experience difficulty or inability bending to the ground.

As increasing numbers of hospitals host a community garden on or near their campus and with a Master Gardener system existing throughout the US and Canada, there are ample opportunities to develop and foster these intergenerational partnerships, and to tie them to the specific needs of AYA cancer survivors and other underserved youthful populations who could benefit from healthier eating and the mentorship of an elder in their surrounding community.

FIGURE 11.1 Picture of one of the plots cultivated by AYA cancer survivors and their mentors

Acknowledgments

The authors would like to thank Rob Holquist for his help in initiating this program, and the Hershey Community Garden for the continued support for the program. In addition, we thank Michael Masiuk (Assistant Director – Horticulture Programs Penn State Extension) and Matthew Kaplan for providing valuable input on an early version of this chapter.

References

Carneiro, T. J. F., Santos, M.-L. P., & Pellegrini, P. L. (2018). Nutritional characteristics of the diets of child and adolescent cancer survivors. *Journal of Adolescent and Young Adult Oncology*, 7(2), 230–237.

Carretier, J., Boyle, H., Duval, S., Philip, T., Laurence, V., Stark, D. P., ... Fervers, B. (2016). A review of health behaviors in childhood and adolescent cancer survivors: Toward prevention of second primary cancer. *Journal of Adolescent and Young Adult Oncology*, 5(2), 78–90.

Chand, V. S., & Shukla, S. (2003). Biodiversity contests': Indigenously informed and transformed environmental education. *Applied Environmental Education and Communication*, 2(4), 229–236.

George, D., Whitehouse, C., & Whitehouse, P. (2011). A model of intergenerativity: How the intergenerational school is bringing the generations together to foster collective wisdom and community health. *Journal of Intergenerational Relationships*, 9(4), 389–404.

George, D. R., Kraschnewski, J. L., & Rovniak, L. S. (2011). Public health potential of farmers' markets on medical center campuses: A case study from Penn State Milton S. Hershey Medical Center. *American Journal of Public Health*, 101(12), 2226–2232.

George, D. R., Rovniak, L. S., Dillon, J., & Snyder, G. (2017). The role of nutrition-related initiatives in addressing community health needs assessments. *American Journal of Health Education*, 48(1), 58–63.

George, D. R., Rovniak, L. S., Kraschnewski, J. L., Hanson, R., & Sciamanna, C. N. (2015). A growing opportunity: Community gardens affiliated with us hospitals and academic health centers. *Preventitive Medicine Reports*, 2, 35–39.

Lalli, V. A., Tennessen, D. J., & Lockhart, K. (1998). *Using Plants to bridge the generations: Horticulture and intergenerational learning as therapy*. Ithaca, NY: Cornell University.

Nathan, P. C., Ford, J. S., Henderson, T. O., Hudson, M. M., Emmons, K. M., Casillas, J. N., ... Oeffinger, K. C. (2009). Health behaviors, medical care, and interventions to promote healthy living in the childhood cancer survivor study cohort. *Journal Clinical Oncology*, 27(14), 2363–2373.

Patient Protection and Affordable Care Act, Section 9007. (2019). Retrieved from http://gpo.gov/fdsys/pkg/BILLS-111hr3590enr/pdf/BILLS-111hr3590enr.pdf.

Pennsylvania Historical & Museum Commission. Pennsylvania Agricultural History Project. (2019). Retrieved from http://phmc.state.pa.us/portal/communities/agriculture/history/index.html.

Robert Wood Johnson Foundation Culture of Health Blog. (2017, March 15). *What you need to know about hospital roles in community investment*. Retrieved from https://rwjf.org/en/blog/2017/03/can-hospitals-defy-tradition.html.

Rovniak, L. S., Sallis, J. F., Kraschnewski, J. L., Sciamanna, C. N., Kiser, E. J., Ray, C. A., ... Hovell, M. F. (2013). Engineering online and in-person social networks to sustain physical activity: Application of a conceptual model. *BMC Public Health, 13,* 753.

Winkels, R. M., Artrip, R., Tupinio, M., Veldheer, S., Dandekar, S., & George, D. R. (2019). Opportunities for growth: A community gardening pilot intervention pairing adolescent and young adult cancer survivors with master gardeners. *Journal of Adolescent and Young Adult Oncology,* October. doi:10.1089/jayao.2019.0035

Young, G. J., Chou, C.-H., Alexander, J., Lee, S.-Y. D., & Raver, E. (2013). Provision of community benefits by tax-exempt U.S. hospitals. *New England Journal of Medicine, 368*(16), 1519–1527.

PART III
Education Settings

12

SCHOOLS AS INTERGENERATIONAL CONTACT ZONES

The Cleveland Case

Catherine Whitehouse, Peter Whitehouse, and Mariano Sánchez

Intergenerational relationships and intergenerational learning are not new concepts, but over time some of these natural bonds and activities have become less apparent in society. Families are more mobile and the frequency of extended families with members of different generations living together under one roof has decreased. As people live longer but find their lives more restricted, they can feel a disconnection from the younger generations. Children similarly may not see grandparents regularly or conversely may live with grandparents due to the absence of the parent generation. In such a context, and perhaps feeling this loss of connection, societies have looked to create places beyond the family setting in which intergenerational relationships can form and intergenerational learning can take place. It is ironic that schools have not been at the center of the interest in developing Intergenerational Contact Zones (ICZ) since they exist as clear examples of spaces for *potential* intergenerational engagement.

Schools are places where people of different generations regularly meet and interact. These include students of a variety of ages, possibly ranging from preschool (3–5) through end of high school (17–18), teachers and staff, parents and extended family members, and community members who may attend special events. Despite this, there is surprisingly, and in our view, disappointingly, little true intergenerational engagement. The very fact of highly segregated age-based grade levels that is generally ubiquitous in all but the more innovative school models, suggests a mindset that it is more important to keep individuals of different ages apart than to design opportunities for true intergenerational learning. So, while most schools are multigenerational spaces, few exhibit the characteristics of Intergenerational Contact Zones. Here we examine how schools can intentionally foster an intergenerational profile, resulting in enhanced student learning and community engagement. In this chapter, we do so through describing the rationale, configuration, and evolution of a school-as-intentional *Intergenerational Contact Zone* model, as approached by *The Intergenerational Schools* (TIS) (see www.intergenerationalschools.org), three Elementary (K-8) public charter schools in Cleveland, Ohio.

The concept of ICZ refers to the many dimensions and characteristics of spaces that serve as "focal points for older adults and younger generations to meet, interact, build trust and friendships, and work together to address issues of local concern" (Kaplan & Hoffman, 2015). In the particular case of TIS, the main concern and motivation to develop meaningful and powerful intergenerational learning opportunities came from a need to improve children's educational outcomes. In 1998, as planning for the school started, the public schools in Cleveland were not serving students well. Throughout Ohio, test scores in the largest eight urban districts were low and not improving. This created an opportunity for educational innovation by starting a public charter school, publicly funded and designed to serve the poorest, most at-risk children living in those urban areas.

BOX 12.1

The mission of TIS was, and is, to develop lifelong learners and spirited citizens who are able to succeed not only in school but also in life.

At TIS, a first focus was on reading proficiency, particularly with regard to the students' development as lifelong readers: "We don't want to just teach you to read, we want to teach you to be a reader," liked to say Cathy Whitehouse, Chief Educator at TIS. Through a combination of rejecting traditional age-based grade levels in favor of a more developmental approach to learning that involves teaching each child based on individual learning progress and recognizing the need for massive adult relationship and support, the founders of TIS began what has become a signature program at all of *The Intergenerational Schools*: Reading Mentors. We will argue that the school's Intergenerational Reading Rooms and other intergenerational programs that organically evolved through an ICZ lens are opportunities to raise awareness of how educational spaces can simultaneously function to enhance intergenerational relationships while developing deep core capacities such as literacy and citizenship.

Connecting Generations: Relationship-based Learning

The Intergenerational Schools see themselves as communities of lifelong learners: "TIS was founded on the belief that adults and children – of all ages, mixed together, embracing the life cycle – could help each other learn about important values, academics, and 'real stuff.'" (Learning Network Associates, 2009, "Lesson 4," para. 1). There is no question that effective learning is relationship-based and children who have disrupted families or have experienced trauma in all its manifestations, are most in need of stable, caring adult relationships with teachers and other adults in the school setting. More than just another school devoted to education and learning, TIS considers itself the seed of an intergenerational wisdom center, i.e. a space and community within which generational knowledge, experience, and engagement flow and cross in all directions, both through planned activities and spontaneous and flexible meetings.

While there are the occasional bright spots, there is no doubt that urban schools in the United States generally are failing large numbers of children. This leads to undereducated youth, who face a dismal future. A core competency for all future learning is literacy and any school serving at-risk children must seek innovative ways to promote literacy learning. According to its founders, at TIS "no other pursuit receives as much attention as reading. Reading is ubiquitous." (Learning Network Associates, 2009, "Lesson 21," para. 2). To this purpose, TIS develops multiple strategies, one of which is the Reading Mentor Program.

In 2000, when TIS opened, there were three reading mentors and the program seemed to grow spontaneously from there. Through this program volunteer adult/senior reading mentors commit to at least two hours per week with students "for one-on-one reading, sharing stories and building relationships" (TIS, 2015). For the 2017–18 school year at three schools, 67 mentors spent over 2500 hours with students and many others engaged off site in assisted living facilities and other community locations.

Who are these mentors? They are mostly retired local citizens age 60 and over, "representing a variety of cultural and professional backgrounds, from Civil Rights activists to retired FBI agents" (TIS, 2015). What do these mentors actually do? They do not "teach" students to read but they listen to them read and read to them. Most importantly, they discuss the stories; together, they share and compare perspectives. The design of this program is based on the well-documented importance of relationships in the learning process. Though usually examined in the context of the need for strong teacher-student relationships, it is our contention that all regular, dependable and close student-adult relationships (and even student-student relationships when the students are of different ages), promote better learning. Hence, the training for reading mentors emphasizes the need to take the time to get to know each other and build that relationship through a shared experience around books. When does this reading mentoring happen? During class time, on the presumption that the time spent one-on-one with a reading mentor is at least as valuable to the student as what is happening in the classroom.

It was immediately evident that the extra time spent reading in a one-on-one setting was invaluable. Children had someone who came to see them regularly, and much time was spent conversing about topics inspired by the wonderous books they were sharing. If a mentor saw a need to "just talk" with their mentee, they were encouraged to do so. Children loved this reading time, and mentors enjoyed the experience enough to recruit friends and to come back week after week, year after year. One of the first mentors served children in this capacity for 15 years until he passed away. He was as beloved by the children as they were by him. This program has endured, expanded and can be credited with helping TIS students become true readers, including as measured by state proficiency tests.

This tremendous success led to the development of other intergenerational learning programs in diverse settings and involving many areas both curricular and extra-curricular. These have included oral history projects, gardening, drama, music and dance, chess, computers, investing, knitting as well as a variety of community service projects.

It should be stressed that ICZ demand more than simply putting seniors and children in proximity to one another or even engaging them in a common activity. Unless carefully planned, such situations may lead to parallel activity rather than transactional activity. For example, offering a yoga class to a group comprised of children and older adults may result in each individual doing yoga, but without any meaningful interaction between them. Two of the authors observed an intergenerational preschool activity where the children dressed as princesses and princes and the older participants joined them for lunch and dancing. However, the children danced only with each other and when encouraged to ask an older participant to dance, expressed fear of doing so. Similarly, intergenerational activities where one party is a passive recipient are not powerful. Children performing a concert for residents at an assisted care facility would not constitute an intergenerational learning activity. In a transactional or reciprocal interaction, both parties are *necessary* for the activity, which leads to mutual benefit.

Environmental Design Considerations

Where do the reading and other intergenerational activities take place? They take place in school, in assisted living facilities and in community facilities such as museums or gardens.

When you walk into any of *The Intergenerational Schools*, you are likely to see hallways with comfortable couches or chairs, small nooks and crannies with places for two people to sit and read together or even rooms filled with bookcases and a variety of seats and tables for intergenerational engagement. In one school, specially commissioned reading benches were made. Spaces are designed to look and function as "living rooms" or "family rooms" rather than as traditional "classrooms." Much attention is paid to the choice of furniture so that there is adequate support for seniors who might have difficulty getting up and down (firm cushions and armrests, for example).

BOX 12.2

The spaces are intended to mimic the intimacy of reading together at home, while also meeting the requirements for student safety. Toward that end, the activities must always be fully visible, while simultaneously affording opportunities for one-to-one conversations and connection.

You will also see books everywhere so that everyone can see, share and remember their favorite stories and authors. Spaces were designed to create niches close to the classrooms so that students and mentors could move back and forth efficiently. Because of the large number of intergenerational pairs doing various kinds of activities, the space was designed with comfortable chairs and tables to allow both reading and, as needed, writing and other activities. Moveable panels in some niches allow subdividing the space. The space has good natural light and is wheelchair accessible for older mentors with mobility and/or visual challenges. Direct face-to-face interaction minimizes the effect that hearing impairments might have on intergenerational communication. Policies and expectations throughout the school are aligned with the goal of having these intergenerational niches encourage quiet, respectful forms of communication. Some spaces contain school mementos like school team trophies but in general decoration is kept to a minimum to avoid distraction.

Some activities take place at assisted care facilities, as long as transportation is available. This enables residents with less mobility to engage in intergenerational learning. A wide variety of abilities and disabilities, among both children and adults, can be accommodated with careful planning. In these activities, it is critical that each organization has an "intergenerational programming champion" and that planning is done collaboratively between staff from the school and from the senior facility. This ensures that each planned activity is beneficial to both parties and not a one-way interaction.

In some cases, children and seniors visit a community organization together. A favorite activity is "museum explorers" where child/senior partners visit a museum and participate as pairs in docent led activities. Some favorites include arts and culture organizations such as art and natural history museums, a botanical garden and nature center. A special location is the nearby nature center which sits on the same watershed as the first TIS school. No matter the site, activities are planned to be of interest to the seniors and to support the school curriculum and learning standards of the children.

In respect of mentors' varying physical capabilities, the spaces are handicapped accessible and assistance is available from staff as needed. In school, intergenerational spaces are located adjacent to areas that are quite active during the school day, yet, they also provide a reasonable level of quiet so that mentors can hear the children even if they have mild hearing loss. Mentors with mild to moderate cognitive or memory difficulties can be accommodated in most cases, although sometimes such mentors are accompanied by an aide or family member. The commitment of the mentors is shown by the fact that most continue in their role year after year, even as their own aging progresses.

The spaces for intergenerational relationship building are important to allowing close relationships to emerge. Reading spaces can support student/mentor pairs. But so too is common commitment to learning in community, and field trips can be valuable to support these activities. Learning in nature about nature is powerful, especially for urban students. For instance, TIS successfully competed for a prize from the Environmental Protection Agency for multimedia intergenerational learning about ecosystems.

Training and Safety Considerations

Reading mentors (and all mentors) receive training so that they understand what is and isn't part of their role. The goal is to create an equal relationship where the child is an equal partner and not just a recipient (which is often the case in tutoring relationships). It is important to have staff who are available to touch base with volunteers at school and be alert for any signs of frustration, inappropriate exchanges (on the part of the adult or the child), or anything that challenges the relationship. In each of the schools, there is an intergenerational coordinator who also plays a role in community outreach.

While the importance of training adult and older adult volunteers may seem obvious, it is equally important to explicitly teach the children about aging and how to engage with older people. Children need to learn what it means if a person is frail, hard of hearing, or experiencing memory challenges and how to adjust their own behavior accordingly. Children adapt well and become very caring and protective of their older "friends" and learning partners.

Beyond Reading – Lessons Learned

Recognizing the need to find innovative ways to support literacy learning, the founders of *The Intergenerational Schools* developed the reading mentoring program as the first intergenerational initiative. However, they quickly saw that the power of these relationships and the richness of the resulting learning had influences far beyond just literacy. Students, many of whom lacked stable, positive adult relationships in their own lives, thrived in ways that enhanced their social-emotional development generally. Important benefits also accrue to the adult and elder volunteers who report a sense of usefulness and purpose, for some even a sense of legacy.

The reading mentor program quickly expanded to a plethora of intergenerational experiences at the three Intergenerational Schools, ranging from clubs where volunteers shared their own hobbies to arts (especially dance and theater), math and engineering activities. Computer-based activities often permit the youngsters to take the lead teaching role. Moreover, from the beginning TIS emphasized getting out of the classroom into nature where people of all ages could learn about gardening or stewardship of nature.

BOX 12.3

The core requirements for intergenerational activities remain the same: relationship-based, interactive requiring the active participation and input from both members of the partnership, and joyful.

Even outside the explicit reading program, story sharing is a common activity. Children often gain a sense of historical perspective and elders imagine visions of the future through the eyes of the children. In a world that is demanding more testing and "evidence" for educational outcomes sometimes one needs to just open one's eyes and ears to watch the joy and engagement that occurs when human beings of different ages and life experiences share conversations and stories. It is our belief that once a school puts a toe into the waters of intergenerational learning, the benefits to all participants will become so evident that expansion of the activities will be inevitable, although we recognize that sometimes structural barriers exist to expanding intergenerational education.

Final Remarks

Our international work though *Intergenerational Schools International* has supported these conclusions. The spirit of multiage learning is powerful but so can be the conservative resistance. Public education systems can be quite rigid, and champions are critical. Starting small and building support from teachers, their unions, parents, students, and administrators are key. Sharing stories of success is essential. The TIS model has influenced educators, researchers, and community planners. For instance, in Spain a public-funded research initiative is piloting intergenerational primary schools in two different locations. In Toronto we are working with a public union and the school board to develop an intergenerational alternative high school. In Tokyo our oldest collaborator, St. Luke's School of Nursing, has an afterschool program with a research component.

We remain convinced that when intergenerational relationships are nurtured by the educational system, they emerge in some sense naturally, like extensions of grandparent-grandchild relationships. In that space people can think about human life over longer time periods than each of us can conceptualize alone. Children see the past through the eyes of elders, and elders imagine the future through the eyes of children. In this process we see such intergenerational programs and contact zones as important in fostering democratic citizenship and contributing to a sustainable future.

References

Kaplan, M., & Hoffman, J. (2015, August 19). Intergenerational contact zones: What and why? [Blog comment]. Retrieved from www.ageing.ox.ac.uk/blog/2015-intergenerational-contact-zones-blog.

Learning Network Associates. (2009). *The intergenerational school: Civil learning across the generations*. Retrieved from www.tisonline.org/wp-content/uploads/2012/08/manual.jpg.

TIS. (2015, Winter). Intergenerational programming. *Connect, 2*(2), Retrieved from www.tisonline.org/wp-content/uploads/2015/03/IS-Newsletter-Winter-2015.pdf.

13

COLLEGE CLASSROOMS AS INTERGENERATIONAL CONTACT ZONES

Joann M. Montepare and Mark Sciegaj

The Growth of Campus and Community Partnerships

Campuses and communities have a long and varied history of educational partnerships. With recent shifts in age demographics, new partnerships around learning and living are emerging. In particular, university-based retirement communities (UBRCs) associated with institutions of higher education are growing as housing options for older adults in the United States (Montepare, Farah, Doyle, & Dixon, 2019). Since 1995, approximately 100 UBRCs have established partnerships with nearby colleges or universities, and the aging of populations coupled with an increase in housing needs is expected to generate new ones, especially given their appeal to emerging generations of older adults with advanced educational backgrounds and active lifestyles (Carle, 2006; Senior Housing News, 2017; Smith, Rozak, & Moore, 2014).

In addition to offering older adults a ready way to keep physically and mentally active with convenient opportunities for education, fitness, and recreation, UBRC partnerships offer benefits to institutions. For example, they can strengthen ties with alumni and retired faculty, expand educational training for students, and support faculty research and professional development (Logan, 2012). Partnerships also offer financial benefits through shared resources such as technology and security services, along with convenient employment for students and training opportunities for UBRC staff (Montepare et al., 2019). Beyond pragmatic benefits, UBRC partnerships create valuable opportunities for intergenerational interaction. Indeed, at a time when social isolation and loneliness are a public health concern for older and younger individuals alike (Cacioppo & Hawkley, 2003; Chatters, Taylor, Nicklett, & Taylor, 2018),

UBRCs can be a naturally occurring intervention to enhance social connectedness by providing space and time for intergenerational interactions.

On a broader societal level, UBRC partnerships provide a route for breaking down age-segregation with the age-diversity they bring to a campus. Winkler and Klaas (2012) showed that communities across the United States are age-segregated, especially college towns. Considering the negative implications of segregated living spaces, housing communities built on or near campuses where the young and the old can interact are desirable (Neyfakh, 2014). Intergenerational connections fostered by UBRC partnerships also can have a positive impact on personal age attitudes, which in turn can be of significant consequence for the health and well-being of aging adults, as well as younger adults when they age (Levy, 2009, 2017).

The establishment of the Age-Friendly University (AFU) initiative further supports the value of UBRC partnerships (Montepare et al., 2019). The AFU initiative reflects the work of an international, interdisciplinary team convened at Dublin City University to identify the distinctive contributions higher education can make in responding to aging populations (O'Kelly, 2015). The AFU team identified six pillars of institutional activity – teaching and learning, research and innovation, lifelong learning, intergenerational learning, encore careers and enterprise, and civic engagement – from which a set of ten AFU principles were articulated (see Montepare et al., 2019 for a list of AFU principles). The AFU principles advocate that older adults should be enabled to participate in educational, career, cultural, and wellness activities at institutions of higher education. They also call for institutions to extend aging education to younger students, increase an understanding of the longevity dividend, and promote age-inclusion by bringing younger and older learners together in educational exchange in the classroom.

Creating Intergenerational Contact: The Lasell University – Lasell Village Partnership

In 2015, Lasell University became the first institution of higher education in Massachusetts and second in the United States to endorse the AFU principles. Located in Newton Massachusetts, Lasell University is a co-educational institution enrolling approximately 1,700 undergraduate students pursuing professional degrees in a liberal arts curriculum, of whom 96% are below the age of 25 (64% female). Lasell Village, a continued care retirement community, was built by the University in 2000 on the edge of its campus and consists of 13 buildings adjacent to academic structures and dormitories. Lasell Village is home to approximately 225 residents who range in age from 73 to 104 years (72% female). The Lasell campus is a unique AFU member with its UBRC partnership. Moreover, Lasell Village is a unique UBRC program in that residents are required to complete 450 hours of learning and fitness activities each calendar year (which coincides with the annual in-class credit hours completed by full-time undergraduate students). Learning plans are managed by an Education Office at Lasell Village, headed by a Director and staff experienced in higher education. Accommodations are made if residents are unable to engage in activities because of medical or related issues they experience.

Lasell Village residents can fulfill their learning plans in several ways, including participating in educational, wellness, arts, and cultural activities at Lasell Village and at Lasell University, along with volunteering in the community or maintaining work activities. Promoting intergenerational exchange to facilitate the reciprocal sharing of expertise between learners of all ages is a key AFU principle in practice on the Lasell campus. To encourage participation across the curriculum, a roster of approximately five intergenerational courses is designated each semester (e.g. Global History of Childhood, Ceramics, Wealth and Poverty, Lyric Poetry, Environmental Justice) and several spaces are reserved for residents to enroll. Instructors are given a small stipend for their intergenerational teaching efforts. As described below, residents may also participate in other types of intergenerational activities.

Environmental Features

As a place for intergenerational contact, basic physical features of classrooms can enhance or impede exchange for students of different ages. Many traditional classrooms have had the same design features for generations – desk or podium at the front of the room with rows of individual desks for seating. Such a design can foster isolation and disconnection among students. Moreover, desks are often designed such that older students can experience difficulty sitting, rising, or navigating around them (with a walker). To accommodate age-diverse students, many Lasell classrooms have movable tables with chairs, and many make use of seminar style designs. As well, classrooms are equipped with modern technology systems that allow for presenting visual images at the front (and sometimes side) of a room (e.g. PowerPoint slides) to allow for better readability of text and images. Likewise, some newly renovated classrooms are equipped with sound systems (audio induction loop) that can transmit sound from handheld microphones and a ceiling microphone array to individuals' enabled hearing aids. Headsets are available in these classrooms for individuals of any age without hearing aids to use this feature, if desired. Although a number of classrooms do not yet have these acoustical features, microphones are available upon request. The small size of courses across the curriculum (typically 25 students or less) also makes it easier for students of all ages to see and hear each other, and for instructors to have more direct interactions with all students.

Curricular Formats

Although the 15-week semester is the typical format for intergenerational courses, other formats also bring residents and students together to increase an understanding of the longevity dividend, and the complexity and richness of the aging experience, as advocated by an AFU approach. For example, class projects in sociology, communication, or ethics courses have afforded students the opportunity to interview residents about topics such as family structure and work dynamics, interpersonal relationships and dating, or the personal meaning of truth. A computer science course paired students with residents to create personal digital histories with the resident's pictures and personal reminiscences. In these exchanges, the AFU principles of reciprocal sharing of expertise between learners is emphasized. To this end, faculty work with students to prepare them not to simply interview residents, but to engage with them in an exchange of experiences and perspectives. Information gathered in these exchanges is shared back in final discussions or project presentations. As described below, other curricular formats have been developed with the intent of mitigating potential negative age-related attitudes by bringing together older and younger learners around issues of common interest and mutual personal concern (Montepare & Farah, 2018).

Bridging Age and Generational Diversity

In bringing together different generations in the classroom, instructors need to recognize how psychological differences can challenge and enhance intergenerational teaching and learning. In addition to cohort-related differences, individual age-related differences add to this classroom diversity. In intergenerational classrooms at Lasell, instructors are advised to expect and plan for differences in multiple domains when students can range from 18 to 98 years. As one instructor offered,

> An underlying concept when designing courses for adults who may vary in age, cognitive, and physical levels is to consider a variety of choices in the way information is acquired, demonstrated, and assessed. Choices built into the course give students of all ages agency and diminish the isolating effects of having to create ad hoc concessions to age-related learner variability.

Educational Motivations

Instructors of intergenerational courses have reported differences in students' learning expectations, suggesting that whereas some traditional-aged students may enroll in a course because it meets a degree requirement or fits their schedule, older students may be more likely to seek out courses because they satisfy a curiosity. Divergent motivations can lead to imbalances in course participation and engagement with the course content and fellow students. Instructors have also reported that as more experienced lifelong learners, older students may come more prepared and ready to participate in discussions and challenge content. Left unmanaged, such enthusiasm can result in some older students dominating the discussion, which in turn can be intimidating to younger students who may hesitate to disagree. While differences in engagement are not new to college classrooms, instructors in intergenerational courses may wish to address them differently because of the unique status of the older learners. Several strategies Lasell instructors have found useful is to meet with residents before the course to discuss expectations and practices. Instructors also suggest leveraging these qualities in older learners by engaging them as teaching "allies" who can serve as points of reference or extend information when called upon in class.

Background and Experience

Older students may possess more educational experience than younger students, as is true of Lasell residents. Most residents have undergraduate degrees and many have advanced graduate degrees, whereas Lasell students are high school graduates new to the college environment. As well, many residents have extensive professional backgrounds. Such differences can emerge as skill differences in the classroom (e.g. differences in writing and speaking competency). One way to approach these differences is to be mindful of incorporating topics or activities that draw on different levels of skill or perspectives. Another strategy is to leverage skill differences as a learning opportunity. For example, some instructors build in student presentations to an older audience as a class activity given the observation that students approach these presentations with more seriousness and attention to detail than when students' peers were the audience (Montepare & Farah, 2018). Such observations are consistent with those of scholars who have argued that bringing generations together in higher education can serve as a strategy for sharpening basic academic skills in addition to broadening content knowledge (Sánchez & Kaplan, 2014).

Whether dealing with differences in educational motivations, experience, or expertise, developing best practices for intergenerational exchange is a natural and ongoing challenge, beginning with the realization that bringing different generations together in a classroom is a first step, not an outcome. Furthermore, as Sánchez and Kaplan (2014) have noted "intergenerational learning goes beyond learning about others; there is also the potential for profound learning about oneself and one's own generational and sociocultural bearings" (p. 478).

Acknowledging, Confronting, and Transcending Age Stereotypes

When students of any age enter the classroom, they bring with them a range of assumptions about other groups of students. In intergenerational classrooms, these assumptions can take the form of age stereotypes which the age-segregated structure of higher education perpetuates (Whitbourne & Montepare, 2017). This is of particular concern in the contemporary classroom given that cultural views of age have become more negative, and age attitudes are significant predictors of the well-being of older adults, as well as younger adults as they age (Levy, 2009, 2017; Levy, Zondervan, Slade, & Ferrucci, 2009). Moreover, ageist assumptions "go both ways" – with younger adults holding biased assumptions about older adults, and vice versa.

Although more research has attested to negative stereotypes about older people, ageism is a "two-way street" and negative stereotypes about youth abound (Zebrowitz & Montepare, 2000). Both are barriers to teaching and learning. Beliefs that older adults are "set in their ways" are just as detrimental as expectations that young adults are "constantly-connected yet unengaged." Moreover, given that manifestations of ageism may be socially tolerated (consider humorous birthday cards), students of all ages may be quick to assert ageist assumptions or use age-stereotypic language in classroom exchanges. Our experience suggests several ways to address age biases when they emerge (Montepare et al., 2016). These include embracing teachable moments – and being direct, informative, and nonjudgmental about pointing out biases. In doing so, try to reframe the assumptions and language through examples that draw on mutual experience. Abundant social psychological research for reducing prejudice also calls for utilizing activities with common goals that play to the strengths and expertise of individuals, and in this case intersect with their age.

Issues around age dynamics enter the intergenerational classroom in other ways. For example, Lasell instructors have routinely raised these questions: *Should older adults' age-related backgrounds be acknowledged and leveraged to promote teaching and learning? Is it acceptable to presume differences in experiences, views, and styles of discovery, and to incorporate them directly into discussions and course activities? Is it acceptable to ask older adults specifically about their age-related views, intentionally organize mixed-aged small groups, or separate out same-aged peers to be able to compare age differences?* (Montepare et al., 2016). However, instructors have not agreed on the answers to these questions. On the one hand, the value of intergenerational interaction is seen as an opportunity to draw from varied age-related experiences and skills. However, the direct focus on age can run the risk of provoking stereotypic age comparisons and negative personal age perceptions. With these concerns in mind, we propose several strategies for instructors to consider.

STRATEGIES FOR TRANSCENDING AGE STEREOTYPES IN THE CLASSROOM

- Include opportunities to challenge assumptions.
- Draw on both older *and* younger age vantage points.
- Develop activities that warrant input from different (vant)age points.
- Situate age discussions around "us, as we age" rather than around younger versus older age comparisons.
- Listen carefully, respond respectfully, and model interaction.

Talk of Ages

Over the course of discussions with Lasell instructors, the potential negative consequences of age-focused or age-comparative activities has emerged as a concern. Although research has found that intergenerational exchange in the college context can yield positive age attitudes (Chonody, 2015), not all studies show this effect owing in part to the nature of classroom activities (Lytle & Levy, 2017). We believe that activities that call attention to fears of aging (declining change), historical differences ("older" times that lacked modern technologies), or age group differences ("us" compared to "them") can in some cases lead to negative social and personal age perceptions, as opposed to topics that call for less age-specific references and focus on topics of more mutual concern and individual interest. Indeed, we have found that Village residents often voice disinterest in activities that focus specifically on aging issues, and tire of being invited to be interviewed about the older times and their younger years.

Given these concerns, some courses may be of particular value for intergenerational instruction. For example, courses that allow older and younger students to explore topics of mutual interest (e.g. art, music, culture, social issues), incorporate shared activities (e.g. service), or venture into unique experiences (e.g. chemistry of fashion, the lure of the occult) are all apt alternative options. At Lasell, we have formalized this approach even further with our Talk of Ages programming (Montepare & Farah, 2018). The vision of this approach was to bring younger and older students together around topics of shared educational interest, rather than around issues that brought age or age differences into explicit focus. To this end, an intergenerational Talk of Ages Speakers Series was developed around an annual theme (e.g. Healthy Living and the Environment, People and Politics). Talks are co-hosted with courses related to the theme.

The Talk of Ages approach was extended into the classroom using a "module" format in which older and younger students participate in activities designed by instructors for one- or two-week class sessions (Montepare & Farah, 2018). To encourage participation across the curriculum, instructors receive a small stipend and are advised to use existing course content and planned activities. Using this age-friendly, instructor-friendly framework, a wide range of modules have been implemented. Consistent with the AFU principle of the reciprocal sharing of learning, faculty use varied collaborative strategies including interactive lectures, small group discussions, intergenerational panels, and joint art projects.

Personal Contact

Instructors have routinely noted the importance of building in time for one-to-one interactions between younger and older students. This often takes the form of small group activities. In addition, they recommend making time for younger and older students to develop social connections, early in the course. In a typical classroom, younger students enter with some familiarity with their age peers, having been together in other courses, having similar majors, and engaging in campus events. Such familiarity can facilitate communication and learning in the classroom. However, they do not have this relationship with older students – who are also similarly more familiar with their own-age peers. Thus, it is important to encourage intergenerational personal relationships – beginning with the first class – so that younger and older students "get to know each other." Such relationships are especially important to cultivate in courses that tackle content which may evoke highly charged, strong personal reactions, and differences in perspectives. Moreover, cultivating positive social relationships within the classroom will hopefully generalize to positive intergenerational connections outside of the classroom – and make for more age-friendly, age-inclusive communities.

In conclusion, it is clear that there are many layers to building effective intergenerational college classroom contact zones – beginning with shaping the basic built environment and moving toward fostering a social environment that supports authentic personal relationships. We hope that readers will agree that the intergenerational classrooms described in this age-friendly UBRC case are both a timely response to age demographics and a necessary pursuit to supporting the well-being of students of all ages, campuses, and ultimately communities.

References

Cacioppo, J. T., & Hawkley, L. C. (2003). Social isolation and health, with an emphasis on underlying mechanisms. *Perspectives in Biology and Medicine, 46*(3), 39–52. doi: 10.1353/pbm.2003.0063.

Carle, A. (2006). University-based retirement communities: Criteria for success. *Nursing Homes: Long Term Care Management, 55*(9), 48–51. Retrieved from www.iadvancese niorcare.com/article/university-based-retirement-communities-criteria-success? page=3.

Chatters, L. M., Taylor, H. O., Nicklett, N. J., & Taylor, R. J. (2018). Correlates of objective social isolation from family and friends among older adults. *Healthcare, 6*(1), 24. doi: 10.3390/healthcare6010024.

Chonody, J. M. (2015). Addressing ageism in students: A systematic review of the pedagogical intervention literature. *Educational Gerontology, 41*(12), 859–887. doi:10.1080/03601277.2015.1059139.

Levy, B. R. (2009). Stereotype embodiment: A psychosocial approach to aging. *Current Directions in Psychological Science, 18*(6), 332–336. doi:10.1111/j.1467-8721.2009.01662.x.

Levy, B. R. (2017). Age-stereotype paradox: Opportunity for social change. *Gerontologist, 57*(S2), S118–S126. doi: 10.1093/geront/gnx059.

Levy, B. R., Zonderman, A. B., Slade, M. D., & Ferrucci, L. (2009). Age stereotypes held earlier in life predict cardiovascular events in later life. *Psychological Science, 20*(3), 296–298. doi:10.1111/j.1467-9280.2009.02298.x.

Logan, M. (2012). When providers and universities partner, seniors, students and research benefit. *Leading Age Magazine, 2*(4). Retrieved from www.leadingage.org/magazine/julyaugust-2012/when-providers-and-universities-partner-seniors-students-and-research.

Lytle, A., & Levy, S. R. (2017). Reducing ageism: Education about aging and extended contact with older adults. *The Gerontologist*. doi:10.1093/geront/gnx177.

Montepare, J. M., & Farah, K. S. (2018). Talk of ages: Using intergenerational classroom modules to engage older and younger learners across the curriculum. *Journal of Gerontology & Geriatrics Education, 39*, 385–394. doi:10.1080/02701960.2016.1269006.

Montepare, J. M., Farah, K. S., Doyle, A., & Dixon., J. (2019). Becoming an Age-Friendly University (AFU): Integrating a retirement community on campus. *Journal of Gerontology & Geriatrics Education, 40*, 179–193. doi: 10.1080/02701960.2019.1586682.

Montepare, J. M., Zeek, C., Lowenstein, S., Abbott, S., Gerardo, H., & Kennedy, R. (2016, May). *Challenges and triumphs of intergenerational classrooms*. Medford, MA: Poster presented at the meeting of the New England Faculty Development Consortium.

Neyfakh, L. (August 31, 2014). What "age segregation" does to America. *The Boston Globe*. Retrieved from www.bostonglobe.com/ideas/2014/08/30/what-age-segregation-does-america/o568E8xoAQ7VG6F4grjLxH/story.html.

O'Kelly, C. (2015). *Age-Friendly University annual report*. Dublin: Dublin City University. Retrieved from www.dcu.ie/sites/default/files/agefriendly/afu_annual_report_complete.pdf.

Sánchez, M., & Kaplan, M. (2014). Intergenerational learning in higher education: Making the case for multi-generational classrooms. *Educational Gerontology, 40*(7), 473–485. doi: 10.1080/03601277.2013.844039.

Senior Housing News. (2017). *What senior living residents really want from university partnerships*. Retrieved from https://seniorhousingnews.com/2017/12/07/senior-living-residents-really-want-university-partnerships/.

Smith, K., Rozak, E. K., & Moore, K. D. (2014). Creating SPOTs for successful aging: Strengthening the case for developing university-based retirement communities using social-physical place over time theory. *Journal of Housing for the Elderly, 28*, 21–40. doi:10.1080/02763893.2013.858091.

Whitbourne, S. K., & Montepare, J. M. (2017). What's holding us back? Ageism in higher education. In T. Nelson (Ed.), *Ageism: Stereotyping and prejudice against older persons* (2nd ed., pp. 263–290). Cambridge, MA: MIT Press.

Winkler, R. L., & Klaas, R. (2012). Residential segregation by age in the US. *Journal of Maps, 8*(4), 374–378. doi: 10.1080/17445647.2012.739099.

Zebrowitz, L. A., & Montepare, J. M. (2000). Too old, too young: Stigmatizing adolescents and elders. In T. Heatherton, R. Kleck, & J. H. Hull (Eds.), *The social psychology of stigma* (pp. 334–373). New York: Guilford Press.

14

ADDING EXCITEMENT AND RELEVANCE TO SECOND LANGUAGE LEARNING

Imagining a School-based English Language Center as an Intergenerational Contact Zone

Alan Lai

Introduction

There are over 500 secondary schools in Hong Kong, and all secondary schoolchildren are given access to school-based English Language Centers (ELCs) (Education Bureau, 2012, 2014). Since ELCs were first introduced by the Education and Manpower Bureau of Hong Kong in 2001, the intention was for these settings to function as "self-access centers," with the main objective being to promote autonomous learning so that students could be more self-directed in their efforts to learn English as a second language (ESL) outside the classroom (Education and Manpower Bureau of Hong Kong, 2004).

Recently, I visited an ELC located inside a school which had plans for implementing a broader intergenerational (IG) language learning program based on the IG-ESL model piloted at secondary and tertiary school levels throughout Hong Kong, in partnership with Hong Kong Polytechnic University's Institute of Active Aging (Lai, 2017; Lai & Kaplan, 2016).

The school was in a working-class community, on the outskirts of downtown Hong Kong. Upon my site visit to the school's ELC facility, I encountered a modern, well-furnished, brightly lit, air conditioned room, filled with long tables, comfortable chairs, walls covered with cheerful decorations and posters and pictures with famous quotes (in English), numerous laptop computers, headphones, a DVD player, a projector, a large screen, a large flat-panel TV, and a front desk presumably for staff members to provide on-site assistance. Along the walls were numerous bookshelves, filled with stacks of English language movies (in DVD format), neatly kept English language books, magazines and newspapers, and half a dozen Scrabble board games. There were also several small cabinets with mini-drawers filled with vividly labeled, laminated worksheets that the students were expected to access and study.

This ELC was clearly well stocked with plentiful, multimedia English language stimuli. However, after observing how students used the room and listening to how they described their feelings and experiences in this English language learning setting, several limitations came to light.

A student lamented to me that "it is a space of loneliness" and "it is so hard to find anyone to speak to … . Even if we do, we prefer using Cantonese or silence."

Another student who frequented the ELC room told me, "We better stay quiet. One time, something not happy happened. A student quarreled with the center manager who tried to enforce the English-only speaking policy."

As a way of gaining a sense of the extent of student agency in setting the bounds of endorsed social interaction within this setting, I asked about a range of activities, including opportunities to create or play games of interest. One student responded, "The only time we played was for school competition only. I never see anyone play if not that."

The ELC setting and its policies seem to have driven students to a socially isolated way of pursuing and experiencing their own English language learning. Students tend to simply show up, select a worksheet, complete the exercises, check answers on their own, and leave. I was also told that very few students choose to spend time there unless they must for some mandatory activities or need a quiet place to do homework.

Such asocial, routinized experiences run counter to what linguists who study second language learning processes (Van Lier, 2004) recommend for establishing settings that promote meaningful, motivated practice and enhance learner agency and competence in drawing upon their acquired second language skills in real world, daily activity.

This encounter with a school-based ELC in Hong Kong has convinced me of the need to redesign and reprogram such settings in order to enrich students' second language learning experience. Accordingly, since my ELC site visit, I have been working with school administrators, teachers, groups of older adult volunteers, and students at this school to find ways to add excitement, relevance, and additional layers of social support at this ELC room. Below, I lay out a multidimensional intergenerational framework and provide examples for modifying the social ecology of the ELC setting in ways that stimulate student interest and motivation to develop and practice their English language skills.

Reconceptualizing the ELC as an Intergenerational Contact Zone

The challenge of modifying this and similar ELC sites can be framed as an exercise in reimagining these settings as "Intergenerational Contact Zones"

(ICZ)[1] for second language learning. An ICZ for second language learning is conceptualized as an intergenerational approach to help address the types of limitations noted in the ELC described above, including facility underuse, asocial contexts, overemphasis on routinized, repetitive exercises, and limitations to autonomous learning (i.e. lack of student voice and initiative in determining how activities outside the classroom are designed and implemented).

Here are several conceptual cornerstones that might be useful in guiding efforts to incorporate intergenerational engagement ideology and opportunity, so that the learning environment could be reinvigorated in ways that facilitate planned and spontaneous activities and stimulate and sustain English language conversation.

1. Creating an *intergenerational milieu*: A milieu refers to a real place, one where co-inhabitants thrive in social or cultural activities they experience and with which they become familiar. By "intergenerational," emphasis is given to the "real" quality arising from the interplay between or investment of energies across generations. A "rich" intergenerational milieu in an ELC setting would incorporate a variety of visual cues, resources, and entry points for engaging in planned and unplanned opportunities for intergenerational exchanges cast within a second language learning/practice context.

2. Promoting *meaningful intergenerational contact*: Older adult volunteers who are well-versed in English could help foster an English language speaking culture in the ELC by drawing upon their life experience to emphasize connections and relevance to real-world contexts. School- and community-based activities could be planned to stimulate authentic discourse related to ways in which older adults' English language skills have contributed to their careers, recreational pursuits, family life dynamics, major life decisions, and acquired wisdom.

3. Establishing a *zone for mutual development*: In ELC settings, there should be recognition of how all generations benefit insofar as there are reciprocal learning processes at play. For older adults, it is where they engage the young while taking this opportunity to learn how to communicate with, understand, and contribute to younger generations. For students, opportunities are there to encounter older adults as "peers" and "partners" with whom they can take action together, with shared goals in collaborative contexts. At the same time, the older adults add depth and breadth to what and how the students learn, so in this sense, they might be considered "more capable" peers. According to Vygotsky (1978) and Van Lier (2004), positioning the learner alongside a more experienced or capable peer is essential for second language development.

Examples of ICZ-oriented Strategies for Stimulating English Language Conversation in ELC Sites

This section describes several intervention strategies for modifying school-based ELC settings in Hong Kong, though some of these intergenerational engagement approaches are also applicable to other types of language learning settings and cultural contexts.

To aid in creating more of an ICZ atmosphere in the language center, various alternatives are explored for providing "choice" in the content and format of student exposure to the English language (in both, written and verbal forms), while also aiming to promote contact and conversation between generations. "Choice" in this context means that the students and the adult volunteers are empowered to choose the topics they want to discuss, the flow of their conversations, how these conversations are mediated, and the extent to which conversation is extended on certain topics. The students and the volunteers are viewed as active agents; they are encouraged to explore, discover and make decisions together; they are partners. Emphasis is thus placed on stimulating vibrant intergenerational conversations that are authentic and relevant to participants' lives.

Three distinct strategies are described: creating toolboxes filled with conversation-sparking activity cards and placing them throughout the classroom; engaging participants in mobile web ("smart phone") activities designed to stimulate unscripted conversation about shared interests; and co-constructing and playing games of mutual interest.

The Toolbox Approach

Our project team developed a "toolbox" approach which stands in stark contrast to the reliance that many English Language Centers place on having students work in social isolation, filling out an abundance of worksheets with closed-ended response options (of the type described in the Introduction section).

By design, the ECL "toolbox" is as simple as a handy box housing a collection of activity cards. The opening of the box is space wide enough, with a swiveling lid and no lock, to allow easy access to contents inside. The box is made of see-through plastic, so that participants can readily view the contents.

The cards function as *tools* or activity *portals* for bridging generational experience, skills, wisdom, and imagination. They are intended to optimize intergenerational contacts in an unscripted way.

Toolboxes typically hold 50 cards, each representing a distinct activity designed to generate some form of small group intergenerational sharing and conversation. As a set, the cards offer a variety of activity choices to select from. To jumpstart, one card could be selected randomly. Each card is an independent idea, offering suggestions for members to consider and take actions such as setting specific goals, drawing up a schedule, making a plan, and determining outcomes they like.

Here are a few examples. One card is labeled, "iG-clouds." The instructions read: "Together with your younger and adult partners:

- Look out the window (or step outside) and look up to the sky.
- Focus on the clouds and take notice of their shapes and colors.
- Now take a snapshot of them.
- Co-author a story/poem based on the cloud shapes."

Another card is labeled, "ESL Secrets." The instructions read: "Interview at least two adult members. Ask them if they could offer you any "secret" ways of helping you improve your English. Consider:

- Interviewing more.
- Coming up with songs, poems, jokes, etc. to help remember the secrets.
- Inviting some other student partners to practice together."

One other card is labeled, "Time Machine." The instructions read: "Retell a story based on an adult partner's childhood. Consider:

- Using PowerPoints slides.
- Creating a five-minute drama."

Mobile Web ("Smartphone-friendly Websites")

One way to extend the second language learning affordances of the ECL environment, beyond the four walls of the ECL room, is to create or access websites with content that could ignite new lines of conversation. Smartphones are prevalent in Hong Kong; recent statistics indicate that 99% of youth and 96% of adults have smartphones (Census and Statistics Department, 2018). With access to websites designed to fit the smartphone interface (which we like to call, "smartphone-friendly" websites), smartphones could be turned into conduits for accessing and generating new realms of intergenerational communication, collaboration, and language practice.

An example of a particularly attractive digital site that could be used in several ways to bring new content and capability into intergenerational engagement and language learning processes is *Innovative Garage* (http://igconnect.in/). This mobile web platform, described by the website creators as an "Innovation Garage," provides resources and a structure to help people work collaboratively to develop and implement new project ideas. As noted on the website,

> Ever since its inception in 2015 it [the Innovation Garage site] has given rise to lots of projects, friendships, mentors, startups and reasons for many to work harder than ever before. Join IG [Innovation Garage] and come find a reason to turn procrastination into innovation.
>
> *(Innovation Garage, n.d.)*

Any ESL participant, whether a student or adult volunteer, could put up content (perhaps in the form of a new project idea) and invite other participants to join. Those with similar interests would then sign in and confirm joining. This process is conducive to establishing dynamic projects consistent with participants' talents, skills, and interests in communicating with one another. A program staff person or technologically savvy volunteer (or student) could help customize website applications to create distinct project design experiences.

The Finger Soccer Game: Co-constructing and Playing Games of Mutual Interest

When thinking about environmental features or objects in ELC settings that could generate intergenerational conversation in English conversation, it is not only a question of how the facility is designed and equipped, but also a matter of opportunities (afforded by policies, curricular activities, participatory philosophy, and materials) that participants have to modify the environment.

In another IG-ESL program, during the "time machine"/fantasy sharing activity, the conversation between one senior volunteer and four students, shifted to the question, "What toys or games did you play when you were young?" The volunteer shared that he and his friends used to spend hours playing a finger soccer game.

He was so surprised and inspired by the profound interest expressed by the students that he purchased the supplies, built the frame of a finger soccer set at home, brought it into school, and finished up the construction process with the students. The game was made of simple pieces of paper including two teams of players, two goalies, and a soccer ball. The game was then played over a rectangular shaped table outside of the classroom. A group consisting of three older adults and two students set up the game on the long table that was used as the tiny soccer field (see Figure 14.1). As they played, they actively communicated (in English) about the game rules, their playing skills, their favorite shots, winning strategies and so on. They were fully immersed in the co-sharing environment through a tiny, simple yet interesting game.

FIGURE 14.1 The older adults and the students actively engaged one another in conversation as they played one of the senior volunteers' favorite childhood game, *finger soccer*

This was a turning point in the program insofar as these students had been far less talkative than previous cohorts of students with whom the adult volunteers had worked. This was somewhat disconcerting to the program team (which included the volunteers, a college student intern, and myself as project coordinator).

Fortunately, as they played (finger soccer) together, the students loosened up, as did the volunteers. There was less pressure on them to speak, teach, practice, and promote correct English language usage. The floodgates of enthusiastic communication had opened. The spark was this childhood game which showed the students the fun side of this older adult. Seeing him so animated and joyful in reminiscing about his childhood glory days humanized him in the eyes of the students. He now could be seen as one of them, someone they could trust not to be overly critical or judgmental if they made a mistake in trying to express themselves in English.

Over time, the volunteers began to view the entire game-based effort as an integral part of their teamwork strategy for contributing to the students' English language skill development. They had seen, up close, the relationship-building significance of this finger soccer game. In emergent curriculum development fashion, during one of the activity planning sessions, they came up with a strategy for having this finger soccer game play a prominent role in the subsequent activity of writing a short story together. Accordingly, shortly following the end of several series of finger soccer games, the older adults signaled the students to the work bench located right next to the game to further discuss the game and begin outlining a story which they would further co-construct.

The older adults created an actual finger soccer game set and used it to engage the students over a tactile mode of second language practice through the mediation of the game as a teaching tool. In this specific milieu, the older adults managed to provide an enriched social context for meaningfully communicating in English. Through playing and discussing various facets of the game, the students could easily and directly pick up necessary information to further their meaning-making actions. In other words, the older adults created a stimulating environment for students to experiment, discover, and explore; the students' meaning-making actions were socially mediated and thusly promoted.

Discussion

What all these intergenerational engagement strategies have in common is that they effectively generated second language conversation that they viewed as meaningful and compelling enough to broaden and prolong.

In some ways, it appeared that the "active ingredient" for generating animated English language conversation in the ELC setting was the mere introduction of novel objects into the environment. However, what we found to be at least equally significant was the manner in which such items were integrated into the social ecology of the ELC setting. When considering the intergenerational engagement affordance of the finger soccer set, for example, its allure was as much tied to the participatory way in which it was introduced as to the engaging nature of the game itself. There was activity choice, agency on the part of the team of older adult volunteers to create and introduce this game, agency on the part of the students to influence how they played and discussed this game, and enough unstructured time and opportunity for participants to extend conversation and joint activity beyond playing the finger soccer game.

Another set of instrumental factors not previously considered in this chapter relates to the school context, particularly policies and values with regard to building school–community linkages, eliciting older adult contributions to student learning, pedagogical orientation for ESL instruction, and teacher/staff training/support for facilitating intergenerational ESL-oriented activities.

All of these factors have a discernable role in affecting the degree the school embraces efforts to reimagine, reprogram, and redesign this ELC facility as an ESL Intergenerational Contact Zone.

Note

1 In the Introduction chapter of this book Intergenerational Contact Zones have been defined as "spatial focal points for different generations to meet, interact, build relationships (...), and, if desired, work together to address issues of local concern". The ICZ conceptual framework draws attention not only to the characteristics of a setting's physical environment, but also to the programs, policies, and values that influence how that environment is designed, built, perceived, modified and utilized by those who inhabit the setting.

References

Census and Statistics Department. (2018). *Women and men in Hong Kong key statistics.* Hong Kong: HKSAR.

Education and Manpower Bureau of Hong Kong. (2004). *Collaborative research and development ("seed") project: Self-access language learning (SALL) in Hong Kong secondary schools (2001–2003).* Hong Kong: Government Logistics Department of the HKSAR.

Education Bureau. (2012). *Development of support measures for student adaptation in English-medium schools.* Hong Kong: HKSAR.

Education Bureau. (2014). *Overview on primary education.* Hong Kong: HKSAR.

Innovative Garage. (n.d.). Website, Retrieved from http://igconnect.in/.

Lai, A. (2017). Intergenerational-ESL activities: Lessons learned and corresponding actions. In A. Kusano, K. Mizobe, H. Uchida, & M. Yasunaga (Eds.), *The theory and practices of intergenerational learning; Series 2: Future of the intergenerational exchange as the world standard* (pp. 77–92). Japan: Sangaku Publishing Co., Ltd.

Lai, A., & Kaplan, M. (2016). Weaving intergenerational engagement into ESL instruction: Case study of a university-based program in Hong Kong. *International Journal of Teaching and Learning in Higher Education, 28*(2), 254–264.

Van Lier, L. (2004). *The ecology and semiotics of language learning: A sociocultural perspective* (Vol. 3). New York: Kluwer Academic Publishers.

Vygotsky, L. S. (1978). *Mind in society: The development of higher mental functions.* Cambridge, MA: Harvard University Press.

PART IV

Residential Settings and Family Life

15

INTERGENERATIONAL LIVING IN COHOUSING COMMUNITIES

Lisia Zheng

FIGURE 15.1 A cohousing community gathering before dinnertime

There is still time before the dinner bell rings but as usual neighbors have started to gather in front of the Common House in anticipation. A few older kids, apparently practicing their "outdoor voices," are racing each other up and down the play structure off to the side of the porch. The younger ones have (wisely) opted out of this relay and are playing among the scattered toys and tricycles on the courtyard in front. Their parents and neighbors loiter and banter on the porch as others stroll by or stop by on their way home from work. One neighbor, as often happens, has his guitar out and is strumming and chatting in between songs. A few others seem to have arrived earlier and have settled comfortably into the lounging chairs happily bantering with each other. Everyone is warming up and catching up before the common meal starts.

(Fieldnotes from a cohousing community, 2014)

Unlike most residential developments, many cohousing communities are explicitly designed to support and encourage intergenerational living. A typical cohousing community combines private homes of different sizes and styles alongside shared facilities such as gardens, playgrounds, workshops, gyms, and usually a common house enclosing a large kitchen and dining room. Beyond the physical space, these communities often feature busy social rosters that include weekly (or more) community meals, retreats, movie nights, and other social gatherings. This is on top of the ongoing tasks involved in co-managing the community – Home Owners Association (HOA) meetings, committee meetings, "work parties," cleaning groups and so on – that further encourage and sometimes oblige interaction among residents.

Within these communities, busy young families live alongside older neighbors who often become "surrogate grandparents" while their own grown children and relatives live far away. While smaller communities may be more flexible and intimate, larger communities (sometimes with as many as 30 to 40 households) benefit from the wider range of professions and skills among their residents. The norm here is that everyone contributes time and skills to the governing and upkeep of the community and neighbors often generously support and assist one another. The mix of different generations in one community ensures that residents can benefit from varying schedules, skill sets, and physical abilities, often in a physical setting intentionally designed to encourage social interaction. Many residents fondly liken their communities to a kind of "extended family" or "modern day village."

FIGURE 15.2 Porch around common house in one cohousing community

Cohousing as Design Concept

The idea behind cohousing comes from Denmark, where, in the 1960s, growing dissatisfaction with single-family housing inspired more collaborative experiments called *bofllesskah* (living-togetherness).[1] In the 1980s, a pair of American architects, Kathryn McCamant and Charles Durrett, visited these housing cooperatives and returned to the U.S. to adapted the idea in their first book *Cohousing: A Contemporary Approach to Housing Ourselves* (1988). The book came out two years before the term "McMansion" was coined. As American homes and American mortgages inflated across the country, a small number of people looking for something different found both inspiration and guidance in McCamant and Durrett's book. Cohousing communities started popping up across the country beginning with the first one, Muir Commons, in Davis, CA. Today, according to the Cohousing Association of America, there are more than 160 built communities in the US and more than 125 in some stage of construction. Cohousing is also found in other countries including Australia, England, Japan, and of course Denmark where it is estimated that nearly 10% of households live in such communities.

Depending on where it is located, one cohousing community can look very different from the next. There are thriving cohousing developments throughout every state, from urban condominium-like buildings to suburban clusters of townhouses or detached homes, to rural developments with generous open space. Some are retrofitted old buildings, some are simply single-family homes that have torn down their abutting backyard fences, while others are completely new developments designed and built upon previously undeveloped properties.

Whatever the form, most cohousing communities share a few general characteristics: participatory planning, community-oriented design, shared common facilities, resident self-management, nonhierarchical organization, and separate household incomes (McCamant & Durrett, 1988, p. 38). By design and in practice, cohousing communities also share a vigorous commitment to intergenerational living.[2] Many feature a variety of household structures – young couples with children, older as well as retired couples, single parent and even single person households. This diverse composition, according to many residents, is what makes possible well-functioning and well-managed cohousing communities. Residents with more free or flexible time contribute to the organizing of events and meetings; younger residents contribute labor; and everyone puts in whatever skills and expertise they have towards the community "brain trust." The mixture and mingling of such age-diverse neighbors – of young and old, working and retired, and those with needs and those with skills – generate vibrant and engaged communities.

It is easy to see the appeal of this housing option. But how does it feel to actually live in cohousing? How does daily life *look* and *feel* in such communities? As an anthropologist, I conducted fieldwork on cohousing for nearly three years and visited more than 20 communities on both coasts, including one community in MA that we came to call home. For over a year, my family, with two young children, lived and worked and played alongside our fellow neighbors in our lively intergenerational community. Among the 32 households in our community, there were five of us with young children, many professionals without kids, several single senior residents, and many "surrogate grandparent" households. Our lives in this setting were rich, and busy, and sometimes challenging. It was a little like stepping into a modern day village with its own distinct spatial, social, and cultural configurations.

Cohousing as Intergenerational Contact Zones

Cohousing communities tend to be as diverse and varied as their inhabitants. While each community has its own norms and rules and routines, there is generally some set of spatial features, regular gatherings, and tools and resources that form the core infrastructure of all well-functioning, intergenerational communities. The following section offers some examples of these attributes.

Spaces and Places

> Cars are generally left in the parking area near the entrance of the community, next to the common house. Inside the common house, a brightly lit hallway lined with mailboxes and bulletin boards led past a laundry room and a children's art room (currently unoccupied but bore telling signs of recent activity). The hallway opens up to a bright, expansive kitchen and an even larger dining room (currently set up with chairs for an upcoming meeting). A grandmother and a toddler played nearby (and said hello). In one corner of the dining room was a piano and along one wall, a fireplace that looked as if it had just been used. Off to the side of the dining room was a cozy room with a television and bookshelves and inviting couches and chairs – the TV/small meeting room which is remarkably quiet, I'm told, when the glass doors are closed. The common house is large and features a second floor with guest rooms (occupied as usual), a rather sequestered "teen room" (momentarily empty), and the soon-to-be community office space by the balcony windows in the back. Outside the common house was a large brick patio that led to a sand box and the community pool (encircled in locked metal fence to protect young children and animals, I'm told). Elsewhere and dotted throughout the community were shared vegetable gardens, bike sheds, a tool shop (to which neighbors donated their own collections), a potter's studio (where an elderly resident sat glazing tiles), and play areas with various play structures (some for younger and some for older kids). Each home had a front as well as more private (and sometimes fenced) backyard. Most homes are not large by design, one resident explained, but there is ample community space to socialize and "store their stuff." They also don't need as much stuff, many claim, as neighbors frequently borrow and share with each other.
>
> *(Fieldnotes from a community tour, 2011)*

I remember the first time I visited a cohousing community. On a warm Sunday afternoon, I arrived at my prescheduled tour of one community in a suburb of California and was immediately taken by the scene of cheerful houses and gardens with friendly neighbors and kids milling about. In the years since that first encounter, I've visited communities of many different sizes and designs but all featured a similar general layout and facilities. The common house in our MA community was generously sized and enclosed a mailroom (a daily meeting place for neighbors), a kids playroom (separate but visible through a window from the dining room), a laundry room (plus space for indoor laundry racks), a pair of guestrooms (managed through an online signup sheet), a "library"/pool lounge, a basement with an exercise room and bike storage, and most importantly for a cohousing community, a large kitchen that opened onto several connected dining rooms and lounge areas. As in every other cohousing community, our common house was rarely unoccupied. Even outside formal meal times and events, neighbors used the space for social gatherings, held meetings in the various lounge areas, worked in the dining rooms or library, and popped in and out for one reason or another. On the weekends and at the end of workdays, neighbors converged and lingered around the mailroom and porch and, if the weather was nice, the brick-paved courtyard surrounding the porch. At these times, it was nearly impossible to have a quick visit to the common house and not get embroiled in whatever conversations or activities were taking place. Even outside of shared meals and activities, the common house was the central meeting place for the community.

Like many other cohousing communities, ours also featured gardens, a workshop, and various meeting nodes – a bench here and picnic table there – throughout the rest of the community. It is easy, and often nearly impossible not to, encounter and linger and chat with neighbors out and about. One can imagine how these spaces enliven and intensify the social atmosphere in the community.

Routines and Rituals

On meal days, the community kitchen would be abuzz with activity – often frantic in the hour leading up to the meal. The head cook and two assistant cooks would chat and banter as dishes bubbled in the pots and vegetables roasted in the ovens. Depending on the menu – and the inclination and commitment of the cooks – preparation often started the day before with shopping and precooking. Around 6:00pm – delays and/or undercooked dishes were not uncommon – someone rings the meal bell outside the common house to announce the beginning of the meal. This is more performative than practical as the size of the community means the bell is rarely heard by most of the houses located at a distance from the common house, especially during cooler months when windows are shut. Nonetheless, the children would often jostle each other for a chance at this privilege and those who do hear the bell immediately scurry to the common house if they haven't already. Inside the common house dining room – the Great Room as it's called here – neighbors gather in a circle while the menu is described (although most diners already know this when signed up for the meal) and cooks and assistants are acknowledged. Hosts introduced any visiting family or friends, and other neighbors with important announcements take their turns. This is often the time when neighbors remind each other of upcoming events – both in the community and beyond, when birthdays, anniversaries or other significant family dates are announced, and when teenagers in the community unveil yet another school fundraiser – for track or band or the library – and promise to "come around the tables" later to collect donations. (Not surprisingly, the children of the community are champion fundraisers among their peers at school.) With this quick round of announcements over, everyone scatters to their tables, already set up with "family style" dishes and platters. Each table seats six to eight and there is always a rush to reserve seats at desired tables in the minutes preceding a meal. The dining room hums with chatter as the dishes and platters are passed around. Everyone quickly settles down to eat, and the food goes quickly. There are usually seconds available but popular tables – some accommodating an extra friend or family member – often run short and have to send out "scavengers" who circulate among others tables looking to appropriate leftovers. The whole affair lasts no more than 30 minutes before the kitchen is bustling again with cleanup activities. Diners clear their own plates and help wipe down their tables. Cleared plates and utensils are passed to the dish crew in the kitchen and the dining room is quickly swept and restored to order.

(Fieldnotes from common meal, 2013)

Communities are often defined by the routines and rhythms of their social life. For cohousers, eating together – whether casual meals with one or a few neighbors, regular potlucks, or more formal "common meals" – is the "glue" that holds the community together. So much more happens at these meals than the mere sharing of food. Many residents remark that cohousing would not be possible without these routines and rituals around food.

In most cohousing communities there are also a myriad of other regular social gatherings such as retreats, festivals, group activities, holiday celebrations, "work parties," and, always, meetings of one kind or another. Our community in MA also held frequent music concerts that often drew not only community members but also neighbors from further afield together for lively Friday evenings. The occasions made interaction among neighbors easy, sometimes necessary, and almost habitual. After living in cohousing for a period of time, one gets accustomed to, and hopefully more skilled at, interacting and engaging with one's neighbors on a daily basis.

FIGURE 15.3 Spring Festival with puppets and music

Tools and Resources

It is easy to get cohousers to start talking about all the ways they share with neighbors – sharing resources, ideas, and time. A lot of the sharing appears to be arranged online or over email. Many communities have long-established internal list serves or online portals. Among my neighbors in MA, technology-facilitated sharing was commonplace. All resident had access to an internal database of information and resources as well as various list serves that dished out announcements, requests, and general information. Our emails were perpetually abuzz with neighbors making requests for rides or seeking favors or offering (or requesting) news and advice. Many emails circulate daily asking if "someone out there" might have an extra something or another – a stick of butter, a particular kind of spice, a Philips wrench, a cardboard box of a certain dimension for shipping something. Almost always, a follow-up email with a quick "all set" and acknowledgement of the benefactor pops up within hours of the request. Alongside favors arranged online, similar exchanges take place offline just as often. Every resident expects and is expected to participate and partake of this circulation of support.

As expected, communities often feature varied talents and skills. This is something many cohousers like to point out about their community – the "deep pool" of expertise. Many are happy and eager to contribute what they can towards the betterment of their community and their neighbors, and they in turn benefit from whatever expertise their neighbors might have. These resources, facilitated by technology, naturally feed into the cycle of interaction and mutual support among neighbors.

Lessons for Creating and Sustaining Residential Intergenerational Contact Zones

Living in cohousing offers a variety of benefits – material as well as social. Many of these come from its commitment to bringing together residents of different ages. As such, cohousing offers valuable lessons in building as well as sustaining intergenerational *living* zones.

Participatory Design

The involvement of future residents in every stage of the design process is believed to lead to stronger, more cohesive communities. The experience of discussing, debating, negotiating, and finally deciding together the features and layout of their future community not only makes for a better, more suitably customized design but also build relationships and communications skills that will figure critically in community life after move-in. This process also creates communities that better serve the needs of all their residents, both young and old.

Communal Spaces

Generous shared spaces and facilities make possible frequent and easy socialization among neighbors. In many cohousing communities, these spaces are intentionally *intergenerational*. A "common house," for example, typically includes a multipurpose dining room, a TV room or lounge, a playroom or studio, and various other mixed-use and mixed-age spaces. These spaces both combine and, at times when necessary, serve separately the needs of different age groups (such as locating a playroom off the dining room). They also, by design and in practice, serve multiple purposes and evolve over time as community members themselves age and change.

Elsewhere in the community, especially in larger, less urban communities, gardens, gathering nodes, and playgrounds abound. The addition of benches and tables, plus their typically central locations, ensure that such play areas and gardens become meeting places for neighbors of all ages. Even the areas between houses – the pedestrian pathways – allow for, and indeed encourage, spontaneous gatherings.

Privacy and Choice

While cohesive community life certainly benefits from cozy neighborhood design and neighborly relations, the quality of life in these communities also depends on maintaining privacy and choice. Cohousing design emphasizes access to shared spaces as much as to private and secluded spaces. For example, individual homes in larger cohousing communities often feature "private" backyard spaces (fenced or not) alongside more "public" front yards. Many common houses offer quiet or adult-only areas where residents can seek refuge from the bustle (and mess) of community life. While homes tend to include such community-friendly features such as glassed entry doors (often leading directly into kitchens where, it is assumed, we spend most of our time), as well as patios and "lounge" areas in front of each house, the norm in many communities tend to be well-shaded doors (and windows) and patios that are landscaped or otherwise marked off as extensions of private homes. This built-in versatility makes community life much happier (and sometimes quieter) for residents of all ages.

Rituals and Routines

While cohousing design aspires to encourage spontaneous neighborly engagements, it is the regular, routine social events that more importantly strengthen and sustain community life. Almost all cohousing communities make efforts to regularly hold "common meals," potlucks, holiday celebrations, festivals, and retreats. These frequent gatherings, often elaborately planned and meticulously managed, help nurture and reinforce the neighborly relationships that underlie all community life. They are also, frequently, opportunities for residents of all ages to mingle and mix.

Technology and the Social

Cohousing communities, thanks to their demographic diversity, often feature enviable technological infrastructure and in-house IT support. Resources such as community-maintained servers and internal websites (for circulating news or signing up for common meals or guestrooms) effectively create *virtual* community spaces alongside the concrete *physical* ones. These realms offer additional (and even more convenient and inclusive) opportunities for neighbors to interact. They supplement and bolster real world interactions and even, sometimes, make possible and manageable elaborate systems of sharing and communication (such as reserving popular guestrooms or shared equipment, or signing up for meals and community jobs). For residents of all ages, these parallel environments make the benefits of community even more accessible and convenient.

Notes

1 The idea was first introduced in Denmark by a young architect named Jan Gudmand-Hoyer who drew inspiration from his studies of American utopias while a student at Harvard. His article based on his studies, "The Missing Link Between Utopia and the Dated One-Family House" (1964), drew over 100 interested families eager to try out his proposed housing alternative. This was the beginning of cohousing in Denmark.

Two decades later, McCamant and Durrett studied these Danish communities and brought the idea (back) to the U.S. (Christensen & Levinson, 2003).

2 While most existing cohousing communities are still intergenerational, there has been increasing interest in adapting cohousing principles to building "senior cohousing." Durrett himself addresses this market demand in his book, *The Senior Cohousing Handbook* (2009).

References

Christensen, K., & Levinson, D. (Eds.). (2003). *Encyclopedia of community: From the village to the virtual world.* New York: Sage.

Durrett, C. (2009). *The senior cohousing handbook.* Gabriola Islands, BC: New Society Publishers.

Gudmand-Hoyer, J. (1964). The missing link between utopia and the dated one-family house. *Information, 26.*

McCamant, K., & Durrett, C. (1988). *Cohousing: A contemporary approach to housing ourselves.* Berkeley, CA: Ten Speed Press.

16

COCKTAILS IN CARE HOMES

An Intergenerational Strategy For Bridging the Care Home–Community Divide

Phoebe Grudzinskas and Susan Langford

FIGURE 16.1 A volunteer and resident joining the dancefloor

"When you come, we know we are not forgotten" – Care Home Resident.

> I think it has improved my understanding for those who might no longer be living in their own homes, and to be more sympathetic to them. I think it is easy to forget – out of sight, out of mind – but meeting residents has really encouraged me to be more considerate, especially living in London when it is so fast paced.
>
> *(Volunteer,* Cocktails in Care Homes *Annual Survey 2018)*

Cocktails in Care Homes (*Cocktails*) is a project run by Magic Me (MM), an intergenerational arts charity, based in East London in the UK. *Cocktails* is an intergenerational project connecting predominantly young adult volunteers with older people 60+ who live in care homes and extra care schemes, through monthly evening parties.

In the UK a care home (residential or nursing) provides personal care and accommodation for older people with a range of needs for example living with a dementia, with physical, sensory or other impairments (Care Quality Commission, 2018a). The median period from admission to the care home to death is 15 months (Age UK, 2018).

An extra care scheme is designed for more independent older people with varying support needs – residents have their own self-contained homes and their own front doors (Housing Care, 2019). In this chapter the term care home covers both the extra care scheme and care homes that participate in *Cocktails*.

London – The Care Sector and Loneliness

In 2016 there were 8.78 million people living in London (World Population Review, 2019), of whom over 980,000 people were aged 65+, a number estimated to grow to 1.2 million by 2024 (Age UK London, 2011). The population are living longer with a greater variety of care needs in their later life. In London there are 367 care homes and 175 extra care schemes for older people, run by private, public, and charity organizations.

All is not well in the UK care sector. The Care Quality Commission, the independent regulator of all health and social care services in England, ended their *State of Care 2017/18* report concluding that

> The urgent challenge for Parliament, commissioners and providers is to change the way services are funded, the way they work together and how and where people are cared for. The alternative is a future in which care injustice will increase and some people will be failed by the services that are meant to support them, with their health and quality of life suffering as a result.
>
> *(Care Quality Commission, 2018b)*

Despite living surrounded by others, 22–44% of older people living in care homes experience loneliness, compared to 10% of those living in the wider community (Davidson & Rossall, 2015). The importance of addressing loneliness across the lifespan has been climbing up political agendas in the UK, with the government introducing its first strategy on loneliness in October 2018. The Campaign to End Loneliness UK has highlighted the health risks – loneliness is as bad for your health as smoking 15 cigarettes a day (Holt-Lunstad, Smith, & Layton, 2010), is worse than obesity (Holt-Lunstad et al., 2010) and is likely to increase your risk of death by 29% (Holt-Lunstad, Smith, Baker, Harris, & Stephenson, 2015).

Care Homes as Intergenerational Contact Zones

Care staff are from different generations to the residents, however, the relationship between them is functional, located in a service user/service giver environment and not celebrated. Due to the fragility of the sector, with low budgets and poor staff retention, time to form relationships is often limited.

BOX 16.1

Cocktails encourages involvement of the community around a care home, recruiting and bringing in local people through regular parties, people of a different generation to residents who actively want to visit. The project and parties allow space and time for relationships to be formed, thus creating genuine social interactions within an Intergenerational Contact Zone. *Cocktails* also demonstrates to the care staff, residents' appetite and capacity to develop and enjoy positive intergenerational relationships.

What is Magic Me?

MM is an arts charity based in Tower Hamlets, east London, founded in 1989, which has pioneered intergenerational work in the UK. MM works with and serves local communities in the East End of London, characterized by poverty, cramped housing, poor mental and physical health, and with a diverse and ever-changing cultural mix. People of different generations and cultures live parallel lives, rarely mixing outside their peer group, which increases the sense of social isolation and loneliness for many.

MM designs and delivers creative ways to bring together people of different generations and cultures. Children or young people 8+, and older people 60+ enjoy creative arts projects together. They exchange skills and points of view, understand one another better, building stronger communities. MM uses an asset-based model, valuing what people can do, not focusing on what they cannot do.

MM has been working in care homes since its inception and over 30 years has developed a strong creative practice, informed by evaluation and research. For example, 'Getting Everyone Included' (1998–2001), MM's report on an action research project involving people with dementia and those who work with them, focused on the challenges that artists face working in a care environment. It found that creative activity could become a form of communication between the people with dementia and care staff.

From 2015–2017, MM led a two-year program of Artist Residences in care homes in partnership with Anchor, England's largest not-for-profit care home provider and four arts partners, all leaders in their field: Punchdrunk Enrichment, Lois Weaver, Upswing and Duckie. The key point of learning was that being a guest in a care home is never simple, confirming MM's belief that artists, guests and volunteers, as well as staff, need the right framework and tailored support in order to do emotionally challenging work.

What is *Cocktails in Care Homes*?

Cocktails grew from conversations between MM's Director, Susan Langford and care home residents during the evaluation of an intergenerational arts project linking them with local school children and artists. The older people really

FIGURE 16.2 Volunteers and residents enjoying a drink and chat

valued this activity but asked what MM could offer them in the evening, the loneliest part of the day for them. Activities Coordinators finish work at 5 pm, dinner is served at 6 pm and then residents go to bed at 7 pm, waking early and waiting until the staff helped them get up again. MM was also being approached by adults who worked 9–5 and wanted evening opportunities to volunteer with the charity.

As a result, in Autumn 2011, MM designed and piloted *Cocktails*, working with residents and staff at three care homes and adult volunteers, to throw early evening parties during the Cocktail Hour. This new model, in effect, expands and diversifies the intergenerational footprint woven into MM's work in care homes; residents and staff encounter new opportunities to engage young adults (18+) as well as children and youth. This helps to further bridge the care home–community divide. It extends upon the care home's capacity to function as an "intergenerational contact zone" (ICZ) that is meaningful, welcoming, and appealing to all who enter its front doors.

HOW DOES IT WORK?

Each participating care home receives a monthly *Cocktails in Care Homes* party, between 6 pm and 7.30 pm on a Wednesday or Thursday evening. Residents, their family members and friends are invited by the home staff and with MM providing promotional posters with the dates and time. The parties take place within a communal space, often the lounge or dining room. A range of alcoholic and non-alcoholic drinks and nibbles are served and those attending enjoy music, conversation, and maybe a dance. "Last orders at the bar" are called at 7.15 pm and the party finishes at 7.30 pm. In February 2019, 15 care homes across London were hosting monthly *Cocktails* parties.

Volunteer Party Managers

Volunteer Party Managers (VPM) are a dedicated team of volunteers who help MM to run the parties. VPMs go to the same care home each month, arriving early to set up the space, host the party, manage the volunteers, serve drinks and pack everything away. They are integral to the running of the project and champion our intergenerational work within their community and networks. Some VPMs have been in this role for over five years.

> This one evening a month is a chance for me to put things in perspective and learn from people older and wiser than me, with lives as rich as you can imagine. If I've had a stressful day at work or I'm feeling a bit

low, the experience always brings me into the present, allows me to reflect and realize the things I often take for granted.

(Zosia, Volunteer Party Manager)

In February 2019 a team of 32 VPMs were supporting 15 parties across London.

Volunteers

MM recruits volunteers who are 18 years old or older, the legal age to drink alcohol in the UK. *Cocktails* attracts much media attention which enables easy recruitment. People are also recruited through volunteer recruitment websites and via their employers through corporate and business partnerships. There were 450+ inducted, active volunteers in February 2019.

Volunteers come to the parties as guests to socialize with residents and other volunteers. They must each attend a 90-minute Volunteer Induction run by MM which combines an introduction to the project with exercises and training on communication and dementia. MM understands that going into a care home can be an overwhelming or upsetting experience. Volunteers may meet people living with a dementia, loss, or health conditions that they may not previously have experienced.

As *Cocktails* has continued and expanded MM has developed its induction process to ensure that all volunteers are introduced, trained, and supported properly in their volunteer journey. Quarterly training sessions led by dementia specialists are offered. In some cases, the project is not right for the volunteer. MM acknowledges this and understands that this can be down to the volunteer's personal experiences.

Safeguarding

Cocktails works with vulnerable care home residents and protecting them is a governance priority for MM, reflected in its Policy & Procedures for Safeguarding Vulnerable People. This procedure includes a Disclosure and Barring Service (DBS) check on all VPMs. In the UK the DBS prevents unsuitable people from working with vulnerable groups by checking for any criminal convictions and conditional cautions.

Volunteers are not DBS checked because they are treated and expected to behave as would any other guest in the care home. They sign a visitors' book and VPMs show them areas where they may visit: the room where the party is held, a place to store their personal belongings and the visitors' toilet. Volunteers are trained not to go anywhere alone with a resident and to seek help from care staff, should an individual need, for example, to move from a wheelchair to a chair.

The Relationship with the Care Home/Scheme

MM understands that each relationship with a care home is a bespoke partnership. A standard agreement and risk assessment are given to all care partners, however despite this, the most challenging and essential part of the project is the day to day administration and communication with the care partners.

Also vital are the relationships between MM staff and the care staff who work at the parties supporting the residents. In some homes the same members of staff are assigned to work at every party, in other cases, it might be a different staff member each month. Either way, MM is able to support the VPMs in this relationship with the staff, to ensure that the residents are supported to attend and enjoy the parties and practical arrangements about furniture, equipment, and stock go smoothly.

Financing the Project

Cocktails is supported by grants from local and national charitable trusts and foundations. In addition, to grow *Cocktails* in a sustainable way, MM has gained support from participating partners and individuals, extending the engagement of volunteers and others.

Since 2017 MM has requested an annual contribution from care home providers, towards the cost of parties. Care homes have all agreed to pay this, from very tight budgets, with care home managers arguing the case with their regional directors, demonstrating how much care homes value *Cocktails*.

Corporate and business partners offer financial and in kind support. When employees attend a party they make a financial contribution per volunteer hour. They also donate venues with refreshments for volunteer inductions. Businesses recognize the benefits of volunteering for individual staff and for team building: One volunteer said, "I feel more in touch with the community where I work – it's no longer where my office is!".

Cocktails in Care Homes Growth: 2010–2019

When *Cocktails* began in 2010 it was piloted in three care homes run by three different care providers, where MM already had good working relationships with residents, care staff, and managers. This trust enabled MM to positively disrupt the status quo: to shift the work patterns of the care staff by running an activity in the evening, introduce alcohol into care home activities, and welcome groups of volunteers "after hours." MM staff also had to be more flexible with their working hours, usually 9.30 am–5.30 pm, to host the evening events.

By 2016 Magic Me had grown *Cocktails* to serve nine care homes. It was no longer possible to manage nearly 300 volunteers through emails and lists. *Cocktails* launched its own bespoke website for volunteers to sign up, create profiles, book onto induction events and then parties, completely automating the processes behind volunteer management. To better support the residents, care staff and volunteers, the decision was made to have two VPMs at each care home. In January 2017 two full time members of staff were employed to manage the project – a Project Manager and a Project Coordinator – and to grow it from nine to 18 care homes across London by September 2019.

Creating an Intergenerational Contact Zone

In order to grow *Cocktails* successfully, MM had to examine and hone these key elements: the care home audience; the volunteer experience; and the extension of the intergenerational contact zone.

The Care Home/Scheme Audience

"I am so filled with joy at seeing you again" – Resident to a VPM.

Understanding and catering for residents' individual and varied needs is essential. Residents may have a variety of needs: physical frailty, sensory impairments, and a lack of confidence. Depression affects 40% of older care home residents, whilst up to 80% of people at some homes may live with a dementia (Age UK, 2018). Before introducing parties at a care home MM meet with staff who know residents well.

FIGURE 16.3 Volunteers and a resident enjoying the Solar System Soirée party

Party decorations and themes are designed to create an immersive experience, stimulating engagement using all five senses. A volunteer DJ creates Spotify playlists for each theme. Table games, party poppers, dancing, themed nibbles and drinks enable volunteers and residents to communicate nonverbally. Volunteers are encouraged to use their mobile phones to share their own lives e.g. photos, apps or find references to older people's stories.

Some residents speak English as a second language. Dementia can affect languages acquired in adulthood and residents may revert to their mother tongue leaving them unable to communicate with many, if any, other people in their care home. MM recruits bilingual volunteers in order to engage residents who speak for example Farsi, French, Portuguese, and Spanish.

MM's partnership with the Royal Academy of Music, one of the leading music conservatoires in the world, enables non-verbal communication through music. MM trains students and supports them to perform at the care homes enabling them to perform in a completely different context, whilst giving the residents, volunteers, and care staff an opportunity to listen to professional classical musicians.

Volunteer Experience

London can feel quite lonely and unfriendly at times. This program makes me feel the opposite. I always leave feeling so happy, and I imagine if you were new to the city this would be a great way to start meeting people and seeing a softer side to life!

(*Volunteer,* Cocktails in Care Homes *Annual Survey, 2018*)

Loneliness in the UK is not just an older person issue. Young adult volunteers have told MM that they come to *Cocktails* because having moved to London, for education or employment, they find themselves living and working within their own generation, missing intergenerational contact with older relatives.

For some volunteers with relatives living in care homes far from London, visiting other older people through *Cocktails* can make them feel less guilty about not visiting family and that they are doing something to address the needs of lonely care home residents.

Extending the Intergenerational Contact Zone

The project provides me an opportunity to interact with members of my local community that I would not normally have (a) chance to interact with.

(*Volunteer,* Cocktails in Care Homes *Annual Survey 2018*)

One of the aims of *Cocktails* is to get volunteers on their way home, to stop into a care home for a drink and have a chat with a resident, rather than go to their local pub, essentially to open the doors of the care home to the community around it.

MM works to add new engagement possibilities to the ICZ of the care home by connecting with other local organizations, for example local theatres and cultural institutions. *Cocktails* has held volunteer inductions in theaters, with their contacts invited, to ensure volunteers are from the local community.

MM has invited residents, care staff, and volunteers to join *Cocktails* events in cultural institutions such as the Southbank Centre, joining with members of the public. MM's corporate and business partners also hold events for the residents. For example, *Cocktails* volunteers from one law firm invited residents to their workplace and now host twice-yearly tea concerts for 40 residents and carers at their city office headquarters. Such events widen the ICZ, taking it beyond the care home. They also showcase and celebrate the intergenerational relationships between residents and volunteers, for a wider audience, raising the profile of intergenerational work.

Building an ICZ in a care home is not simple. Magic Me is shifting ingrained working patterns and behaviors to host regular parties, supporting and preparing all participants to enjoy and benefit from genuine social interaction in a transformed environment. The benefits of *Cocktails* then push the boundary of the ICZ beyond the walls of the care home and into the everyday lives of the younger adults.

References

Age UK London. (2011). Facts and figures. Retrieved from www.ageuk.org.uk/london/about-us/media-centre/facts-and-figures/.

Age UK. (2018). Later life in the United Kingdom. Retrieved from www.ageuk.org.uk/globalassets/age-uk/documents/reports-and-publications/later_life_uk_factsheet.pdf.

Care Quality Commission. (2018a). Service types. Retrieved from www.cqc.org.uk/guidance-providers/regulations-enforcement/service-types.

Care Quality Commission. (2018b). Summary: The state of health care and adult social care in England. Retrieved from https://webarchive.nationalarchives.gov.uk/20190112070317/https://www.cqc.org.uk/publications/major-report/state-care.

Davidson, S., & Rossall, P. (2015). Age UK loneliness evidence review. Retrieved from https://www.ageuk.org.uk/globalassets/age-uk/documents/reports-and-publications/reports-and-briefings/health–wellbeing/rb_june15_lonelines_in_later_life_evidence_review.pdf.

Holt-Lunstad, J., Smith, T. B., Baker, M., Harris, T., & Stephenson, D. (2015). Loneliness and social isolation as risk factors for mortality: A meta-analytic review. *Perspectives from Psychological Science, 10*(2), 227–237. doi:10.1177/1745691614568352. Retrieved from www.ahsw.org.uk/userfiles/Research/Perspectives%20on%20Psychological%20Science-2015-Holt-Lunstad-227-37.pdf.

Holt-Lunstad, J., Smith, T. B., & Layton, J. B. (2010). Social relationships and mortality risk: A meta-analytic review. *PLoS Med*, 7(7), e1000316. doi:10.1371/journal. pmed.1000316. Retrieved from https://journals.plos.org/plosmedicine/article? id=10.1371/journal.pmed.1000316.

Housing Care. (2019). *Extra care housing*. Retrieved from www.housingcare.org/jargon-extra-care-housing.aspx.

World Population Review. (2019) London population 2019. Retrieved from http:// worldpopulationreview.com/world-cities/london-population/.

17

SENIOR HOUSING AS A COMMUNITY HUB FOR INTERGENERATIONAL INTERACTION

Nancy Henkin and Taryn Patterson

Why Senior Housing?

Housing is an important element of the built environment and a key issue for individuals and families throughout the life course. For older adults who tend to spend a great deal of time in their neighborhoods and may experience physical challenges, the type and location of housing can affect independence, social connection, self-esteem, and life satisfaction (Molinsky & Forsyth, 2018). Research on person–environment fit emphasizes that the relationship between a person's capacities and physical space evolves as needs change. For older adults, access to retail, parks, supportive services, and activities that foster social connectivity, as well as an infrastructure that is safe and convenient, have been identified as important housing features (Frochen & Pynoos, 2017).

The Joint Center for Housing Studies of Harvard University (2016) projects that by 2035, 50 million households in the United States will be headed by someone age 65 or older and the number of people 80 + will double to 24 million. Many older adults are likely to face disabilities that pose challenges to living independently. The Department of Health and Human Services estimates that 70% of people who reach age 65 will need some type of long-term care in their later years. Although the majority of older adults prefer to age in place in their own homes, others choose to age in place in "congregate settings" due to health, financial, and social concerns, and/or the need for improved housing quality and security (Redford & Kochera, 2005; Sergeant & Ekerdt, 2008).

This chapter focuses on *senior housing* broadly defined, which includes both subsidized and market-rate independent living (IL) for adults typically aged 50+, assisted living (AL), which provides assistance with activities of daily living such as bathing, dressing, and eating, "service enriched" IL that provides services and supports such as transportation, congregate meals, and social activities, and Continuing Care Retirement Communities (CCRCs) that provide housing and health care on a continuum of needs for older adults. The National Investment Center for the Seniors Housing and Care Industry estimates that 710,000 older adults are living in IL communities (Joint Center for Housing Studies of Harvard University, 2016). Benefits of living in independent senior housing include access to an array of services in one place, accessibility, and a network of peers who may have similar experiences and can share memories. However, age-restricted housing also presents challenges to individuals and to local communities.

Research suggests that when individuals transition into senior housing, many find it difficult to establish new social connections and/or become integrated into the broader community (Carroll & Qualls, 2014; Mitchell & Kemp, 2000). Such factors may result in a sense of being "left behind," affecting an older adult's quality of life (Blaschke, Freddolino, & Mullen, 2009; Wright, 2000). Loss of social connections, physical separation from familiar places and routines, and resulting emotional distress can combine to affect the mental and physical health of residents (Ball et al., 2000). Feelings of loneliness and a loss of social capital can be consequences of living in an age-segregated environment.

Loneliness in Older Adulthood

A growing public threat to health and well-being across the lifespan, but particularly still prominent in older adulthood, is *loneliness*, defined as "the psychological embodiment of social isolation, reflecting the individual's dissatisfaction with the frequency and closeness of their social contacts and the discrepancy between the relationships they have and the relationships they would like to have" (Steptoe, Shakar, Demakakos, & Wardle, 2013). Recent studies by Goyea, Curley, Melekis, Levine, & Lee (2018) and Taylor, Wang, and Morrow-Howell (2018) suggest that adults living in low-income senior housing are particularly at risk of feeling lonely because they are more likely to live alone, have significant health and/or mental health problems, and have smaller social networks as compared to market-rate housing and community-dwelling older adults. Goyea et al. (2018) found that one out of three older adults in senior high-rise buildings reported feeling lonely. Similarly, Taylor et al. (2018) reported that 70% of the residents they surveyed in three senior housing communities were classified as moderately or severely lonely. They also indicate that individuals who participated in group or community-focused activities at least weekly reported being less lonely, suggesting the need for housing providers to develop partnerships with local organizations to engage residents in meaningful experiences.

Loss of Social Capital

Research suggests that access to social capital, defined as the resources available to individuals and groups through their social connections to their communities (Cannuscio, Block, & Kawachi, 2003), declines for many older adults. For senior housing residents, decreased contact with social network members outside the housing community, in combination with the social constraints of institutional settings, can affect the quality and quantity of their social interactions (Cannuscio et al., 2003). Age-restriction can reinforce ageist attitudes primarily by limiting opportunities for older and younger persons to form stable, interdependent, cross-age relationships. The growing racial generation gap adds complexity to issues of age-restriction and the forming of cross-generational networks (Brown & Henkin, 2018).

It is becoming increasingly important for senior housing providers to not only deliver supportive services to their residents, but also to develop opportunities for residents to connect with and contribute to their local communities. Intentionally diversifying the social networks of older adults and fostering the development of meaningful cross-age relationships can increase resources for social support and encourage people of all ages to work toward the common good. Promoting the integration of residents of senior housing into their local communities can also create opportunities for them to be "generative" by transmitting their skills, knowledge, and experiences to younger generations. Research suggests that engagement in high quality intergenerational programs has been shown to decrease social isolation and increase older adults' sense of belonging, self-esteem, and well-being (Seeman, Lusignolo, Albert, & Berkman, 2001). In addition to benefiting individuals, intergenerational programs and practices can address the pervasive ageism that threatens to undermine the social compact – the obligations we have to each other over time (Pastor & Carter, 2012; Robbins, 2015).

Senior Housing as a Physical Hub for Intergenerational Work

Although many senior housing communities are built in close proximity to or on the same campus as schools, YMCAs, youth organizations, and/or family housing, a 2017 study by Generations United and LeadingAge (Henkin & Patterson, 2017) suggests that there is a major gap between the potential and practice of making community connections and building intergenerational relationships. With some exceptions, connecting with educational institutions and community youth organizations has not been an integral part of senior housing programming or services. Although many senior housing sites offer discrete intergenerational activities, most are short-term and not focused on building meaningful relationships between residents and community youth.

There is a dearth of information on how housing sites use their indoor and outdoor spaces to promote cross-age interaction. In order to explore this issue further, the authors interviewed leadership staff from housing organizations and architects who have intentionally used environmental design concepts to foster connectivity between older residents, youth, and the community more broadly. The following are three models that emerged, with examples of each.

Senior Housing Communities that Open Their Space to the Community

2life Communities (Formerly Jewish Community Housing for the Elderly), Boston, Massachusetts

2Life is a non-profit provider of affordable senior housing in the Boston area. Roughly 1,500 residents, representing 26 different countries and 22 primary languages, currently live in one of 2Life Communities' four campuses in Brighton, Newton, and Framingham. 2Life's approach to new development or rehabilitation embraces the notion of senior housing as "village centers," or a space that can create social connections within the building as well as connect the housing site to the broader community. As an organization, they recognize the potential the built environment has to foster social connections and are strategic about how they balance the intersection between public and private.

2Life and Congregation Kehillath Israel (KI) in Brookline, MA will soon break ground on a multigenerational village center that simultaneously addresses the issues of social isolation and housing affordability. KI has leased space for 2Life to develop 62 units of affordable senior housing, physically and programmatically connected to KI. Additional community partners will offer social, cultural, religious, and educational programming to the wider community, welcoming people of all ages and backgrounds.

FIGURE 17.1 Congregation Kehillath Israel (KI) will be leasing space on its Harvard Street campus to 2Life to create a multigenerational village center that simultaneously addresses the issues of social isolation and housing affordability

The building will include:

- 62 affordable rental apartments for seniors aged 62 and older.
- Resident-only common spaces and exercise room.
- A café or eatery in the senior community open to the public.
- A multipurpose room in KI open to the public.
- A ground floor commercial space for community-oriented retail.
- A public "pocket park" in the front of the senior community and a private landscaped courtyard for residents.
- Programs and supportive services including educational classes, intergenerational programs, senior-specific fitness classes, cultural events, etc.

McGregor, Cleveland, Ohio

The McGregor Home is a senior housing community mostly comprised of affordable and market rate independent living units, assisted living, and hospice. According to McGregor CEO, Rob Hilton, "the housing community should be a source of pride for the community. We want East Cleveland to feel welcome here and we want them to be proud of us."

McGregor planned from the start to share several elements of their community with the surrounding community. These include:

FIGURE 17.2 McGregor residents, family, staff, and the broader community can participate in the "Planting Partners" program at their community garden

The Community Garden and Orchard, located in a space that is easily accessible to the public, offers an opportunity for residents, community volunteers, and area school students to work with a horticulture therapist to grow vegetables that are harvested by residents and volunteers.

The Auditorium (called The Community Room), the largest air-conditioned and well-lit space in East Cleveland, is used to host monthly town hall meetings, mayoral and city council inauguration, and an annual "Senior-Senior Prom" with high school students from the community.

The Bistro café, officially called *Tootie's Tea Room*, is open to the community for breakfast, lunch, and early afternoon snacks and is a favorite daily gathering spot for residents, housing staff, and community employees.

Shared Campuses that Include Senior Housing and Schools, Childcare Facilities, and/or Universities

Hebrew SeniorLife

Intergenerational work is an integral part of programming at Hebrew SeniorLife (HSL), a non-profit, non-sectarian provider of health care and housing for older adults in the Boston area. On their seven campuses of affordable and market-rate housing, there are multiple activities designed to bring older adults and young people together. The long-standing partnership between New Bridge on the Charles senior living and The Rashi School, a Jewish day school that is co-located on the same campus in Dedham, MA, is an excellent example of intentional use of physical space to promote cross-age interaction. Although an internal road separates the school from the housing units, linking the two communities are paved walking paths and an intergenerational sculpture. The paths facilitate

FIGURE 17.3 Residents from New Bridge on the Charles senior living and students from The Rashi School walk on the paved paths that link the two entities and facilitate regular visits

regular visits from classrooms and make it easier for older residents to volunteer in the school. A shared garden and numerous courtyards are used as gathering places for formal intergenerational activities. Plans are underway to develop an after-school program that would take advantage of the campus's wooded area.

Indoor spaces are also used to promote both formal and informal interaction. The New Bridge Community Center, located in the middle of the campus, is the site of many events and has a café that is open to teachers, families of residents, and the community. Recently, children and residents worked together to beautify an underground parking garage that connects residents to the community center. The mural of outdoor scenes and art panels have made this a more welcoming space.

Schowalter Villa, Hesston, Kansas

Schowalter Villa Communities is comprised of independent and assisted living units, a nursing home, short-term rehab, and dementia care. Connected to Hesston Community Childcare and neighboring Hesston College via walking paths, the setting is intentional in its pursuit to provide opportunities for life-long learning, intergenerational relationships, and meaningful community.

The childcare center (now licensed for 99 children) is attached to the nursing home so the least mobile residents can have the closest proximity. Every day, residents and children walk through a hallway called "Main Street" which has a glass viewing wall that looks onto the daycare center, a bank, an ice cream parlor, and a gift shop. Several independent living residents serve as childcare assistants in the childcare center. The intergenerational program coordinator organizes five intergenerational activities per week, open to everyone, but conducted in the assisted living or nursing home communities.

FIGURE 17.4 Viewing wall at Schowalter Villa. A ramp connects the nursing home to the childcare center

FIGURE 17.5 Every morning, residents and children from the day care center engage in playtime in the shared courtyard

Additional intentionally planned shared spaces include:

- Public cafés in the independent living and assisted living communities.
- A shared patio between the new assisted living building and the childcare center designed by a Kansas State landscape architecture student.
- A shared wheelchair and child-friendly courtyard that also hosts Hesston College music department students for performances, singalongs, and bonfires.
- Walking paths that connect all of the elements (independent and assisted living, childcare center, college, arboretum).

Intentional Intergenerational Communities

Bridge Meadows, Portland, Oregon

Bridge Meadows is a multigenerational affordable housing community in Portland, Oregon, consisting of nine homes for families (29 children) who have agreed to adopt children and youth from the foster care system and 27 older adults who contribute 100 volunteer hours/year to support families in exchange for reduced rent. From its inception, the developers of Bridge Meadows were very intentional about using the physical environment to foster relationship building. Connection and safety are pillars of the community. To foster informal interaction, the houses for families and older adults are intermixed. They open onto a central courtyard where children play, and residents of all ages interact informally. In the courtyard there is a community garden with structures that enable all ages to participate in gardening. Sidewalks crisscross the community and connect various gathering places.

FIGURE 17.6 Bridge Meadows central courtyard with raised garden beds, surrounded by intermixed houses for foster families and older adults

A large community room with an attached kitchen and a variety of smaller gathering spaces provide indoor spaces for residents to share weekly community dinners and hold activities (e.g. art classes, reading groups). In addition, all mailboxes are located in the lobby of the main building, increasing the likelihood of residents interacting on a daily basis.

In order to connect with the broader community, Bridge Meadows also offers use of its space to the Neighborhood Association and other groups that are connected to residents.

Cathedral Square Corporation (CSC), Burlington, Vermont

Cathedral Square owns or manages 30 affordable-housing communities in the greater Burlington area. It has three intentionally designed intergenerational communities and one forthcoming mixed-use community.

- *McAuley Square Housing Community* is part of a multigenerational community providing 55-apartments for low-income older adults, as well as a group of seven studio apartments for young mothers and parents returning to school called *Independence Place*. Residents share a communal living space, community kitchen for group meals, and a playroom for the children.

FIGURE 17.7 Independence Place, pictured here, is one of three buildings that make up the McAuley Square community in Burlington, VT. Independence Place provides young parents with children the opportunity to stand on their own feet, and is located next to McAuley Square, housing for older adults. A third building on the campus, Scholars House, provides housing for young parents who are continuing their education

- *Wright House* is a USDA Rural Development/Section 515 36-unit community for seniors and individuals with disabilities. The community is intentionally located across the street from two Habitat for Humanity single-family homes, and adjacent to a HUD-subsidized multifamily community. The properties are connected by walking paths, shared social activities, a community garden with raised garden beds, and a public common room with a fireplace and kitchen.
- *South Burlington Community Housing (SBCH)* is mix of HUD Section 811 housing (eligible residents are disabled individuals 62 years and under) co-located with single-family homes and duplexes. The community offers a non-institutional setting where residents can live independently in a group setting. It is intentionally located near transportation and local colleges for easy access.
- *Cambrian Rise*, a new development slated to open in the fall of 2019, will first include 70 units of subsidized senior apartments and 76 multifamily units.

A courtyard with raised garden beds, a playground with intentionally placed benches, bike paths, and a walking loop will create opportunities for passive observation and active integration to accommodate everyone's level of and desire for engagement.

EMERGING PRINCIPLES

Although the aforementioned senior housing sites differ in the way they use their physical space to foster cross-age interaction or increase opportunities for social interaction, the following are some principles that can be useful to others interested in doing this work.

- Both indoor and outdoor spaces should promote informal interaction as well as formal intergenerational programming.
- Spaces should be designed to be enabling and accommodate variations in participants' abilities, perceptions, and preferences for active vs passive experiences.
- Residents, housing staff, and community partners (when available) should be involved in designing spaces that promote meaningful interaction.
- Space should be used to promote intergenerational values (e.g. interdependence, reciprocity, inclusion, social connectedness, etc.).
- If possible, large rooms should be adaptable, using moveable walls or lightweight furnishings to create quiet, intimate spaces that facilitate self-disclosure as well as spaces for large group activities.
- The use of physical space should be aligned with programming and policies that intentionally promote relationship building across generations.
- New developments should be intentional about proximity to public transportation to support intergenerational programming.

Conclusion

There is growing evidence that senior housing can facilitate service coordination, wellness interventions, and other efforts to help older adults, particularly low-income older adults, age successfully in their community. In this role, it has the potential to serve as a major hub for intergenerational and community interaction. However, in order for that potential to become a reality, efforts are needed to increase awareness and knowledge in relevant fields (e.g. housing organizations, local youth-serving groups, real estate developers, design and architectural firms) about the benefits of intergenerational practice, effective programming, and concrete strategies for using the physical environment to connect older residents and members of the local community in mutually beneficial ways.

References

Ball, M. B., Whittington, F. J., Perkins, M. M., Patterson, V. L., Hollingsworth, C., & King, S. V. (2000). Quality of life in assisted living facilities: Viewpoints of residents. *Journal of Applied Gerontology, 19*, 304–325.

Blaschke, C. M., Freddolino, P. P., & Mullen, E. E. (2009). Ageing and technology: A review of the research literature. *British Journal of Social Work, 39*(4), 641–656.

Brown, C., & Henkin, N. (2018). Communities for all ages: Reinforcing and reimagining the social compact. In P. B. Stafford (Ed.), *The global age-friendly community movement: A critical appraisal* (pp. 139–168). New York: Berghahn.

Cannuscio, C., Block, J., & Kawachi, I. (2003). Social capital and successful aging: The role of senior housing. *Annals of Internal Medicine, 139*, 395–399. doi:http://dx. doi.org/10.7326/0003-4819-139-5_Part_2-200309021-00003.

Carroll, J., & Qualls, S. H. (2014). Moving into senior housing: Adapting the old, embracing the new. *Generations, 38*(1), 42–47.

Frochen, S., & Pynoos, J. (2017). Housing for the elderly: Addressing gaps in knowledge through the lens of age-friendly communities. *Journal of Housing for the Elderly, 31*(2), 160–177.

Goyea, J. G., Curley, A., Melekis, K., Levine, N., & Lee, Y. (2018). Loneliness and depression among older adults in urban subsidized housing. *Journal of Aging and Health, 30*(3), 458–474. doi:10.1177/0898264316682908.

Henkin, N., & Patterson, T. (2017). *Intergenerational programming in senior housing: From promise to practice. A report of Generations United and LeadingAge.* Retrieved from https:// leadingage.org/sites/default/files/Intergenerational_Programming_in_Senior_Hou sing_Full_Report.pdf.

Joint Center for Housing Studies of Harvard University. (2016). *Projections and implications of housing on aging population: Older households 2015–2035.* Cambridge, MA: Joint Center for Housing Studies.

Mitchell, J. M., & Kemp, B. J. (2000). Quality of life in assisted living homes: A multidimensional analysis. *Journal of Gerontology: Psychological Sciences, 55B*, P117–P127.

Molinsky, J., & Forsyth, A. (2018). Housing, the built environment, and the good life. *Hastings Center Report, 48*(53).

Pastor, M., & Carter, V. (2012). Reshaping the social contract: Demographic distance and our fiscal future. *Poverty & Race, 21*(1), January/February 2012, 5–6.

Redford, D. L., & Kochera, A. (2005). Targeting services to those most at risk: Characteristics of residents in federally subsidized housing. *Journal of Housing for the Elderly, 18* (3–4), 137–163.

Robbins, L. A. (2015). The pernicious problem of ageism. *Generations, 39*(3), 6–9.

Seeman, T. E., Lusignolo, T. M., Albert, M., & Berkman, L. (2001). Social relationships, social support, and patterns of cognitive aging in healthy, high-functioning older adults: MacArthur studies of successful aging. *Health Psychology, 20*(4), 243.

Sergeant, J. F., & Ekerdt, D. J. (2008). Motives for residential mobility in later life: Post-move perspectives of elders and family members. *The International Journal of Aging and Human Development, 6*(2), 131–154.

Steptoe, A., Shakar, A., Demakakos, P., & Wardle, J. (2013). Social isolation, loneliness, and all-cause mortality in older men and women. *Proceedings of the National Academy of Sciences*, *110*(5), 5797–5801.

Taylor, H. O., Wang, Y., & Morrow-Howell, N. (2018). Loneliness in senior housing communities. *Journal of Gerontological Social Work*, *61*(6), 623–639. doi:10.1080/01634372.2018.1478352.

Wright, K. (2000). Computer-mediated social support, older adults, and coping. *Journal of Communication*, *50*, 100–118.

18

THE JAPANESE TEAPOT

Objects at Home that Possess Intergenerational Contact Zone Generating Properties

Yoshika Yamamoto and Leng Leng Thang

Introduction

In Japan, green tea is the most frequently consumed beverage at any time of the day (MAFF, 2005). Japanese tea culture brings to mind the unique way of appreciating tea through formal tea sessions at *chano-yu* or the Japanese tea ceremony promoted through major traditional schools of tea, such as Urasenke, Omotsenke and Enshu (Sadler, 2011). Nonetheless, it is also important to recognize the significance of Japanese tea culture in everyday social practice at home. In fact, the space for tea is equivalent to the home space: a Japanese living room is called a *chanoma* – a space for tea; a traditional Japanese dining table is called a *chabudai* – a platform for tea. A family getting together to share a teapot of brewed Japanese tea at the *chanoma* provides the prospect to promote family communication and thus signifies the ideal scenario of multigenerational family togetherness (Zojirushi Corporation, 2018; Shimobiraki, 1999). Conceptually, we refer to such a tea-drinking space as one that creates intergenerational connections – an ICZ (Intergenerational Contact Zone) made possible through the sharing of Japanese tea in a teapot.

Although it may seem straightforward, the act of brewing tea from a teapot requires technique commonly transferred from one generation to the next as part of Japanese tea culture at home. The making of Japanese tea in a teapot requires a steaming process to prevent oxidization of the freshly picked tea leaves. This unique method produces the desired Japanese tea color and flavor. Because of this process, control technique learned from the older generation to attain appropriate temperature and timing for brewing in a teapot is necessary. However, with recent decades of generational segregation accelerated through the process of family nuclearization, it has become increasingly difficult to expect generational succession of Japanese tea culture at home as multiple generations of family members make less efforts to get together.

In this chapter focusing on ICZ as a conceptual approach, we contend that as a symbol of Japanese tradition, the Japanese teapot at home is an example of home objects that come to possess ICZ-generating properties by way of promoting values and restoring opportunities for family communication in a modern era context. In the following section, we first briefly discuss the factors leading to a decline of Japanese tea culture at home. Following which, we introduce two case studies conducted in Nara Prefecture aimed at exploring the efforts of 'Yamato-cha' in the reviving of Japanese tea culture among the younger generations. 'Yamato-cha' refers to tea leaves that are produced on the Yamato highland situated in the northeastern region of Nara Prefecture.

Nara Prefecture is a part of the Kinki region in west central Honshu, the biggest island of Japan. Nara Prefecture is situated just next to Kyoto.

The Decline of Japanese Tea Culture at Home

Green tea is one of the main agricultural products in Japan. The 'Current Outlook of Japanese Tea' Report prepared by MAFF (2017), however, has shown several dilemmas challenging the industry, such as slowdown in demand affecting the crude tea price, the decline in the population of tea farmers and a reduction in the production volume. Nonetheless, with increasing awareness of the desirable health properties of green tea, the export of Japanese green tea has seen a rapid rise over the years, increasing from 599 tons in 2001 to 4108 tons in 2016 (MAFF, 2017). In the domestic market, there is however a diversifying trend of a decline in consumption volume of green tea (in the form of leaf tea) and the contrary increase of green tea beverage consumption in plastic polyethylene terephthalate (PET) bottles. Since 2007, the expenditure for tea beverage products has been exceeding that of green tea leaf (Ministry of Internal Affairs and Communications, 2007). In 2001, the proportion of annual expenditure for green tea leaf/green tea beverage product per household was about 60%/40%, but this proportion was reversed in 2016 (Ministry of Agriculture, Forestry and Fisheries, 2017). The decline in the consumption of green tea leaves shows a gradual shift in consumer preference away from the social practice of brewing tea in a teapot at home. Obviously, the easy availability of bottled green tea introduced since 1984 by Ito En, a Japanese tea company has greatly contributed to the shift in preference (Nikkei Asian Review, 2017).

The green tea leaf/tea beverage preference also differs among different generations. The periodical report on the monitoring of food consumption (Ministry of Agriculture, Forestry and Fisheries, 2005) shows that younger generations prefer tea beverages rather than green leaf tea. Yamamoto and Shimizu (2018) further point to the generation gaps between older and younger generations about tea-drinking custom at home: while the younger generation prefers bottled tea beverages and tea bags, those who are in their sixties and older prefer brewing tea from a teapot. Tsunoyama (2005) has cautioned that the convenience of consuming bottled green tea beverages is negatively affecting everyday customary tea culture. At the same time, he is wary of the gradual disappearance of family get-togethers as families spent less time socializing and drinking tea in the Japanese living room. The characteristics of households with persons aged 65 and over have changed drastically in the last three decades. As shown in the Comprehensive Survey of Living Conditions (MHLW, 2018), while 44.8% lived in three-generation households in 1986, the proportion has declined to 11% by 2016. During the same period, the proportion of those living alone or with a spouse only has risen from 28.8% to 49.6%. It is a reality that more of the older generation are drinking their tea brewed in the teapot without the presence of the younger persons, or any other people. Families are spending less time dining and drinking tea together as more women have joined the workforce, and more children are spending time in their own bedrooms. The ideal of tea culture at home as a socializing platform for both the old and young generations seems to be disappearing in everyday practice.

Efforts to Promote Japanese Tea Culture and the ICZ of Tea

'Yamato-cha' and the Act on the Promotion of Tea Industry and Tea Culture *(Ocha no shinkou ni kansuru houritsu' (2011)*

Nara Prefecture is among the top ten prefectures in the production of tea leaves in Japan (see Figures 18.1 and 18.2). However, over the last three decades, the tea industry in this area faced serious problems relating to the decline in the tea price, the decline in the population of tea farmers and the reduction of tea plantation fields. To counter these problems, many organizations are cooperating to ensure the sustainability of Yamato-tea growing.

In a way, the dilemma facing Yamato-cha is typical among the Japanese tea-growing regions. In 2011, such challenges have led to the establishment of the 'Act on the Promotion of Tea Industry and Tea Culture' (Ocha no shinkou ni kansuru houritsu' (2011) by the Japanese government. The Act aims to

> take various measures such as securing stable business management of tea producers, expanding consumption, promoting food education using tea to contribute to such consumption, promoting export and disseminating knowledge on tea tradition, so as to contribute to the achievement of sound development of tea industry and healthy and affluent lives of nationals.
>
> *(Ministry of Agriculture, Forestry and Fisheries, 2017)*

FIGURE 18.1 The location of Nara Prefecture

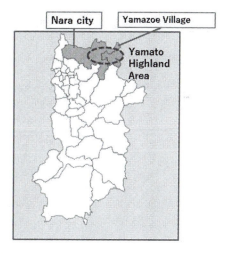

FIGURE 18.2 The Yamato-cha area in Nara Prefecture

Under this Act, the Ministry of Agriculture, Forestry and Fisheries and local governments have proactively promoted a tea culture through various events that promotes intergenerational interaction in a direct or indirect manner. In the following section, we discuss two of these activities called 'A Yamato-cha class at an elementary school' and 'A Yamato-cha promotion event'.

Yamato-cha Classes at Elementary Schools

To promote the tea culture of drinking green tea from a teapot, Nara city has collaborated with the 'Yamato-cha' tea producing farmers and tea specialists to offer a lesson on drinking Yamato-cha to elementary school children. The lesson is usually offered to fourth and fifth graders as a part of the local studies curriculum. During the lesson, students learn about Yamato-cha and are given a chance to taste Japanese tea brewed in a teapot. Tea specialists qualified as 'Japanese tea instructors' first demonstrate how to brew tea using a Japanese teapot with appropriate temperature and timing. The children then have hands-on opportunities to try to make Japanese tea in a teapot by themselves and taste the tea. In a report by Yamamoto and Shimizu (2018) who had conducted a survey with 236 students from five elementary schools who participated in the lesson in November 2017 to February 2018, 40.7% of the students responded that they did not have a teapot at home. Furthermore, 36% answered that they have never drunk tea from a Japanese teapot. Children in families with only younger parents are less likely to have experienced the tea culture of brewing tea in a Japanese teapot.

When the students were asked the question 'When do you want to drink Yamato-cha (defined as Japanese green tea with a Japanese teapot)?' almost all wanted to do it with their family members, with 58.1% answering 'With my grandparents'. About 80% of the students also answered, 'We like to drink "Yamato cha" in the future.' (Yamamoto & Shimizu, 2018, pp. 14–15). By relating the consumption of green tea from a teapot with family gatherings and experience, the Japanese tea class in the school curriculum also promotes motivation for interaction of the younger generation with the older generation. It is likely that in the future, the school education system might assume the leading role in the transfer of Japanese tea culture instead of expecting older generations to impart the culture solely through home education. As school children bring back the knowledge and skill of making Japanese tea from a teapot with the connected idea of intergenerational communication, school thus becomes an agent in enabling the generation of ICZ in the home environment.

A Yamato-cha Promotion Event

The Yamato-cha promotion event first started in the autumn of 2015 with the aim of branding and marketing Yamato-cha. Since then, this event has been held every autumn in Nara Prefecture. The event is a collaboration managed by multiple organizations including the local tea farmers, the land improvement district office, Nara city, Yamazoe Village, the Nara Prefecture, the Kinki Regional Agricultural Administration Office and two universities in the region (St. Agnes Heian Jogakuin University and Kyoto University). From 2015 to 2017, the event was held at the Gyoki-hiroba just in front of Kintetsu Nara station. This is a busy site located in the city center and near to popular tourist spots such as Todai-ji Temple and Nara Park. As a result, it was attractive for both tourists and the locals. In the past three years, thousands of cups of tea were distributed for tasting at the event (4000 cups/2015, 4400 cups/2016 and 6000 cups/2017). Many people regardless of age or gender enjoyed the leaf tea brewed in Japanese teapots. In a street survey conducted at the 2017 event, feedback centered on requests for more information about the characteristics of drinking tea using tea leaves and proper ways to brew good tea with a Japanese teapot (Yamamoto & Shimizu, 2018). The survey shows that this event is effective in expanding public awareness about Yamato-cha in general as well as appreciation of how it tastes, but it has not been able to achieve more to engage people with the tea culture in the long term.

To improve on the annual event, a workshop was then held among the event members to discuss a strategy for the 2018 event. In this workshop, tea farmers in their sixties and university students in their twenties got together to exchange views. When tea farmers served tea brewed in a Japanese teapot during the workshop, the aroma of the tea, completely different from that of bottled tea beverages, seemed to change the flow of the conversation. The attendants became interested in how to make such good tea with a Japanese teapot. The university students were especially in awe and began to ask the tea farmers what were the features of the tea leaves used, and the technique of brewing the tea. They grew to have great respect for the tea farmers. The older generation tea farmers also seemed to enjoy talking about their own tea and sharing their skills for making good tea. The workshop ended up as an effective platform for intergenerational exchanges. At the end of the workshop, it was also decided that the event would move from the city center to the suburbs of Nara to reach out to more locals.

Subsequently, the 2018 Yamato-cha event was held at the farmers' market in Kashihara city in a Nara suburb. The farmers' market is a popular shopping place among the locals with more than 1000 visitors during the weekend. With more spaces, the tea farmers were able to brew their own tea in a Japanese teapot and engage more deeply with the visitors about how to make good tea. Young parents with small children were especially enthusiastic and listened intently. Moreover, for educational and fun purposes, the 'Yamato-cha quiz' was organized in a family friendly way to test the visitors' knowledge of Yamato-cha. Many children were excited about the quiz, and attempted the questions with the help of their parents and grandparents. The quiz consisted of ten 'yes' or 'no' responses relating to the basic knowledge of Yamato-cha, such as: 'Is May the best season for picking new tea leaves?', 'Are black tea and green tea produced from the same tea leaves?', 'Is there more caffeine in green tea brewed from cold water?', 'Is 100 degree Celsius ideal for brewing Japanese green tea?'. Parents and grandparents were seen having fun engaging with the young children in determining the right responses, while at the same time sipping Japanese tea brewed in a teapot. Although all participants received small participation awards, those who obtained perfect scores also received premium Yamato-cha products as special prizes.

At the 2018 event, many university students were positioned alongside the tea farmers to help serve tea to the visitors. To prepare for this partnership, the students stayed one night at the tea farmers' houses before the event. During the stay, they learned the differences in the lifestyles of the generations and about the older generation's passion for Japanese tea. This experience enabled the students to gain more knowledge about tea farming and the skills required to brew good tea with a Japanese teapot. Besides gaining tea-brewing skills from the tea farmers, the students were also presented with finest Japanese tea to brew in a teapot and share with their family in the *chanoma* (living rooms) in their homes.

During the event, these university students appeared to serve as a 'bridging generation' between the school children, parents and grandparents. While they belong to the younger generation that generally prefers bottled tea beverages, they have learned how to make fine tea from the older generation that they have respect for. As servers, they tried to express the essence of Japanese tea culture in their own words and contributed towards turning the event into an ICZ through tea sharing from a teapot. Through interest and communication centered on the teapot, the revamped event in 2018 has contributed towards building deeper intergenerational connections between the students, tea farmers and visiting families.

FIGURE 18.3 University students and the tea farmers at the 2018 Yamato-cha event

Discussion and Conclusion

A recent survey conducted every 12 consecutive years since 1982 by Corporation (2018) (a Japanese household produce manufacturer) has revealed interesting facts that Japanese people consistently perceive drinking tea during family get-togethers as a mode of enhancing social bonding and communication. This problematizes the reality that such scenarios of ICZ where family members of all generations get together over a pot of tea are fast disappearing in today's culture where bottled tea beverage consumption and small nuclear households are the norm.

This chapter considers how such ICZ contexts can be sustained and expanded through a revival – or at least an increase in awareness – of the traditional everyday tea culture. Through two case studies focused on efforts to promote interest and engagement of younger generations in the restoration of Japanese tea culture in Nara Prefecture, we identified several effective components and interventions that contributed to deepened intergenerational exchanges at community events, in school, and at home. They include: (i) inviting farmers and tea specialists to elementary schools to conduct demonstrations on preparing Yamato-cha tea, and provide students with hands-on opportunities to make and taste Japanese tea made in a teapot, (ii) basing tea promotion events outside of the city center in order to get closer to where most residents spend the majority of their time, (iii) including family engaging activities at tea promotion events, such as the 'Yamato-cha quiz' which was organized in a family friendly way to increase visitors' knowledge and stimulate interest in preparing and consuming Yamato-cha tea, and (iv) making sure that all residents have ample opportunity to enjoy the aroma and taste of traditionally prepared, high quality green tea. Although it may seem too simplistic to assume that serving tea from a teapot is enough for the creation of an ICZ, drinking from the 'same' teapot should at least hope to symbolize the creation of a sense of solidarity among the generations as they share from the 'same' teapot.

To conclude, the case of a Japanese teapot provides evidence of how the resurgence of a culturally significant practice could activate the potential for related objects to take on ICZ generating properties. Parallels in other cultures that have ICZ-generating properties are worth exploring. For example, there has been a resurgence of slow cooking in Indian food in recent years (see for example, Singla, 2010; Paniz, 2014). If this indeed becomes a trend, and if growing sales of an object like a slow cooker (necessary for slow cooking of Indian food) is a parallel trend, could the slow cooker be noted as an object that connects generations in a manner similar to the Japanese teapot but in a different cultural context?

The discovery of ICZ generating properties in objects such as the Japanese teapot, which serve as symbols of intergenerational as well as cultural continuity, can further our understanding of their potential for regenerating and recreating culturally distinct social practices in multigenerational households and community settings.

Acknowledgment

We acknowledge funding from Tobacco Academic Studies Center Foundation, Japan (2017). We wish to thank the Research Institute of Science and Technology for Society, Japan Science and Technology Agency for the opportunity to discuss this paper at the World Social Science Forum held in Fukuoka, Japan in September 2018.

References

Japan Soft Drink Association. (2017). *Soft drinks statistics*. Retrieved from http://j-sda.or.jp/about-jsda/english/sd-statistics.php.

MAFF (Ministry of Agriculture, Forestry and Fisheries). (2005). *Shokuryohin shohi monita. Dainikai teikichosa kekka* [The second periodical report on the monitoring of food consumption]. Retrieved from http://www.maff.go.jp/j/heya/h_moniter/pdf/h1702.pdf.

MAFF (Ministry of Agriculture, Forestry and Fisheries). (2017). *Current outlook of Japanese tea*. Retrieved from http://www.maff.go.jp/e/policies/agri/attach/pdf/index-1.pdf.

Ministry of Health, Labour and Welfare. (2018). *Graphical review of Japanese household from comprehensive survey of living conditions, 2016*. Tokyo: Author. Retrieved from https://www.mhlw.go.jp/toukei/list/dl/20-21-h28_rev2.pdf.

Ministry of Internal Affairs and Communications, Household Statistics. (2007). *Family income and expenditure survey*. Retrieved from http://www.stat.go.jp/data/kakei/index.html.

Nikkei Asian Review. (2017. October 25). *30 billion bottles and counting: Japan's green tea titan*. Retrieved from https://asia.nikkei.com/Business/30-billion-bottles-and-counting-Japan-s-green-tea-titan3.

Ocha no shinkou ni kansuru houritu [Act on Promotion of Tea Industry and Tea Culture]. (2011). April 5, Act No. 20. The House of Representatives. Japan.

Paniz, N. (2014). *The new Indian slow cooker: Recipes for curries, dals, chutneys, masalas, biryani, and more*. Berkeley, CA: Ten Speed Press.

Sadler, A. L. (2011). *Cha-no-yu: The Japanese tea ceremony*. North Clarendon, VT: Tuttle Publishing.

Shimobiraki, C. (1999). Ocha to Kazoku ni kannsuru chosa kenkyu [The research on tea and family]. *LDI Report, 108*, 31–53.

Singla, A. (2010). *Indian slow cooker: 50 healthy, easy, authentic recipes*. Chicago: Agate Publishing.

Tsunoyama, S. (2005). *Cha to motenashi no bunka – Tea and culture of hospitality*. Tokyo: NTT Publishing.

Yamamoto, Y., & Shimizu, N. (2018). Jizokukanouna chagou wo mezashita tiikishigen manejimento: Yamato-cha wo jireitoshite [Challenges for sustainable local resource management of Japanese tea farming: A case study of Yamato-cha]. *The Report of Research Grant of Tobacco Academic Studies Centre, 2017*, 133–161.

Zojirushi Corporation. (2018). *Ikkadanran ni kansuru ishiki to jittaityousa* [A survey of facts and perceptions of family get-together]. Retrieved from https://www.zojirushi.co.jp/topics/danran2018.html.

19

THE VIRTUAL ENVIRONMENT AS INTERGENERATIONAL CONTACT ZONE

Play through Digital Gaming

Eyu Zang

Introduction

Following societal digitization, social interaction has been widely extended beyond physical spaces to digital realms. Literature has drawn emphasis on how digital inclusion benefits both the young and old, such as facilitating social inclusion and overall well-being of older adults (Bailey & Ngwenyama, 2011; Kaletka, Pelka, Diaz, Rissola, & Rastrelli, 2012; Kaplan, Sánchez, & Bradley, 2015; Smith & Chilcott, 2013), as well as enhancing academic performance, employability, and social integration of youths (Kaletka et al., 2012; Loos, 2014; Ter Vrugte & de Jong, 2012).

Digital platforms have further shown potential to bridge generations, often on the basis of equitable participation, along with goals such as knowledge transfer, greater family cohesion, and joint participation in community improvement projects (Sánchez, Kaplan, & Bradley, 2015). In proposing that the virtual environment is a pertinent dimension to be recognized as a new category of Intergenerational Contact Zone (ICZ), this chapter contends that it is important to consider ways to design digital platforms for intergenerational contact and relationship building, and addresses digital gaming as part of this discourse.

Although digital gaming is traditionally seen as the domain of the young (particularly male users), in recent years gaming industries and researchers have branched out to target other user groups such as females and the elderly. There has also been an increased attention to gameplay designs with substantial intergenerational (IG) interaction components, although in general, digital games for IG play and bonding remain a novel idea.

The remainder of this chapter puts forth a series of design principles with relevant examples deemed to be critical for inclusion in digital gaming platforms intended to serve as ICZ.

Digital Game Pre-development Stage: Participatory Design Process

Prior to game designing, involving the target users during the pre-development stage through participatory design is a viable strategy for addressing the socio-psychological preferences and needs of the different age groups, which could vary across sociocultural or economic backgrounds. The participatory aspect also allows for an investigation of gameplay motivations, which might help sustain players' interest if addressed (de la Hera, Loos, Simons, & Blom, 2017). Participatory design can come in forms of both passive and active involvement ranging from surveys and interviews to focus group discussions, co-designing sessions, and prototypical testing.

For example, *Blast from the Past*,[1] a digital game specifically designed for gameplay between grandparents and grandchildren, employed player-centered design methodologies. The design team involved seniors and children from the start through sessions of brainstorming, co-design, focus group discussions and prototypical testing. Through iterative developments, the target audiences contributed recommendations for game design adjustments at each stage (De Schutter, 2008; De Schutter & Vanden Abeele, 2014).

A more passive pre-development stage game design process was adopted in developing the *Distributed Hide and Seek* game.[2] Building upon observations of playgroups between grandparents and preschool grandchildren, as well as cultural probe analysis of IG activities, the developers explored how the nature of interaction (episodic and open-ended creative play) and diverse IG roles (with seniors as "Organizer, Instructor, Carer, Co-player, Entertainer or Observer," and kids as "Accomplice, Apprentice, the Cared-for, Co-player or Audience") can be translated into technological form (Vetere, Nolan, & Raman, 2006).

Gameplay Design Content: Social Dynamics

Designing to Leverage and Bridge the Different Generational Capabilities

IG gameplay builds upon or caters to the experiences and capabilities of each age group. Consider, for example, the game *Age Invaders* that targets grandchildren, parents, and grandparents. While the game element of avoiding laser beams and rockets, which requires speed and proprioceptive awareness, might favor younger participants, the feature that draws on players' acquired knowledge (involving detection and use of visual cues for solving cognitive problems) might favor the older participants.

Furthermore, the game's "hyperspace mode" with combined quiz and movement gameplay makes it more effective for the players to adopt collaborative play strategies that draw upon the strengths of each generation (Figure 19.1) (Khoo, Cheok, Nguyen, & Pan, 2008).

Additionally, IG digital games can incorporate supportive or adjustable elements that assist to bridge age-related limitations (de la Hera et al., 2017). For example, the laser beam speed in *Age Invaders* is an adjustable game parameter to help leverage the playing field, which could be helpful for some elderly players who might have slower physical reflexes.

Designing for Diversified IG Gameplay Patterns

Game mechanisms that allow a player to partake in the IG digital game in various manners can facilitate more dynamic IG interactions. *Minecraft* and *Pokémon Go* are excellent examples, despite not being specifically designed as IG digital games.

In *Minecraft*,[3] there are diverse modes and sub-games that encourage different ways of gameplay. Players can experience the game single-handedly or compete and collaborate with each other. The open-ended playing style that emphasizes creation allows players to showcase their personalities, which greatly enriches the gameplay

FIGURE 19.1 An illustration of the hyperspace mode whereby gameplay taps on the different strengths of generations to make meaningful collaborative play (Source: Khoo et al., 2008). Reprinted by permission from Springer Nature: Springer Nature, *Virtual Reality*, Khoo et al., Age invaders: social and physical intergenerational mixed reality family entertainment, Copyright 2008

interaction. For example, in a collaboration case of the IG Minecraft workshop (under the Age-Friendly Honolulu Youth Engagement Initiative), youths and older adults partnered up to discuss how their neighborhood should be redesigned for age-friendliness. They jointly coordinate the design details using *Minecraft*, such as building a community gathering area with benches and shade (Nishita & Terada, 2019). Families and even an entire neighborhood can come together on the same server to build on the same game world in *Minecraft*, and the game also serves as a teaching tool since players are able to learn and participate in architectural planning and programming (Morris, 2017; Popper, 2014). Through these processes, players could have a deeper understanding of each other's character and thinking, which helps to provide quality bonding between generations.

Pokémon Go[4] has also been observed to enhance family bonding time and increase IG communication within many families (Sobel et al., 2017; Sung, Sigerson, & Cheng, 2017; Tran, 2018). The gameplay system allows for both structured and unstructured play, and this flexibility accommodates diverse family roles and relationships as well as gameplay interests and routines. For example, parents can create a structured play environment for children by providing guidance on gameplay strategies (Tran, 2018) and monitoring their safety while maneuvering in the physical space (Sobel et al., 2017). Unstructured and spontaneous exchanges can also happen when users play individually and learn from each other thereafter, such as children, parents, and grandparents sharing their experiences over a mobile chat group (Sobel et al., 2017). This versatile IG gameplay is possible from the multitude of online and offline collaborations and documentation on gameplay information, which is accessible to any player.

It is also recommended to design for "vicarious play", referring to co-located gameplay whereby one party is in active control of the game, while others participate mentally at the side. Vicarious play has been observed as one of the most common styles of IG gameplay, but rarely intentionally designed for. For instance, having the side players or observers keep track of on-screen visual hints, or to source for information outside the game while the main player controls the game (De Schutter & Vanden Abeele, 2010).

Designing for Larger Breadth of Generational Involvement

Another recommendation is to pay more attention to intermediary age groups (such as adults or youths) in IG gameplays. ICZ are age inclusive, going beyond just engaging older adults and children. In Voida & Greenberg's (2012) study, it was observed that the intermediary age groups tend to be adept in both gameplay mechanisms and pro-social behaviors, whereas the younger and older generations tend to be more proficient in the former and latter respectively. Incorporating the intermediary age groups in IG gameplays can hence be advantageous as they may assume facilitator roles to bridge capability differences, thus ensuring positive gaming experiences between the young and the aged.

Other than assuming a mediating role, involving intermediary age groups can add a layer of complexity to the gameplay. For example, in *Age Invaders*, parents can participate through operating a computer from a distance in real time (catering to parents who are often absent from home due to work). Grandparents and children play against each other in physical spaces, whereas parents are connected through the virtual world and can choose to help either team (Figures 19.2 and 19.3).

Gameplay Supporting Features

Multigenerational Design Considerations

As a basis to effective IG gameplay, gaming equipment and technological features should be conducive for multigenerational usage. This includes ensuring larger visual interfaces, such as on-screen texts and graphics for the ease of seniors' reading, and the provision of gaming equipment that incorporates lightweight and ergonomic designs that are suitable for multigenerational participation. For example, gaming tools can be made adjustable to fit children's smaller build.

FIGURE 19.2 Illustration of how parents can introduce new elements into the game through remote controls (Source: Khoo et al., 2008). Reprinted by permission from Springer Nature: Springer Nature, *Virtual Reality*, Khoo et al., Age invaders: social and physical intergenerational mixed reality family entertainment, Copyright 2008

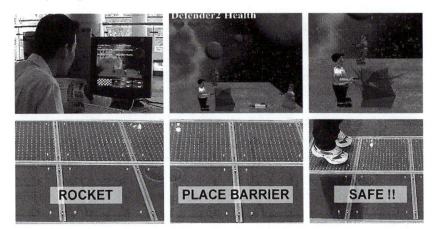

FIGURE 19.3 Parents can participate by placing virtual barriers and dropping bonus items for the game players, with the physical gameplay represented in a virtual space on the parent's computer screen (Source: Khoo et al., 2008). Reprinted by permission from Springer Nature: Springer Nature, *Virtual Reality*, Khoo et al., Age invaders: social and physical intergenerational mixed reality family entertainment, Copyright 2008

Gameplay Configuration Processes that Facilitate IG Role Switching

With legible game configuration processes that are observable to the group of players, transitions between IG gameplay roles can be better facilitated, especially for vicarious players to transit to an active decision maker/game controller. For example, Voida & Greenberg (2012) recommended to make use of larger shared displays, or to include audio feedback in the configuration process. It would also be helpful to allow for both options of having gameplay inputs on a single device as well as on distributed/multiple devices. For example, one gaming console could control all players' inputs if desired, or all consoles used for the game can be individually controlled to enter separate players' inputs. This allows for the initial situation of a single configurer as a model for others to learn from, before transiting to all parties taking control of their own input choices (Voida & Greenberg, 2012).

Language Considerations

For IG digital gaming that transcends geographical boundaries, language proficiency might become a barrier to effective interaction. In that respect, language translation functions, or pre-set gaming comments and phrases are recommended. For example, De Schutter & Vanden Abeele (2010) suggested automated translation tools in gaming chats. Pre-set gaming comments and phrases could also be crafted by game designers such that players can communicate by choosing from a list of responses in their native language with corresponding translations. It is also prudent to introduce relevant digital gaming terminologies with brief explanations alongside chat functions to facilitate effective assimilation of newcomers to the online gaming community.

Online or Offline Community/Administrative Support

It should also be considered to establish an online IG gaming community platform or forum that serves as support to the actual IG gameplay. This allows the ease of identifying suitable gaming partners with similar interests/skillsets, which will be useful if the IG gameplay designed is not tailored to any specific target groups. Typically, a programming function can be used to organize players' profile information, whereby players can be sorted into categories like age, interests, skills, and language, and the system can make autosuggestions and pairings to suitable players. Otherwise, a manual search system can be designed for players to build up their own friend lists. This supporting gameplay feature can also be incorporated into the digital game itself in the event that a separate online portal is not feasible. Online communities also serve to facilitate gameplay discussions and information sharing between generations, empowering players in the process.

Other than online support, offline support in the form of physical places offering access and training for digital games are recommended. Such support can also be intergenerational in nature, thereby offering opportunities for integrated gameplay experiences that are reinforced by both physical and virtual IG interaction. A plausible reference can be telecenters, which are places where digital services are embedded and typically managed by community-based organizations, serving as easy access points that allow for community-wide participation in ICT (Bailey & Ngwenyama, 2011; Kaletka et al., 2012).

Physical and Virtual Space Interplay

Through virtual gameplay, players' attributed meanings and attachment to physical spaces can potentially be influenced. Similarly, gameplay elements in physical spaces can facilitate the meanings and values constructed for virtual gaming environments. This is a compelling relationship which digital game designers can design for. For example, when playing *Distributed Hide and Seek*, new memories and meanings can be formed in the players' houses (the physical playing medium), whereby players can relate certain areas of the house to memorable IG interactions from the game. Although this may not be intended by the game designers, it shows the potential of utilizing digital games to connect to the physical dimension in order to enhance meaningful connections between players, in this case across different generations.

Pokémon Go further extends this notion of constructing collective new meanings for physical places via IG gameplay from homes into public spaces. For example, a player could recall fond memories at a place where he/she captured a Pokémon with their family members, enhanced by the augmented photos taken (Figure 19.4). IG co-learning experiences about educational or historical sites in the community also occurs when such sites are marked as virtual gamestops in *Pokémon Go*, allowing players' greater appreciation of their surroundings (Sobel et al., 2017; Tran, 2018). Such gameplay allows for meaningful development and anchoring of IG relationships over time and place.

Conclusion

Virtual environments as ICZ can serve as enticing and meaningful meeting places for different generations. As this chapter has illustrated, designing digital games as ICZ include the need to consider factors related to both the hardware

FIGURE 19.4 Player capturing a photo of a Pokémon encountered against the real-life scenery in Singapore. February 9, 2019

and software. In the least, gameplay processes, supporting features and equipment should not only be designed to accommodate the differing needs and capabilities of multigenerational groups, but should also facilitate inter-player sharing of gameplay knowledge, skills, and perspectives.

Moving forward, game designers can also consider establishing a formalized online resource and learning hub for IG digital gameplay. An example of such an IG learning network, *Ulm-Network KOJALA*,[5] demonstrates its power as a virtual place of exchange by allowing connections of different age groups on projects of mutual interest. Through this platform, generations learn from each other regardless of time and place, and the ease of both online and offline IG collaboration is achieved. Referencing this system, creating an online resource and learning hub can greatly benefit IG digital gameplay by encouraging players to collectively devise creative content themselves via the collaborative uploading and sharing of information, which can be used to further enhance the IG gameplay experience.

For instance, by having an online resource hub for *Pokémon Go*, players could share information on popular physical game sites in a systematic manner. This gives opportunities for educational learning to be integrated more easily into the IG gameplay, such as users updating each other on sites with educational value (e.g., historical or nature), supplemented with information that players can pick up to share as do-you-know facts during the game.

There is even potential for users to create their own gameplay trails via the shared information, for example parents could bring their children to a series of historical areas within the community as an educational journey while playing *Pokémon Go*. Such combination of online resource and learning hubs with digital gameplay can offer excellent insights to game designers in integrating learning objectives in game design, as well as merge virtual and physical spaces in ways that build more meaningful and lasting intergenerational relationships.

Finally, while this chapter presented principles on IG digital gameplay design, they are not positioned to address specific digital gaming genres or platforms. The recommendations serve more as general applications, and future research with intentions to examine specific IG digital gaming genres or platforms could potentially build upon this basis.

Notes

1 *Blast from the Past* is a Nintendo Wii game featuring two mini-games. Players experience a digitized folklore game and a building game where a 1950s monument is constructed within a time travelling narrative. These are combined with a variety of game mechanics such as physical play and allowing users to create their own quiz content.

2 *Distributed Hide and Seek* is designed to facilitate open-ended play between grandparents and grandchildren who stay apart. The hider allocates virtual gifts in the seeker's house using a touchscreen (pre-installed maps), and the seeker seeks by moving

around the house with a "magic wand" (Bluetooth PDA) that tracks his/her movements. Vocal communication happens throughout the game.

3 *Minecraft* is an internationally popular construction video game that features creation and free-play. In single-player or multiplayer servers, players create or destroy different 3D blocks that form structures and landscapes, such as cars or houses. There are various game modes, for example survival mode where players collect resources and fight off starvation and monsters, whereas in creative mode players are invincible with access to all resources and can also fly. In addition to these, there are sub-games with player versus player and role-playing modes. The variety of gameplay styles and unguided nature facilitate players in setting their own game rules and objectives.

4 *Pokémon Go* has been massively played worldwide by both the young and old. It is a location-based augmented reality mobile game where players capture virtual monsters called "Pokémon" by exploring real physical spaces. The game uses Global Positioning System to track the players' location, and Pokémon appear on the virtual game map when players are near certain physical locations. Points of interest in the physical world are marked out as virtual gamestops on the game map, such as Pokéstops (providing game items) and Gyms (for game battles). Players capture, train, battle, and trade Pokémon with oneself or others, and can be engaged in community gameplay where they join one of the three worldwide teams for collaborative Gym conquests, or in Raid Battles where different team players work together to capture strong Pokémon.

5 *Ulm-Network KOJALA* is an Internet-based competence platform by the Center for General Scientific Continuing Education (ZAWiW – Zentrum für Allgemeine Wissenschaftliche Weiterbildung) at Ulm University. Through a virtual marketplace, users can place and browse offers for collaborative projects. This is supported by the users' visiting cards (similar to profiling), and *Ulm-Network KOJALA* hosts the formation of working groups for users who have connected and agreed to embark on collaborative work (Kaplan, Sánchez, Shelton, & Bradley, 2013).

References

Bailey, A., & Ngwenyama, O. (2011). The challenge of e-participation in the digital city: Exploring generational influences among community telecentre users. *Telematics and Informatics*, *28*, 204–214. doi:10.1016/j.tele.2010.09.004.

de la Hera, T., Loos, E., Simons, M., & Blom, J. (2017). Benefits and factors influencing the design of intergenerational digital games: A systematic literature review. *Societies*, *7*(18), 1–15. doi:10.3390/soc7030018.

De Schutter, B. (2008). *Blast from the past*. Retrieved from www.bobdeschutter.be/blast-from-the-past.

De Schutter, B., & Vanden Abeele, V. (2010, September). Designing meaningful play within the psycho-social context of older adults. Paper presented at the Fun and Games 2010 conference, Leuven, Belgium.

De Schutter, B., & Vanden Abeele, V. (2014). Blast from the past: Applying the P-III framework to facilitate intergenerational play between grandparents and grandchildren. *Gerontechnology*, *13*(2), 163. doi:/10.4017/gt.2014.13.02.129.00.

Kaletka, C., Pelka, B., Diaz, A., Rissola, G., & Rastrelli, M. (2012, June). Escouts: Intergenerational Learning in Blended Environments and Spaces (ILBES) for social inclusion. Paper presented at the EDEN 2012 Annual Conference: Open Learning

Generations – Closing the gap from "Generation Y" to the mature Lifelong Learners, Porto, Portugal.

Kaplan, M., Sánchez, M., & Bradley, L. (2015). Conceptual frameworks and practical applications to connect generations in the technoscape. *Anthropology and Aging, 36*(2), 182–205.

Kaplan, M., Sánchez, M., Shelton, C., & Bradley, L. (2013). *Using technology to connect generations*. University Park, PA: Penn State University & Washington D.C.: Generations United. Retrieved from https://aese.psu.edu/extension/intergenerational/program-areas/technology.

Khoo, E. T., Cheok, A. D., Nguyen, T. H. D., & Pan, Z. (2008). Age invaders: Social and physical intergenerational mixed reality family entertainment. *Virtual Reality, 12*(1), 3–16. doi:10.1007/s10055-008-0083-0.

Loos, E. (2014, April). Designing meaningful intergenerational digital games. Paper presented at the International Conference on Communication, Media, Technology and Design, Istanbul, Turkey.

Morris, A. (2017, July 3). *Minecraft video game used to design public space in more than 25 developing countries*. Retrieved from www.dezeen.com/2017/07/03/minecraft-designed-public-space-more-than-25-developing-countries-un-habitat-block-by-block/.

Nishita, C., & Terada, T. (2019). Building virtual age-friendly communities in Minecraft. *Journal of Intergenerational Relationships, 17*(1), 118–122. doi:10.1080/15350770.2019.1551666

Popper, B. (2014, September 15). *Why parents are raising their kids on Minecraft*. Retrieved from www.theverge.com/2014/9/15/6152085/why-parents-love-minecraft.

Sánchez, M., Kaplan, M., & Bradley, L. (2015). Using technology to connect generations: Some considerations of form and function. *Comunicar, 23*(45), 95–104. doi:10.3916/C45-2015-10.

Smith, A., & Chilcott, M. (2013). An analysis of the potential to utilize virtual worlds to enhance edutainment and improve the wellbeing of the ageing population. In Z. Pan, A. D. Cheok, W. Müller, & F. Liarokapis (Eds.), *Transactions on edutainment IX* (pp. 65–80). Berlin: Springer Berlin Heidelberg.

Sobel, K., Bhattacharya, A., Hiniker, A., Lee, J. H., Kientz, J. A., & Yip, J. C. (2017). "It wasn't really about the Pokémon": Parents' perspectives on a location-based mobile game. In G. Mark, S. Fussell, C. Lampe, M. C. Schraefel, J. P. Hourcade, C. Appert, & D. Wigdor (Eds.), *Proceedings of the 2017 CHI Conference on Human Factors in Computing Systems* (pp. 1483–1496). Denver, Colorado, USA: ACM.

Sung, H., Sigerson, L., & Cheng, C. (2017). Social capital accumulation in location-based mobile game playing: A multiple-process approach. *Cyberpsychology, Behavior, and Social Networking, 20*(8), 486–493. doi:10.1089/cyber.2017.0222.

Ter Vrugte, J., & de Jong, T. (2012). How to adapt games for learning: The potential role of instructional support. In S. De Wannemacker, S. Vandercruysse, & G. Clarebout (Eds.), *Serious games: The challenge* (pp. 1–5). Berlin: Springer Berlin Heidelberg.

Tran, K. M. (2018). Families, resources, and learning around Pokémon Go. *E-Learning and Digital Media, 15*(3), 113–127. doi:10.1177/2042753018761166.

Vetere, F., Nolan, M., & Raman, R. A. (2006, November). Distributed Hide-and-Seek. Paper presented at the OZCHI 2006 Proceedings, Sydney, Australia.

Voida, A., & Greenberg, S. (2012). Console gaming across generations: Exploring intergenerational interactions in collocated console gaming. *Universal Access in the Information Society, 11*, 45–56. doi:10.1007/s10209-011-0232-1.

PART V
Societal Development
National/International Contexts

20

MULTIGENERATIONAL CYCLICAL SUPPORT SYSTEM

Programs in Japan for "Designing a Sustainable Society through Intergenerational Co-creation"

Masataka Kuraoka

Overview

In this chapter, Japan's approach to social issues arising from its declining and aging population is presented from an intergenerational perspective. The objective of this chapter is for readers to understand how measures to deal with long-term care are shifting from service-oriented and segmented to human-based and holistic. In addition, intergenerational practices and research in the areas of elderly health promotion and long-term care prevention are presented to show both positive outcomes and limitations associated with applying an intergenerational perspective in this context. Finally, the chapter introduces the conceptual framework Multigenerational Cyclical Support System (MCSS) and a pilot project of Multilayered Multigenerational Community Building model (MMCB) conducted in metropolitan Tokyo.

Background

Japan faces an unprecedented demographic change with a growing number of older adults and a declining birth rate. This change has challenged the nation socially and politically to come up with sustainable solutions. This section describes ways in which such demographic trends, as seen through a social and political lens, have contributed to policies and other measures that amount to a national shift from a monogenerational approach to a multigenerational approach for providing health and long-term care services.

In 2018, 12.2% of the population was below 14 years old, 60% between 15 and 64, and 28% 65 and above. However, in 2060 it is estimated that people who are 65 years of age and older will reach 38% of the total population, whereas the young people who are under 14 years old will comprise only 10% of the population

(National Institute of Population and Social Security Research, 2017). The entire population is projected to shrink by about 30% in the next 50 years. The government expenditure on social security has been rapidly increasing due to the augmentation in payouts to older adults. In 2015 it reached 115 trillion yen, that is 960 billion US dollars. The social security expenditure for the elderly consists of about 70% of the total expenditure. On the other hand, the growth in expenditure for children and families has been comparatively lower. This kind of discrepancy has generated *sedaikantairitsu*, generational conflict.

Japanese society used to alleviate such tensions by relying on the traditional family system and roles. However, according to the National Institute of Population and Social Security Research (2017), along with the demographic change, three-generation families comprised 13% of all residences in 1992, but now make up only 8%, and single member families comprised about 35% in 2015. In addition, as the average age of first-time mothers has advanced, more family members now face so-called double care (Soma & Yamashita, 2016), taking care of children and elderly parents at the same time.

These demographic, social, and political changes have escalated the demands for holistic solutions especially regarding health and long-term care service provision. It has become apparent that society cannot pursue interventions aimed at providing a better quality of life for any one generation alone.

Policy Measures

What measures have been taken in order to respond to the issues described above? In this section I would like to introduce a Community-based Integrated Care System (CICS) that is the most influential and substantial initiative promoting intergenerational relations in Japanese communities.

The Ministry of Health, Labor and Welfare of Japan has been promoting CICS since 2003. In this policy framework, the services such as medical care, home- and community-based long-term care, preventative services, and livelihood supports, are provided in an integrated manner in the community for the elderly to live in the community. The concept of integrated care started in 1974 in a rural town in Hiroshima Prefecture (Hatano et al., 2017). This is now a nationally adopted concept that every municipality in Japan embodies in its human services planning and community development process. Under CICS, collaboration among long-term care and medical service providers, governmental agencies, volunteers and nonprofit organizations, and citizens is deemed to be important in order to provide necessary services for the elderly in effective ways. As Morikawa (2014) pointed out, mutual support in the community is essential in Community-based Integrated Care Systems and yet how we design and develop such support in the community has not been established.

In 2017 "*Wagakoto Marugoto*" was introduced in developing the policy "*Chiiki Kyosei Shakai*," inclusive community society. The idea is to go beyond the boundaries of segmentation, "*Taningoto*" (someone else's business), so that those who support and receive support along with various stakeholders in the community engage as if it was their business (*Wagakoto*) and connect with each other as a whole (*Marugoto*) across generations to build a society where each member's living and purpose of life is appreciated in the community (Ministry of Health, Labour and Welfare, 2019). In addition, the Basic Law on Measures for the Aged Society is the base for the elderly health and welfare. In 2018, the guideline of measures for an aging society based on the law added a new amendment mentioning society for all ages for the first time, stating that people of all ages can make use of their motivation and abilities depending on their desire. These new policies approach complex issues of family and community in a more intergenerational manner, instead of the traditional targeting of one generation at a time, each framed as falling in a distinct, bureaucratically defined segment.

Building Intergenerational Community

Community health or long-term care prevention programs with an intergenerational approach have shown various positive impacts as well as limitations. The idea of establishing a community-integrated care system combined with the strength of evidence-based intergenerational programs is at the core of both the Multigenerational Cyclical Support System (MCSS) conceptual framework and the Multilayered Multigenerational Community Building project described below. The design of this practical application of the MCSS framework included developing programs that focused on intergenerational greetings, comfortable places for varied types of intergenerational engagement, and the propagation of values and opportunities for mutual (intergenerational) support.

In 2015, the Tokyo Metropolitan Institute of Gerontology (TMIG) team developed MCSS, a community design conceptual framework, as sketched in Figure 20.1 (Kuraoka, 2015; Kuraoka et al., 2017). There are many excellent intergenerational programs nationwide in various settings; however, it became clear that the impact of a single-activity intergenerational program in a community is limited and there would be value to organizing independent programs in a cyclical way so that anyone who experiences one intergenerational program can experience another with a central platform managing them in the community. We launched a research project that studied 14 innovative intergenerational programs and 14 municipal-based platforms that existed at the time to examine the possibility of MCSS and how we could actually implement the concept in a real community. Figure 20.1 shows how the curly-haired boy experiences intergenerational exchange through his life, from infancy up to his years as an older adult. Formal and informal support systems are in place to expose residents to meaningful intergenerational activities across the lifespan. The MCSS concept was inspired and developed based on the concept of "circle of care" which is rooted in the Hope Meadows project by

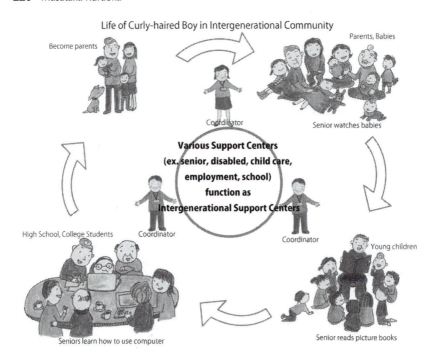

FIGURE 20.1 Multigenerational Cyclical Support System (MCSS) (Kuraoka, 2015)

Generations of Hope (Vojak, Hopping, Eheart, & Power, 2007). Hope Meadows was founded by a University of Illinois professor, Brenda Eheart, in 1994 as an intergenerational neighborhood where older residents support younger families who adopt foster children (Smith, 2001).

After developing the MCSS concept, in 2016 TMIG launched a new project funded by the Japan Science and Technology Agency, Research Institute of Science and Technology for Society (JST-RISTEX) (Japan Science and Technology Agency–Research Institute of Science and Technology for Society, 2019) implemented in two towns, Kita City in Tokyo and Tama Ward in the City of Kawasaki, both in the Tokyo metropolitan area. Based on the concept of MCSS, we targeted mainly two generations, young parents with babies and the elderly in the community, represented in the upper right corner of Figure 20.1. The reasons for targeting these two generations were that they were in the community for long hours and they had similar problems such as isolation and anxiety and need of support from others. This initiative took the form of a series of interventions, each designed to target and benefit specific generations, yet fitting together into a broader "circle of care"/MCSS framework with quality of life implications for all generations living in this small community.

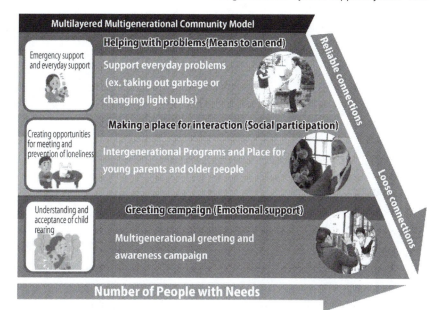

FIGURE 20.2 Multilayered multigenerational community model

The model designed for this project is shown in Figure 20.2 as a multilayered multigenerational community model, which is an operationalized integrated care model pertaining to one segment of the MCSS concept. First, TMIG and the local government in collaboration established councils in each of the two communities to plan and oversee the project. The council members were initially proposed by the partner local government and members were added as the project proceeded. The project team of TMIG and the council developed three main programs. The first one was a campaign program to promote formal greetings and multigenerational support awareness in the community. Second, intergenerational programs and activities were organized in gathering places frequented by young mothers with children and elderly in the community. Lastly, a system was established for providing daily support for community residents participating in the new intergenerational initiatives.

The model indicates the number of people who are involved in each level of activity while also showing the expected strength of the connection of people for each level of intervention. The model promotes and distinguishes between activities that generate strong (or reliable) connections and loose connections, or so-called strong and weak ties. Although each layer represents a different intervention, it is not one-way from bottom to top. It is anticipated that people who meet at intergenerational places and support each other in their neighborhood will also naturally greet each other.

In this project, we also conducted a baseline cross-sectional survey in the two towns and found that promoting intragenerational as well as intergenerational exchanges significantly contributed to enhanced wellbeing, as measured by WHO-5 scores for participants from younger and older generations (Nemoto et al., 2018). It was also found that the older adult participants (age 65–84) were more likely to provide support for children compared to middle or younger generations (Kobayashi et al., 2018).

Intergenerational Greeting

Aisatsu undo, greeting activity, is a very common activity that connects schools and communities in Japan. Murayama, Matsunaga, Kuraoka, Nonaka, and Fujiwara (2017) point out that a long-term plan, having multigenerational engagement, and using tools such as badges and banners are important factors to promote effective greeting activity. Based on this finding, the project established a campaign to promote *aisatsu* in the community that involved requesting local elementary and junior high school students to design a logo to promote awareness of the importance of mutual support and inclusive community. After the committee for the project selected the best logo, a professional designer consulted with the students who designed the original logo to make some adjustments.

In addition, volunteers in the community who are involved in *aisatsu* activity, called *aisatsu-san* (person who greets), were recruited and trained. With name straps saying *aisatsu-san* (see Figure 20.3), the volunteers discussed where they should stand to do greetings and how they might best collaborate with local organizations for extending the greeting campaign in the community.

We have found that the simple act of making eye contact and formally greeting one another is a great way to trigger engagement in a group or assembly that is diverse in terms of age, background, interests, life perspectives, and skillset.

Intergenerational Place and Programs

With integrated care policy and other community health-related policies and practices, in Japan there are many community programs and spaces for the elderly. One of the popular forms is known as *"saron"* (salon) or *"kafe"* (café). They are community-based activities where people gather occasionally and volunteers manage the space (mostly public space) and sometimes run programs. One example is the *"Fureai Ikiiki Salons"* (Side-by-Side and Lively Salons) which are administered by the Japan National Council of Social Welfare in collaboration with local councils and reach 67,903 salons nationwide (Ministry of Health, Labour and Welfare, 2017).

In our project, we opened some of these *saron* spaces to young mothers as well as older adults. Through various public venues, it was made clear that these spaces had been reconceptualized as intergenerational rather than just monogenerational settings. Clarification of this reconceptualization and its

FIGURE 20.3 *Aisatsu-san* in Kita City who wear special volunteer badges and greet people on the street

implications for project planning and site management were key themes in how volunteers for the intergenerational space are trained and supported over time. For example, for the Nakanoshima Family Café in Tama Ward, after the intergenerational space was officially opened on the mornings of the second and fourth Friday each month, two young mothers and three senior volunteer staff who finished the project training program began proactively planning and conducting various intergenerational programs at this site.

As pictured in Figure 20.4, one such activity was centered around physical exercises designed for elderly and young people to enjoy together. Other programs include activities such as picture book reading, laughter yoga, stretching, pelvic correction exercise, seasonal and cultural crafts, etc. Program activities are scheduled for the first hour of the two-hour café session; in the second hour, there is "coffee time" – or "free talk time," which entails unstructured conversation and partaking in refreshments. During this second half, some support corners are set up to help address particular needs that participants might have. During this free conversational time, volunteers help participants to get to know each other. One popular method to help build relationships (and name and face recognition) is to take photos of new participants and place them on the local map so that participants can better recognize and know a bit more about neighborhood residents who are coming to the café.

FIGURE 20.4 Nakanoshima Family Café when the participants enjoy physical exercise as a starter

Mutual Support

The most important intervention in this model and the main purpose of this project was to create a community where people from different generations support each other in daily life. The significance of this was already mentioned in the opening section of this chapter. A shrinking younger population and a growing elderly population in a real-life perspective mean that many older people will have less support with activities such as going shopping, changing light bulbs, and taking out heavy garbage. These are daily activities that some frail people need assistance with but are not supported by the long-term care service providers even for those who are certified recipients of long-term care insurance benefits. These are the types of problems that the Community-based Integrated Care System (CICS) was established to help solve at the municipal level.

In our project, we tried to establish unique intergenerational settings like the Nakanoshima Family Café that would provide the time, opportunity, and place for people to have meaningful and mutually beneficial intergenerational exchanges. Based on this relationship, developed through frequent and varied encounters, it was expected that participants would be more likely to support each other in daily life. However, in interviews conducted in the midst of the project, elderly and young participants expressed some concerns related to attaining the goal of "mutual support," for example, going into someone's house, or taking responsibility for something important to someone else, or fear of forgetting something they promised to help with. As a result, we developed some new ideas. One is conducting "*Otagai-sama* ('same here') Game." In this game, the participants write what they need help with, for example carrying heavy groceries from shopping, on a card, and write as many cards as they wish. When they all finish writing, each person shows one card at a time and explains the need and continues with other cards. When all the participants have displayed their cards, they sort them into categories and discuss whether anyone can help with any of the cards. This game is to make everyone feel that they all have something they need help with and those needs are not so difficult to support. Another idea is to set up a help booth at the intergenerational café. The booth is for easy tasks to be solved during the program so that they can feel comfortable about asking for something and actually see something solved on site. For example, some young staff members helped the elderly participants to use smartphones as shown in Figure 20.5. On a different occasion, the elderly volunteers helped young mothers learn to sew. Helping residents to get used to asking for help (starting with easy and light support) and supporting someone in return are important elements of the intervention strategy for increasing the likelihood of providing support in the future for something at home or more complicated needs.

FIGURE 20.5 A young adult volunteer is pictured helping a few of the older café participants use a smartphone

Spontaneous mutual support outside of the gathering place is still in the development stage. We are expecting daily living support among the participants to happen in the future as more people become involved in these intergenerational programs and build relationships in the community.

Summary

In summary, the goal of MCSS and the multilayered intervention model is to create a community where each generation experiences intergenerational contact throughout the life course cycle provided that a necessary platform to sustain the cycle is established. The project in the two towns in metropolitan Tokyo targeting young parents and the elderly who have problems in common reveals that they may build strong ties to support each other. In order to build such community, key factors are people in the community agreeing on the mission and feeling empowered to take action. Simultaneous program intervention requires a wide range of stakeholders agreeing on the mission, but more importantly each stakeholder needs to enact the mission in their respective roles so that they can extend the message to their networks and earn other people's buy-in. Empowering people is essential in this approach for shifting from service-oriented to more citizen-oriented interventions, driven by the commitment and synergistic partnerships emerging across a wide variety of stakeholders including formal and informal citizens groups, with the support of local agencies.

Kaplan and Sanchez (2014) state that building mutual trust between the parties helps to establish an ethic of mutual caring. This vision is not limited only to the elderly but applies to all the generations in the community. If we can think of ways in which generations are able to do something for each other, pursuing these pathways should lead to a more sustainable society.

References

Hatano, Y., Matsumoto, M., Okita, M., Inoue, K., Takeuchi, K., Tsutsui, T., … Hayashi, T. (2017). The vanguard of community-based integrated care in Japan: The effect of a rural town on national policy. *International Journal of Integrated Care*, 17(2), 2. doi:10.5334/ijic.2451.

Japan Science and Technology Agency–Research Institute of Science and Technology for Society (2019). Designing a sustainable society through intergenerational co-creation. Retrieved from www.jst.go.jp/ristex/i-gene/en/.

Kaplan, M., & Sanchez, M. (2014). Intergenerational programs and policies in ageing societies. In S. Harper & K. Hamblin (Eds.), *Intergenerational handbook on ageing and public policy* (pp. 367–383). Cheltenham, UK: Elgar Publishing.

Kobayashi, E., Nonaka, K., Kuraoka, M., Matsunaga, H., Murayama, S., Tanaka, M., … Fujiwara, Y. (2018). Community child-rearing support scale: Applicability across generations and differences in the supportive behaviors among generations. *Nihon Koshu Eisei Zasshi*, 65(7), 321–333. doi:10.11236/jph.65.7_321.

Kuraoka, M. (2015). Sedaikan koryu katsudo-shinia sedai no ikikatazukuri [Intergenerational activities – senior generation's way of life]. *Fukushi to Kyoiku, 18*, 30–31.

Kuraoka, M., Hasebe, M., Nonaka, K., Murayama, Y., Yasunaga, M., Minami, U., & Fujiwara, Y. (2017). A study of possibilities and requirements for implementation of intergenerational interaction in a multigenerational cyclical society. *Journal of Japan Society for Intergenerational Studies, 6*(1), 69–74.

Ministry of Health, Labour and Welfare. (2017). Annual ministry of health, *Labour and Welfare Report 2017, References*. Retrieved from www.mhlw.go.jp/english/wp/wp-hw11/dl/08e.pdf.

Ministry of Health, Labour and Welfare. (2019). Chiiki kyosei shakai no jitsugen ni mukete. Retrieved from www.mhlw.go.jp/stf/seisakunitsuite/bunya/0000184346.html.

Morikawa, M. (2014). Towards community-based integrated care: Trends and issues in Japan's long-term care policy. *International Journal of Integrated Care, 14*, e005.

Murayama, S., Matsunaga, H., Kuraoka, M., Nonaka, K., & Fujiwara, Y. (2017). Aisatsu undo ni kansuru bunken rebyu-Koka ni kansuru rironteki kosatsu to senshin jireikaramiru katsudojou no kufu to kadai. *Journal of Japan Society for Intergenerational Studies, 6*(1), 75–82.

National Institute of Population and Social Security Research. (2017). Population statistics of Japan 2017. Retrieved from www.ipss.go.jp/p-info/e/psj2017/PSJ2017.asp.

Nemoto, Y., Kuraoka, M., Nonaka, K., Tanaka, M., Murayama, S., Matsunaga, H., … Fujiwara, Y. (2018). [The relationship between intra- and inter-generational exchange and mental health among young and older adults]. *Nihon Koshu Eisei Zasshi, 65*(12), 719–729. doi:10.11236/jph.65.12_719.

Smith, W. (2001). *Hope Meadows: Real life stories of healing and caring from an inspired community*. New York: Berkley Books.

Soma, N., & Yamashita, J. (2016). Daburu kea towa nanika? [What is double care?]. *Chousa Kihou, 178*(3), 20–25.

Vojak, C., Hopping, D., Eheart, B., & Power, M. (2007). Completing the circle of care: Alternative housing at Hope Meadows. Retrieved from http://ghdc.generationsof hope.org/docs/WP_1-2_Circle_of_Care.pdf.

21

EXPLORING DESIGN PRINCIPLES AND STRATEGIES FOR INTERGENERATIONAL PLACES IN AUSTRALIA

Revealing Opportunities and Potential in Beach and Public Pool Settings

Kah Mun Tham, Diane H. Jones, and Ann Quinlan

Setting the Scene

Australia is a dry continent of climatic extremes, unique landscape, flora and fauna with a rich legacy of indigenous culture and custodianship. This legacy continues to intersect with the settler colony heritage of its development as an island nation founded on imperial ambitions (Johnson, Porter, & Jackson, 2018). Achieving settler belonging, civility and self-sufficiency through private land ownership became vital in early coastal settlements like Sydney. Today, 85% of Australians live in a highly urbanized environment of metropolitan cities and suburbs located within 50 kilometers of the coast: the island edge, where the continent and ocean intersect.

Within these cities, it is local government as the oldest of three levels of representative governance, National, State and Local[1], that influences people's everyday lives and their social practices. Initially formed to regulate land ownership and provide public health amenity, over time, local municipalities increasingly responded to citizen demands for places of leisure and recreation such as ocean and urban swimming pools, parks, gardens and welfare programs (Kelly, 2011).

These citizen demands relate to the rapidly changing demographic profile of Australia. Of the 23.4 million people living in Australia, a recent census poll in 2016 revealed age and ethnic diversity, through successful migration, as key aspects of our identity and social vibrancy. While 31.5% of people are aged 24 and under and 15.7% of people are older than 65, by 2030 it is expected that

Australians aged 65 and over will be more numerous than children aged 0–14 (currently 18.7%) (Australian Bureau of Statistics, 2017a).

The same poll revealed that 49% of Australians were either born overseas or had one or both parents born overseas. Second generation Australians aged under 40 are more likely to have Asian ancestry while those aged 40 and over are more likely to have European ancestry (Australian Bureau of Statistics, 2017b). Over 83% of overseas-born people live in a capital city.

56% of migrants, particularly those from North and South East Asia, are apartment residents. More than 20% of Australia's children and young people (0–24 years) live in apartments (Australian Bureau of Statistics, 2017c). When co-located with amenities and services, apartment living is increasingly popular with older Australians.

The growth in high rise residential apartment developments has placed pressure on state, city and local infrastructure, services and places for everyday social and cultural encounters. Privately developed urban places and neighborhoods give rise to a private ownership structure of governance, private sector control of public places and private-public partnership of community services and buildings. With a focus on investment and profitability this approach challenges the citizen rights model of local government as public provider of services, civic buildings and recreational settings for the common good for all (De Magalhaes & Freire, 2017; Liu, Easthope, Ho & Buckle, 2018).

This reflection brings focus to the distinctiveness of national and local contexts when considering how to design places and settings that encourage and support intergenerational relations in an evolving community.

Generations, Places and Settings

The dynamism of changing social mobility, cultural networks, life experiences and aging brings attention to generational segregation and the creation of age homogeneous 'islands of activity' (Aries, 1978 as cited in Hagestad & Uhlenberg, 2006, p. 642; Tham, 2019). In these 'islands' an absence of others different in age, outlook and culture diminishes the community cohesion, conviviality and the intellectual and social capital that comes with interaction and familiarity. They also increase competition for scarce public and natural resources affecting intergenerational equity (Anand & Sen, 2000; Commonwealth of Australia, 2015).

Kaplan, Thang, Sanchez, and Hoffman (2016) note that critical to sustaining aspirations for intergenerational interaction is identifying, designing and implementing physical spaces, places and settings of contact. Thang's research in Singapore and Japan (2001, 2015) brought focus to Pratt's idea of contact zones as 'social spaces where cultures meet, clash, and grapple with each other, often in contexts of highly asymmetrical relations of power' (Pratt, 1991 as cited in Thang, 2015, p. 18). Consequently, researchers have agreed on a working definition of physical contact settings known as Intergenerational Contact Zones (ICZ) as follows:

> Intergenerational Contact Zones serve as spatial focal points for different generations to meet, interact, build relationships (e.g. trust and friendships) and if desired work together to address issues of local concern.
>
> *(Kaplan et al., 2016)*

Intergenerational Contact Zones

For Intergenerational Contact Zones (ICZ) to 'serve as spatial focal points for different generations to meet, interact, build relationships' they need to transcend the abstraction of space as a functional setting to that of a physical place that is embodied with meaning, belonging and emotional bond for all ages. As Kemmis comments, 'citizens cannot be fully healthy, physically and mentally, in isolation, but only as meaningful players in a meaningful community' (1995, p. 152).

Places for shared leisure and recreation are distinctive, meaningful and symbolic settings where generations have opportunity for choice, spontaneity, enjoyment and 'play'; attributes identified as important for ICZ (Kaplan et al., 2016).

> Leisure is a state of mind which ordinarily is characterized by unobligated time and willing optimism. It can involve extensive activity or no activity. The key ingredient is an attitude which fosters a peaceful and productive co-existence with the elements in one's environment.
>
> *(Evans & ACHPER, 1980)*

In settings for leisure, identity transcends age and cultural background to a focus on delight and engagement in a place of shared meaning and memory drawn across time. Such spatial settings enhance generational intelligence; 'the empathetic capacity to cooperatively and emotionally share space across generations' (Biggs & Carr, 2015, p. 108).

The cultural geographer Edward Soja proposed that a setting has three – first, second and third – intersecting 'spatial' conditions (1996).[2] He proposed the term 'firstspace' to describe the physical space that can be seen, measured and reproduced while the 'secondspace' is the perceived, representational or imagined space. For Soja the 'thirdspace' extends and enriches an understanding of real and perceived spaces to characterize a setting or place as 'a space of extraordinary openness, a place of critical exchange wherein perspectives previously considered to be incompatible can be encompassed in our understanding of place' (1996, p. 260).

Recreational Water

For Australians, such 'thirdspaces' are beaches and public swimming pools. While the bush is mythologized as central to Australian's character it is the lived experience of 'being' at the beach or pool that sustains the imagination of our modern 'Australianness' (Fiske, Hodge, & Turner, 2017). For migrants and new Australians, beach picnics and swimming provide an accessible entry for integration into mainstream cultural norms and values to enable their own Australian identity (Walton & Shaw, 2017).

> … Grow up in Australia and you're just meant to know how to swim … Water compelled and horrified my whole family. While other people saw stunning coastlines, we saw picturesque ways to die … I was the skinny kid from the migrant family … It was only in adulthood I fell in love with water … Is it going too far to say swimming is the Australian version of baptism …
>
> To know this country is to know it by the bodies of water into which we can plunge.
>
> Benjamin Law, Foreword, *Places We Swim*
>
> *(Seitchik-Reardon and Clements, 2018)*

Bronte Beach is a Sydney beach of heritage significance, located between Bondi and Coogee beaches. With its parkland setting, gentle surf, rock pool and 30 meter ocean swimming pool it is popular for family and friend gatherings, surfers, swimmers and shore amblers. Over time the beach has proven to be a setting that accommodates intersecting generational groups.

> Hugged by the headlands and surrounded by a perfect picnicking park, Bronte is one of the loveliest and most accessible city beaches. Quiet and unpretentious, it is the perfect place to dive into the water after the coastal walk from Bondi, and if it is too hot you can always nap under the rock ledge.
>
> *(Watts, 2018)*

As 'firstspace' settings of tree-lined picnic parks and headlands leading to sand dunes that cascade to rock formations, the water's shoreline, waves and ocean, they are landscape places where we interact with and appreciate the beauty of nature. Beaches as 'secondspace' are places where we escape conventions of clothed decorum and swim, surf and sunbake.

In synthesis with first and second 'space' experiences is the complex intertwining of memory, attachment and cultural meaning that the beach embodies as a 'thirdspace' setting of lived experience. Accessible, public, inclusive and egalitarian, the beach confers social agreement and freedom, regardless of age,

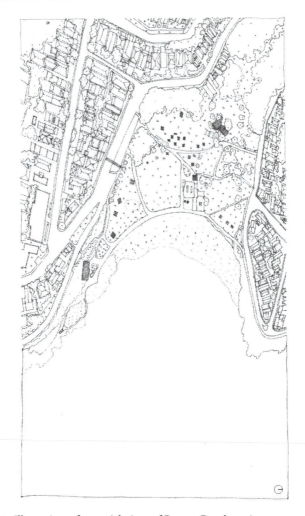

FIGURE 21.1 Illustration of an aerial view of Bronte Beach setting; not to scale

outlook or background. They are places of change and transition between nature and culture as people socialize, picnic, play and exercise. (Ford, 2006; Huntsman, 2001; Walton & Shaw, 2017). For Leonie Huntsman the beach as a setting of transition and an in-between space, is a place of liminality, a threshold between two contrasting spatial and experiential conditions. (Huntsman, 2001; Ng & Lim, 2018).

A unique aspect of New South Wales beaches is the number of ocean swimming pools carved out of beach rock platforms (Larkin, 2019; All into Ocean Pools Inc., n.d.). Although segregated by sex and often race, in the early 1900s swimming for health and recreation was viewed as a citizen right.

FIGURE 21.2 Diagrammatic cross section through Bronte Beach and Park, 2019

FIGURE 21.3 Diagrammatic cross-sectional perspective illustrating a panorama of the 'boardwalk' at Bronte, 2019

Demand for settings for the sport of swimming and swimming instruction saw the early construction of modest local urban pools. The 1950s and 1970s were the halcyon days of government-funded new local public outdoor 50 meter pool settings (Gould, 2010; Lewi, 2017; McShane, 2009). Part of everyday life, municipal community pool facilities as a representation of the beach, are recognized as a cultural institution that embody the values of Australian identity.[3] As Helen Lochhead reflects, 'The Australian pool is the universal leveler, where we all participate. Most of us learn to swim. Many of us in our local pool overcome fear, face challenges, compete and excel' (2016).

As ICZ settings public swimming pools are purposeful places for 'different generations to work together to address issues of local concern'. Increased drowning fatalities in recreational waters emphasize the importance of community-based swimming and water safety education for all (Royal Life Saving, 2018; SBS, 2018a & 2018b).[4] In transcending age and culture public pools are shared places where young migrant children, young adults and families can learn to swim in proximity with the active exercise of older people of European ancestry.

Many local municipal public swimming pools built are now aging, in need of renovation and maintenance and under threat of demolition or closure. At the same time, the social, civic and cultural significance of pools is increasingly subsumed by their financial value for private development (Barnsley, Peden, & Scarr, 2017; Gould, 2010; McShane, 2009). This presents a challenge to municipal councils struggling to meet the demand for new social infrastructure in a neoliberal climate.

Sydney City Council is one municipal council that demonstrates how this challenge may be successfully met by reimagining the public pool as a place of amenity to meet the needs and interests of evolving intergenerational communities in high density urban settings. Since 2004, under the leadership of Lord Mayor Clover Moore and guided by the city vision plan 'Sustainable Sydney 2030 – green, global and connected' a program of design excellence social infrastructure projects has been implemented to meet the needs of Sydney city's growing and diverse community.[5] Monica Barone, the council's general manager explains the reasons for the program as follows:

> The City of Sydney invests in social infrastructure such as pools because we understand that more and more of our life is going to be lived in public. Providing public, accessible facilities as the backdrop for community experiences is one of the ways in which we are tackling affordability, in a city where real estate pressures are real and felt by all. The pool, just like the library, becomes part of a suite of amenities that everyone enjoys.
>
> *(The Pool, Architecture, Culture and Identity in Australia, 2016)*

In the city there are currently five public 50 meter swimming pool civic settings with a sixth under construction.[6] The latter, Gunyama Park Aquatic and Recreation Centre is an ambitious intersection of an urban beach with an outdoor swimming pool within a landscaped park in a high density residential 'revitalization' precinct known as Green Square. The design team for the new pool center credit a close analysis of the physical and social qualities of Sydney's coastal pools for how they reimagined a series of pool and recreational landscapes within the former industrial site of Green Square.[7] One of the Sydney coastal pools referenced in the winning competition entry was Bronte. Referring to the 'playful interaction of natural and constructed landscapes that grafts the beach into the urban pool experience' (Burges, 2019), architect Andrew Burges makes the observation of his team's winning entry, pertinent to discussion of ICZ, that the proposed pool is,

> Not just for fitness fanatics, this is a place for all people to enjoy the center in different ways – even if it's simply reading the paper in the sun and enjoying the occasional dip.
>
> *(City of Sydney, 2014)*

Design Principles and Strategies

Through a series of exploratory and analytical drawings, the natural and constructed landscape of Bronte Beach is observed and analyzed. The key design principles and strategies revealed are:

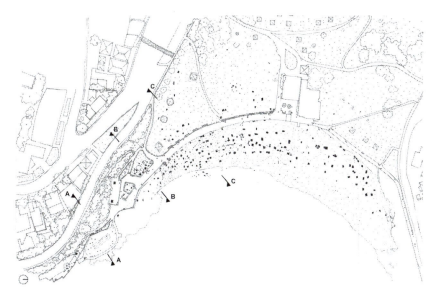

FIGURE 21.4 Diagrammatic plan analysis of Bronte outlining areas of activity (indicated in solid black), 2019

- **Edges and Elevation**
  (articulation, sensory experience)

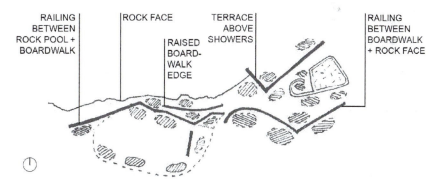

FIGURE 21.5A Diagrammatic plan of Bronte Beach showing the edges (black solid lines indicating the tiered changes in level) against which 'organic' gathering points for activity occur, 2019

These provide a sense of embrace on one side while allowing an openness – always with views out to the water and horizon. 'The environment in itself can also serve as a kind of shelter … provide a sense of belonging, an existential territory and a lived place' (Alerby, Hagström, & Westman, 2014).

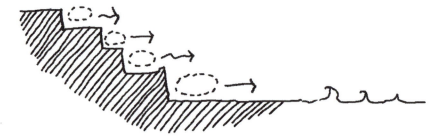

FIGURE 21.5B Diagrammatic cross section drawing, relating to Section A-A in Figure 21.4, showing the edges against which the gathering points occur and the direction of the outlook, 2019

In the Gunyama Park and Aquatic Centre design, the edges become a verandah like structure providing sheltered space and views outward.

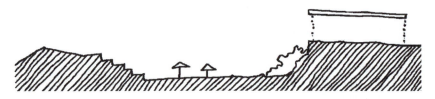

FIGURE 21.5C Diagrammatic cross section showing the verandah and the cascading edge conditions against which gathering points occur in the Gunyama Park and Aquatic Centre competition design, 2019

• Thresholds and Liminal Spaces

(in-between spaces)

Thresholds as transition points naturally present opportunities to create zones of socialization – the organic mediating zone that arises from two intersecting areas. The purposeful installation of bench seating at the threshold between the grass knolls and the boardwalk builds on extant social interactions. Refer to Figure 21.6A.

The different treatments of the thresholds allude to the different activities and inherent qualities of the spaces while still maintaining the views out toward the horizon and water – 'protecting the back' of sun-baking beach goers and the provision of seating for joggers and walkers. Refer to Figure 21.6B.

This proposed configuration at Gunyama Aquatic recalls the spatial sequence found at Bronte Beach – encountering spaces of different materiality as the elevation steps down to the largest body of water (50 m pool). Refer to Figures 21.6C, 21.6D, 21.6E.

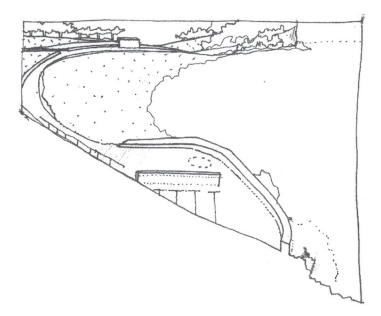

FIGURE 21.6A Diagrammatic sectional-perspective through Bronte rock pool with beach, boardwalk, rolling grass knolls and park in the background, 2019

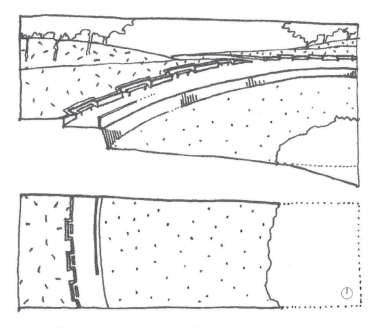

FIGURE 21.6B Diagrammatic cross-sectional perspective and corresponding plan of Bronte, relating to Section C-C in Figure 21.4, showing different thresholds between grass and boardwalk, boardwalk and beach

FIGURE 21.6C Diagrammatic cross section relating to Section B-B in Figure 21.4 showing sequence through ocean, rock ledge, 'boardwalk', planting, sloped parkland setting, road, Bronte. Each threshold creates zones for activity of different kinds, 2019

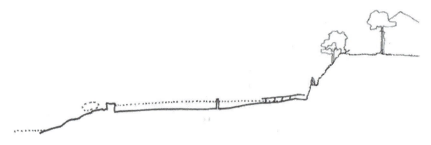

FIGURE 21.6D Diagrammatic sectional perspective sequence, relating to Section A-A in Figure 21.4, showing Bronte Beach, rock pool, cliff wall, road. The topography and constructed landscape create a cascading series of spaces that are both visually and physically connected yet separate, 2019

FIGURE 21.6E Diagrammatic cross section showing constructed sequence from the spectator seating down to the pool in the Gunyama Park and Aquatic Centre competition design, 2019

- **Diagonal Views, Sequence of Spaces and Movement**

  (cues + choice/autonomy + complexity + orientation + awareness)

  The sequence of spaces between which people are drawn to, move along and across, occur along the diagonal both in plan and section in response to the topography. It is this diagonal orientation (rather than straight orthogonal lines) and the difference in spatial qualities within the same location that enable autonomy and a sense of freedom for those who enjoy varying degrees of social connection – young, old, exuberant large groups, quiet reflective individuals etc.

HORIZON

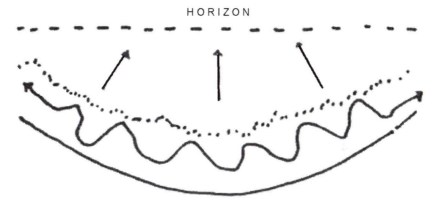

FIGURE 21.7A Diagrammatic plan showing the undulating pattern of movement that draws beach-goers towards the horizon and the surf, Bronte, 2019

FIGURE 21.7B Diagrammatic plan of Gunyama Park and Aquatic Centre competition design showing the sequencing of clearly articulated and differently scaled spaces, 2019, not to scale

The wide range of different scaled spaces, their sense of enclosure or openness, provide a form of complexity which allows intellectual and emotional curiosity. Cues in the form of plantings, walls, paths, trees, rocks, sand and the constant orientation of looking out to the sea give complexity without confusion. However, what the line drawings at a small scale cannot convey adequately is the richness of the sensory experiences – material, texture, density, smells and sounds that contribute to our holistic experience of place.

Reflections

The series of exploratory drawings observe and analyze the natural and constructed landscape of Bronte Beach. The illustrations, sections, plans and diagrams highlight the primary design principles, strategies and elements that distinguish this beach landscape as an 'organic' ICZ – a treasured place where genuine intergenerational contact occurs effortlessly within and across the interconnected landscape of natural and built elements.

The identified design principles and strategies resonate with those which appear in research discourse and guidelines on the design of places for older people and for young children and learning environments. It is supported by the growing body of evidence that reveals the positive effect of elements of the physical environment on people's wellbeing (Goldhagen, 2017).

Informed by analysis and observation of Sydney coastal pools, including Bronte, these strategies are also articulated in the Gunyama Aquatic and Recreation Centre winning competition design in its architectural and landscape representation of the beach.

It is the bringing together of design principles and strategies derived from evaluations of culturally specific and treasured places, informed by qualitative and empirical research in design processes, that leads to enlivening and joyful intergenerational settings.

Acknowledgments

All illustration drawings completed by Kah Mun Tham in April 2019.

Notes

1 In Australia there is one federal parliament, six state and two territory parliaments; and over 546 local government or municipal councils (Christensen, 2018).
2 Edward Soja's spatial theory builds upon the work of Henri Lefebvre published in his 1991 seminal text *The Production of Space*.

3 The pool as a 'lens' to explore Australian cultural identity was the Australian exhibition installation for the 2016 Venice Biennale (Holliday & Tabet, 2016).

4 249 people in Australia lost their lives to drowning and 551 people were hospitalised during 2018–2017 (Royal Life Saving 2018). People born overseas account for 30–40% of drowning fatalities each year (Special Broadcasting Service: SBSa; SBSb, 2018).

5 While the Greater Sydney Metropolitan area is home to five million people living in 650 suburbs governed by 35 local councils Sydney City Council is home to around 250,000 people living in 33 suburbs and welcomes over 600,000 visitors a day (2016).

6 The five existing City of Sydney 50 meter pool complexes are:

- Andrew Boy Charlton pool, originally a harborside bathing pool and developed for the sport of swimming in 1908, refurbished in 2012.
- Victoria Park Pool opened in 1953 was the first in-ground outdoor public pool to be built in Sydney.
- Prince Alfred Park Pool opened in 1954, refurbished in 2013.
- Cook and Philip Park Pool (partially underground) opened in 2001.
- Indoor Ian Thorpe Aquatic Centre opened in 2007.

7 A two stage Architecture and Landscape Architecture Ideas Design Competition was conducted in 2014 by Sydney City Council. 144 entries were received in the first stage. Five finalists proceeded to Stage 2. The team of Andrew Burges Architects in collaboration with Grimshaw and Taylor Cullity Lethlean (TLC) Landscape Architects were selected. The pool is under construction, due for completion in 2020. See City of Sydney Council (2014), *Green Square Design Competition Gunyama Park and Aquatic Centre Jury Report.*

References

Alerby, E., Hagström, E., & Westman, S. (2014). The embodied classroom – A phenomenological discussion of the body and the room. *Journal of Pedagogy, 5*(10), 11–23. doi:10.2478/jped-2014-0001.

All into Ocean Pools Inc (n.d.). Website, Perth Western Australia. Accessed 20 December 2018. https://allintooceanpoolsinc.org/.

Anand, S., & Sen, A. (2000). Human development and economic sustainability. *World Development, 28*(12), 2029–2049.

Australian Bureau of Statistics (2017a, 2017b, 2017c). Australian demographic statistics, June 2017 *Census of Population and Housing: Reflecting Australia – Stories from the Census, 2016.* Cat.no.3101.0, Cat.no. 2071.1, Canberra: Australian Bureau of Statistics. Retrieved from www.abs.gov.au/AUSSTATS/abs@.nsf/DetailsPage/3101.0Jun% 202017?OpenDocument.

Barnsley, P., Peden, A., & Scarr, J. (2017). *Economic benefits of Australia's public aquatic facilities.* Sydney: Royal Life Saving Society – Australia.

Barone, M. (2016). Quoted in A. Holliday, M. Tabet, & I. Toland (curators.) & Australian Institute of Architects, & International Architectural Exhibition (15th: Venice, 2016). *The pool, architecture, culture and identity in Australia*, Red Hill ACT: Australian Institute of Architects. Also see Pool is Cool: www.pooliscool.org/.

Biggs, S., & Carr, A. (2015). Age- and child-friendly cities and the promise of interge-nerational space. *Journal of Social Work Practice, 29*(1), 99–112. doi:10.1080/02650533.2014.993942.

Burges, A. (2019). Quoted in *Gunyama park aquatic and recreation centre*. Retrieved from www.cityofsydney.nsw.gov.au/vision/green-square/city-of-sydney-developments/gunyama-park-aquatic-and-recreation-centre.

Christensen, H. (2018). Legislating community engagement at the Australian local gov-ernment level. *Commonwealth Journal of Local Governance*, issue 21. Accessed 12. Retrieved from https://cjlg.epress.lib.uts.edu.au.

City of Sydney Council (2014). *Green square design competition Gunyama Park and Aquatic Centre jury report*. Retrieved from http://cdn.greensquare.s3.amazonaws.com/finalists/GunyamaParkandGreenSquareAquaticCentrejuryreportweb.pdf.

Commonwealth of Australia (2015). *2015 Intergenerational report: Australian in 2055*, Can-berra: The Treasury. Retrieved from https://static.treasury.gov.au/uploads/sites/1/2017/06/2015_IGR.pdf.

De Magalhaes, C. S., & Freire, T. S. (2017). 'Clubification' of urban public spaces? The withdrawal or the re-definition of the role of local government in the man-agement of public spaces. *Journal of Urban Design, 22:6*, 738–756. doi:10.1080/13574809.2017.1336059.

Evans, P. R. & Australian Council for Health, Physical Education and Recreation & Royal Australian Institute of Parks and Recreation (ACHPER) (1980). Recreation working paper, Kingswood, S. Australia: Kingswood, p. 3.

Fiske, J., Hodge, B., & Turner, G. (2017, first published in 1987). *Myths of Oz: Reading Australian popular culture*, London: Routledge.

Ford, C. (2006). Gazing, strolling, falling in love culture and nature on the beach in nine-teenth century Sydney. *History Australia, 3*(1) 08, 1–14. doi:10.2104/ha060008.

Goldhagen, S. E. (2017). *Welcome to your world: How the built environment shapes our lives*. London: HarperCollins.

Gould, S. E. (2010). *A pond in a park: Social geographies of adolescents at public swimming pools in Tasmania*. Master's thesis, Department of Geography, University of Tasmania, Hobart.

The Guardian (2019). Presenter Gabriel Wilder, *Ocean pools are making a comeback – And not just for their seductive beauty (13 April 2019)*. Retrieved from https://www.theguardian.com/environment/2019/apr/13/ocean-pools-could-make-a-comeback-and-not-just-for-their-seductive-beauty.

Hagestad, G. O., & Uhlenberg, P. (2006). Should we be concerned about age segrega-tion? Some theoretical and empirical explorations. *Research on Aging, 28*(6), 638–653. doi:10.1177/0164027506291872.

Holliday, A., Tabet, M., & Toland, I. (curators.) & Australian Institute of Architects, & International Architectural Exhibition (15th: Venice, Italy) (2016). The pool, architec-ture, culture and identity in Australia, Red Hill ACT: Australian Institute of Architects.

Huntsman, L. (2001). *Sand in our souls: The beach in Australian history*. Melbourne: Mel-bourne University Press.

Johnson, L., Porter, L., & Jackson, S. (2018). Reframing and revising Australia's planning history and practice. *Australian Planner, 54*(4), 225–233. doi:10.1080/07293682.2018.1477813.

Kaplan, M., Thang, L. L., Sanchez, M., & Hoffman, J. (Eds.). (2016). *Intergenerational Con-tact Zones – A compendium of applications*. University Park, PA: Penn State Extension.

Kelly, A. H. (2011). 'The development of local government in Australia, Focusing on NSW: From road builder to planning agency to servant of the state government and developmentalism'. Paper presented at the World Planning Schools Congress 2011, Perth, 4–8 July.

Kemmis, D. (1995). *the good city and the good life*. Boston: Houghton Mifflin Co.

Lewi, H. (2017). From segregation to celebration: The public pool in Australian culture, *The Conversation*. Retrieved from https://theconversation.com/from-segregation-to-celebration-the-public-pool-in-australian-culture-82916.

Liu, E., Easthope, H., Ho, C., & Buckle, C. (2018). Diversity and participation in private apartment buildings: A review of the literature. *Geographical Research*, *56*, 401–409. doi:10.1111/1745-5871.12282.

Lochhead, H. (2016). Quoted in *The Pool makes a splash at Venice Biennale*, presenter, Fran Strachan. Retrieved from https://newsroom.unsw.edu.au/news/art-architecture-design/pool-makes-splash-venice-biennale.

McShane, I. (2009). The past and future of local swimming pools. *Journal of Australian Studies*, *33*(2), 195–208. doi:10.1080/14443050902883405.

Ng, V., & Lim, J. P. (2018). Tracing liminality: A multidisciplinary spatial construct. *Journal of Engineering and Architecture*, *6*(1), 76–90. doi:10.15640/jea.v6n1a8.

Royal Life Saving Society Australia (2018). *People drowned in Australian waterways research and policy highlights*, Royal Life Saving National Drowning Report, Sydney. Retrieved from www.royallifesaving.com.au/facts-and-figures/research-and-reports/drowning-reports.

Seitchik-Reardon, D., & Clements, C. (2018), *Places we swim: Exploring Australia's best beaches, pools, waterfalls, lakes, hot springs and gorges*, Richmond Victoria: Hardie Grant Publishing.

Soja, E. (1996). *Thirdspace: Journey to Los Angeles and other real and imagined places*. Oxford: Blackwell.

Special Broadcasting Service (SBSa) Radio (English), Presenter, Manpreet K Singh (2018). *Migrants and tourists account for a third of drownings in Australia: Lifesavers want better education (1 January)* Retrieved from www.sbs.com.au/yourlanguage/punjabi/en/article/2018/01/03/migrants-and-tourists-account-third-drownings-australia-life savers-want-better.

Special Broadcasting Service (SBSb) Radio (Punjabi), Presenter, Ruchika Talwar (2018). *Migrants face higher risk of drowning in Australia (2 October)*. Retrieved from www.sbs.com.au/yourlanguage/punjabi/en/audiotrack/migrants-often-die-because-they-cant-swim.

Sydney City Council (2016). Retrieved from www.cityofsydney.nsw.gov.au/learn/research-and-statistics/the-city-at-a-glance. Accessed 18 January 2019.

Tham, K. M. (2019). *Age-scapes for a new ageing demographic*, Byera Hadley Travelling Scholarship 2018 report, NSW Architects Registration Board, Sydney. Accessed August 13, 2019. https://www.architects.nsw.gov.au/download/BHTS/Kah-Mun-Tham-AgescapesForNewAgeingDemographic_BHTS-2018.pdf?v=2

Thang, L. L. (2001). *Generations in touch: Linking the old and the young in a Tokyo neighborhood*. Ithaca & London: Cornell University Press.

Thang, L. L. (2015). Creating an intergenerational contact zone: Encounters in public spaces within Singapore's public housing neighborhoods. In R. Vanderbeck & N. Worth (Eds.), *Intergenerational spaces* (pp. 17–32). London, UK: Routledge.

Walton, T., & Shaw, W. S. (2017). Land-beach-risk-scape: Deciphering the motivators of risk-taking at the beach in Australia. *Social & Cultural Geography*, *18*(6), 869–886. doi:10.1080/14649365.2016.1239755.

Watts, M. (2018). The ten best beaches in Sydney, *Concrete Playground*. Retrieved from https://concreteplayground.com/perth/author/madeleine-watts.

22

INTERGENERATIONAL CONTACT ZONES IN CONTESTED PLACES AND SPACES

The Olive Tree as Entity and Symbol

Suzanne H. Hammad

Background

While program and infrastructure are being intentionally designed to promote intergenerational and cohesive communities (Beth Johnson Foundation, 2011), spaces in the natural environment that are naturally created to perpetuate this very thing are under threat. People–place relationships within such places are also central to promoting consistent and healthy intergenerational encounters. Yet, despite the potentially powerful role of the physical environment in sustaining intergenerational engagements (Kaplan, Thang, Sánchez, & Hoffman, 2016; Vanderbeck & Worth, 2015), the agency of these places and those who live and interact with them have yet to be better understood and utilized. This paper takes Kaplan et al.'s (2016) working definition of Intergenerational Contact Zones (ICZ) as '*spatial focal points* for different generations to meet, interact, build relationships, and, if desired, work together to address issues of local concern', to scrutinize the olive tree in the contested Palestinian landscape as socio-economic and political entity and symbol around which communities and generations engage. The multiple significances of the olive tree to Palestinians are brought to the fore and its natural role as an ICZ exemplified. In the context of systematic uprooting of historic olive trees among other factors, the various modes of 'undoing' of this intergenerational entity, physical space, and sociocultural space is then outlined, followed by the ways people have tried to reclaim it through political and civic engagement. The chapter concludes with lessons and practical considerations in regard to ICZ that can be extracted through the case example of the olive tree.

The Multiple Meanings of the Olive Tree to Palestinians and Natural Role as an ICZ

> The olive tree isn't like any other tree. It's special.
>
> *(Manal, a 35-year-old mother of four[1])*

The Palestinian geopolitically defined landscape, though often portrayed in the news as a land devoid of people, is much more than geography or politics. Its land, villages, and olive groves represent 'lived spaces' that are invested with strong emotion, and intense political, deeply rooted sociocultural meanings passed down from one generation to the other (Hammad, 2011; Miftah, 2018). The olive tree, in particular, and the social, economic, and political activities that revolve around it as entity and symbol, holds a strong significance and multiple meanings for Palestinians. On the one hand, the olive tree is known to be a tree that can live for hundreds of years, sometimes even thousands, providing an economic resource and bearing the

FIGURE 22.1 The olive tree as a source of livelihoods for Palestinians. Photo by Abed Qusini – Palestine

fruit for generations of Palestinians (see Figure 22.1). It has dotted the landscape for centuries and is a key feature in Palestinian art and cultural representations. The olive tree has multiple functions: it produces olive oil, provides heat in a fire, is harvested for soap, has medicinal functions, and provides protection from the sun to peasants and travelers. In fact, olive oil has been a key product of the Palestinian national economy, and olives are the main crop of local agricultural production.[2]

The olive tree and its products also hold religious value to Muslims world-wide; it is one of the few trees mentioned in the Holy Quran and its prod-ucts – olives and olive oil – are often cited for their therapeutic properties. The olive tree is drought-resistant and able to grow in poor soil and condi-tions; this has enabled it to stand tall across time and across historical and polit-ical conquests in Palestine up until the present day. It signifies continuity, history, and identity attached to place (Miftah, 2018). It has also been known to function as a focal point for perpetuating social bonds and socio-economic livelihoods (Swedenburg, 1990). Today, despite the decreasing economic sig-nificance of the olive tree in Palestine, the olive tree has gained more of a symbolic significance in political discourse (Graham-Brown, 1983; Sweden-burg, 1990).

The role and spaces created (naturally) by the olive tree are indisputably aligned with the notion of ICZs. This is evident at a number of levels and poignantly cap-tured through Kaplan et. al's (2016) conceptual framework of typical ICZs. Table 22.1 (below) illustrates in detail and through the voices of different generations of Palestinians, how the olive tree and its associated practices manifest various inter-generational expressions, functions, and outcomes as an ICZ. Understanding the naturally occurring role of the olive tree and olive harvest season as an intergenera-tional space is critical as it juxtaposes the shifts that transpired in response to the threat of loss of that very entity.[3]

Shifting Generational Encounters with the Olive Tree: A Spatial Site and Symbol of Resistance

Where are the goats that trimmed my weeds as they feasted?
Where are the garlic-scented hands that pruned my twigs?
Where are the rhythmic voices that sang to me in the language of the hills and the seas?
(Extract from poem: Rest in My Shade[4])

The olive tree has been shown to be a site and space for sustained intergenera-tional encounters and potential for cultural and economic continuity in which various generations are 'naturally' involved. Yet, due to the highly contested geopolitical nature of the Israeli–Palestinian conflict, this 'special tree' and communal space is under threat. The 'separation barrier', together with a regime of permits, closures, curfews, military check points and Israeli only

TABLE 22.1 ICZ dimensions of the olive tree and harvest season illustrated

ICZ dimensions	Role of the olive tree and olive harvest season	Illustrative voices and facts
Physical – the location	A characteristic feature of the Palestinian landscape A place to relax, play, rest, picnic	'The elderly come along even if it's just to sit under the shade of a tree and just be with everyone, men and boys' (Halima, 34) 'We wait for *el-zatun* season by the minute. We all do our bit, we sing, or take a radio with us while we're up on the ladder' (Sara, 14)
Physical – the economic	Olive harvest is a means of livelihood for young and old A season everyone takes part in some way: cross-generational support is a given	'Children and *el-zatun* are one. One [her emphasis]. Without your land, can you raise your son? It's our livelihood. Our children's livelihood' (Um-Jamal, 60) 'We've never needed anything as a family because of our *zatunat* (pl. of *zatun*). They've given us all the olive oil we need and much more. Because of *el-zatun*, I was able to get married. If it hadn't been for *el-zatun*, I couldn't have' (Abu-Jamal, 68)
Physical – the history	Olive trees date back thousands of years and are passed down from generation to generation	'[My father] would tell me more stories about the olive trees and their connection with the people of Palestine and all the civilizations that governed it over the ages' (Ahed, 16) Palestine has some of the world's oldest olive trees, dating back 4,000 years. Some families have trees that have been passed down to them for generations and the olive harvest season in October bears a sociocultural meaning where families come together to harvest olive trees bearing in mind that their forefathers and mothers had tended to the same trees several years ago (IEMU, 2019; Miftah, 2018)
Physical – geopolitical	A discourse of place-identity and resilience passed down across generations	'As a young girl, my father would tell me the history of the olive tree and how the Romans brought it to Palestine when they ruled here. And

Sociocultural	Olive harvest season is marked by numerous traditions and festivities and demonstrates the connection of Palestinians to their olive groves. The olive tree is a key socio-political signifier in representations of Palestine in art and culture	Palestinians have adopted the olive tree as a symbol of their attachment to their land. This tree is a resilient tree and likewise, the Palestinians draw their strength from its strong roots and resilience' (Ahed, 16) 'The olive harvest season in October bears sociocultural meaning where families come together to harvest the trees. I still remember those days when we came home from school and then going out to the field to pick the olives, then coming back home to finish our homework … once complete we would take the olives to our family factory where the olives are pressed to make olive oil' (Ahed, 16) 'We would help out, play, argue, run around … it was fun being there. We'd watch our father sweating in his land, do whatever he asked, then we would sit all together in *el-khala* under the shade of the olive tree and eat what our mother had prepared. Sometimes we went every day. It was such a treat. This is a big part of my childhood memories and just the way things are and ought to be' (Mohammad, 14)
Psychological-perceptual	Olive harvest is perceived as a celebration for everyone across the generations Olive harvest is perceived as more than an economic activity Symbiotic relationship with nature – the olive tree as 'giving' and 'kind'	'Did I tell you that when we go to *el-zatun*, it's as if we're going to a wedding. I swear I am not joking. It has a totally different feeling to it. It's nice. Really, you know. Seriously, it's like they are going to a wedding' (Zahra, 44) 'I remember standing next to my dad to have a taste of the freshest olive oil along with my pita bread. He used to say that once you drink olive oil it becomes part of your soul. I will never forget and miss always miss the smell of olives on those days' (Ahed, 16) 'You know [the olive tree] is like a friend or a relative you live with and you find it hard to be far away from her. It's not an economic relationship

(*Continued*)

TABLE 22.1 (Cont.)

ICZ dimensions	Role of the olive tree and olive harvest season	Illustrative voices and facts
Psychological-emotional	Attachment to participating in olive harvest season and related rituals and celebrations across old and young An emotional connection – the olive tree in need of care and love	at all! It's part of our identity, our life, and we were ordered to take care of it by God – that's why it will never disappear' (Abu-Mohammad, 50) 'People love *el-zatun*. I wonder why. There is something that binds us to it, without us feeling … from the day you were born, there was something about it, something that keeps us attached … we've always, as far as I can remember, cared for *el-zatun*' (Sara, 14) 'The olive tree needs me to care for it, just like a child, maybe even more because it is what will feed my children' (Rabhia, 40)
Psychological-cognitive	A sense of duty towards olive harvest season that all generations engage in, despite laborious olive-picking The olive tree represents resilience and resistance (known as *sumud* or steadfastness) maintained across generations A social belief system transmitted across generations regarding the religious significance of the olive tree	'People go energized and refreshed, seriously, they wake up early, they get tired, extremely exhausted, especially the women, they go, work get tired, then go back to work some more in their homes, and despite that they are willing to go olive-picking the next day … We reach out for that olive between the thorns and under the rocks so that we can make our olives. I swear to God' (Halima, 34) 'It's mentioned in the Quran, not from me, since Adam and Eve. It's a holy tree. The oil is used if your hand hurts you, as it says in the Quran "eat it and apply on your skin". We use it for everything, for cooking, for healing – put some corn oil on some hummus or some olive oil on the hummus. Which tastes better? Hahaa' (Abu-Mohammad, 48)

highways, have restricted mobility of Palestinians and barred them from accessing their olive orchards and inhibit access to their traditional livelihoods and way of life (B'tselem, 2018). This transformed the olive tree and the cultural spaces for human engagement that revolved around it into an entity and symbol that was imbued with strong emotions – anger, a sense of violation, nostalgia, place-attachment, among others (Hammad, 2011). In my view, other factors have contributed to the 'undoing' of the olive tree as an ICZ, including increasing urbanization and globalization influences; decreased reliance on rural way of life as source of livelihood; shifting interests of youth and greater apathy towards culture and politics; waning intensities in place attachment and attitudes towards elders; and migratory movements. These factors are important to take note of as they challenge notions that second and third generation Palestinians are attached to Palestine as a homeland by default (Peretz, 1993) as well as assumptions that political consciousness across generations is natural and hereditary (Hammad, 2011).

Despite this trend, there has been a parallel revival of resistance to place and place identity embodied in the olive tree and the land it was uprooted from. This has been manifested in a number of ways including: replanting olive trees as an act of defiance; participation in popular protests, instilling memory among younger generations of what was lost and must be reclaimed, engagement in virtual spaces, and advocacy through art and culture. All of these acts of resistance, discussed below, involve a transmission of physical or symbolic meaning and action between older and younger generations aimed at maintaining that connection with the olive tree as entity and symbol. These have transformed the olive tree into a locus for cross-generational resistant acts.

1. *Political participation and popular protest.* The olive orchards blocked off by the separation barrier or to be uprooted, have become the spatial site for resistance actions in defense of all the above. The role of youth and transnational actors has been central in these protests, rooted in a cross-generational sense of responsibility towards the olive tree and political redefinition of the significance of the olive tree among younger generations of activists.[5] For this same reason parents and grandparents engage younger generations in olive picking harvest season despite restrictive measures (see Figure 22.2).

2. *Replanting olive trees as an act of defiance,* such as replanting trees that have been uprooted by settlers or no longer accessible without permits due to annexation of land[6] in backyards of homes or in the confiscated land itself. One grandmother explains that involving children and grandchildren and maintaining the attachment and the memory is a way of resisting these violations across the generations – 'perhaps they do not see [the olive trees] but they will not forget'.

3. *The role of memory in sustaining the significance of intergenerational places.* There are multiple levels of memory that families use to mobilize younger generations

FIGURE 22.2 Father and son picking olives during olive harvest season despite restrictive measures. Photo by Abed Qusini – Palestine

to resist the violation of the olive tree and land: its profound importance in their lineage and ancestry, memories of sociocultural practices and their importance, repeated emotional accounts of parents and grandparents about their attachments to the land and olive trees ('the land was everything to my father'), romanticized memories of what the original landscape used to be that younger generations no longer have access (Hammad, 2011, 2020).

4. *Virtual spaces of engagement.* Much activism has been taking place online through social media, alternative news channels, and this has resulted in a stronger global justice movement. Such campaigns advocating for the olive tree and what it signifies has indeed moved across borders to become more transnational in nature in support of this cause.[7]

5. *The role of art, poetry, and music in resistance* cannot be overlooked as it has been a growing area of resistance among older and emerging artists. The olive tree continues to feature as a strong representation and symbol.

Concluding Remarks and Possibilities for Reinstating the Olive Tree as an ICZ

In this chapter, I have outlined a different perspective on ICZ by focusing on an entity and place of engagement viewed to be a naturally occurring spatial focal point for intergenerational cohesion – the olive trees and orchards. The multiple meanings that this entity has held for people across generations was traced along with its transformation from a primarily sociocultural, psychological and economic site to a symbol and focal point for political civic engagement in defense of the olive tree and all that its loss represents.

In doing so, this chapter draws attention to the disabling factors that could undermine or violate naturally occurring cross-generational zones such as sites, land or symbolic entities within them such as the olive tree. It also points to the intentional acts that aim at holding onto these spaces and resisting their annihilation. This contributes to discussions that could raise our awareness of how ICZ that stimulate meaningful and positive intergenerational connections in some contexts might also exist at the epicenter of broader conflicts over space and place. It also applies to struggles over public spaces at risk of being 'undone' due to rapid urbanization or expansionist plans of the private sector. There are also instances where naturally occurring ICZ are impacted by lack of responsibility towards our own environment or changing uses of landscape that warrant further research through the ICZ lens. Thus, the perspective offered in this chapter reinforces the notion that ICZ could be utilized as a tool for social and political cohesion in a variety of contested neighborhoods and contexts, while emphasizing the importance of people–place relationships (Kaplan, Sánchez, & Hoffman, 2017; Vanderbeck & Worth, 2015). A number of lessons and practical considerations in regard to ICZ can be extracted through this case study that is applicable to various other contexts and sites:

1. ICZ can be naturally existent spaces that are under threat because of globalization or social transformation or political strife, or they can be spaces that are being reclaimed or recreated.
2. We must capitalize on naturally occurring ICZ and preserve the social bonds that they generate and actively seek to sustain them. This necessitates raising awareness among the public of their significance, and creatively utilizing resources to engage younger generations.
3. This case has shown that ICZ are more than physical spaces; they are spaces that represent a common interpretation and attachment across generations. When those who inhabit an ICZ hold a shared ethical or political commitment, virtual mobilization can be an equally effective way of bridging generations, potentially as strong as physical interactions.
4. ICZ are not passive spaces that are unchanging; they have an inherent agency and significance in and of themselves in bringing together, breaking apart and stirring resistance across generations.

5. The inhabitants of ICZ are not passive recipients of environmental influence. They are active in constructing and refining meanings associated with ICZ and in determining which intergenerational engagement possibilities to pursue and how these settings could function.

6. As the extended family dilutes into nuclear families and social ties loosen, education campaigns are needed to instill the value of intergenerational spaces and interactions, together with a respect for history, culture and elderly members of the family and society. There is also a distinct role among parents and grandparents in perpetuating these notions to support ICZ.

7. Bringing together different generations is an opportunity to enhance not only social cohesion but also political cohesion in communities and contexts that are ethnically or politically divided.

8. ICZ should not be romanticized: It is important to pay attention to threads of tension and conflict as well as harmony in the interpersonal and intergroup relations occurring within and around settings with effective and not-so-effective ICZ spaces.

In relation to the ICZ conceptual framework proposed by Kaplan et al. (2016), the following considerations are proposed:

o ICZ dimensions must be seen as interrelated and mutually reinforcing as agents of that 'intergenerational glue', and this entanglement of the psychological, political, emotional, etc. (as in the case of the olive tree) is a crucial consideration when designing and sustaining ICZ.

o The temporal dimension of the ICZ conceptual framework is a cross-cutting element; it represents the continuity of this experience and attachment over time and across the generations.

o The ethical and virtual dimensions of this framework are significant in relation to the defense of contested places as in the case of the Palestinian olive trees – framed as a political responsibility and ethical commitment against injustice.

o The sustainability of ICZ needs to be integrated within conceptual framework.

Notes

1 Quotes in this paper are derived from my PhD research conducted in 2010–2012 in a contested Palestinian village called Bil'in. It is to be published as a book entitled *Toward a theory of emplaced resistances: 'it all starts and ends with the land'*, due for publication in 2020. Due to the contested nature of this site and place, the 'physical' dimension is broken down into history, location, economics and politics.

2 According to UN figures, around 48% of the agricultural land in the West Bank and Gaza is planted with olive trees. Olive trees account for 70% of fruit production in Palestine and contribute around 14% to the Palestinian economy. 93% of the olive

harvest is used for olive oil production while the rest is used for olive soap, table olives and pickles. Much of the olive production is for local consumption with a small amount of olives being exported primarily to Jordan.

3 Sources of these voices include recent research in Bil'in village (Hammad, 2020), an interview with Ahed Tamimi, a 16-year-old Palestinian female activist (Abu Bakr, 2018), and advocacy factsheets from UN and civil society organizations that advocate Palestinian land rights (IEMU, 219; Miftah, 2018).

4 From *Rest in My Shade: A Poem about Roots*, published by Olive Branch Press, an imprint of Interlink Publishing Group, Inc. Text copyright © Nora Lester Murad and Danna Masad, 2018. Reprinted by permission.

5 Examples of intergenerational activities centered around the olive tree include: Youth Against Settlements (https://hyas.ps/activities/olive-harvest/) which has engaged youth in Hebron olive harvest season alongside generations of Hebronites. Bil'in weekly protests towards separation wall that blocks them from their ancestral olive orchards (https://jfjfp.com/get-stuck-in-planting-olive-trees-in-palestine/); Stop the Wall (www.stopthewall.org).

6 In the land where the olives are planted lies in Area C, 60% of the West Bank, which according to Oslo is under full Israeli control, the farmers need permits from Israeli authorities to access their land and to tend to their trees. The same regulation applies to those farmers whose lands are in the 'seam zone' i.e. the area between the Green Line and the Separation Wall. (Miftah, 2018). Jewish settlers have also been known to uproot or burn Palestinian olives trees seen to be both a political and a criminal act (Hass, 2018).

7 Examples of transnational campaigns and programs that mobilize and advocate for the protection of the olive tree online include: Plant an Olive Tree campaign of Human Appeal (http://atg.ps/programs/olive-campaigns).

References

Abu Bakr, W. (2018). *The Palestinian olive tree and Ahed Tamimi.* Shehab News. Retrieved from https://shehabnews.com/post/33438/the-palestinian-olive-tree-and-ahed-tamimi.

B'tselem (2018). *Olive harvest, 2018: Israeli settlers injure Palestinian farmers, harm trees and steal olives* Retrieved from https://www.btselem.org/node/212224.

Beth Johnson Foundation (2011). A guide to intergenerational practice. Stoke-on-Trent, UK: Author. Retrieved from: www.emil-network.eu/a-guide-to-intergenerational-practice-beth-johnson-foundation.

Graham-Brown, S. (1983). The impact on the social structure of Palestinian society. In N. Aruri (Ed.), *Occupation: Israel over Palestine* (pp. 230–256). Belmont, MA: Association of Arab-American University Graduates.

Hammad, S. (2011). Senses of place in flux: A generational approach. *International Journal of Sociology and Social Policy, 31*(9/10), 555–568.

Hammad, S. (2020). *Toward a theory of emplaced resistances: 'Everything starts and ends with the land'.* London: Rowman and Littlefield Publishers.

Hass, A. (2018, October 15). *Hundreds of trees destroyed in West Bank Palestinian villages,* Israeli rights groups report. Retrieved from www.haaretz.com/israel-news/.premium-hundreds-of-trees-destroyed-in-west-bank-palestinian-villages-rights-groups-say-1.6555686.

IEMU (2019). *Palestine: 2018 in review – Factsheet.* Institute for Middle East Understanding. Retrieved from https://imeu.org/article/palestine-2018-in-review.

Kaplan, M., Sánchez, M., & Hoffman, J. (2017). *Intergenerational pathways to a sustainable society*. New York, NY: Springer.

Kaplan, M., Thang, L. L., Sánchez, M., & Hoffman, J. (2016). *An introduction to intergenerational contact zones*. University Park, PA: Penn State Extension. Retrieved from https://aese.psu.edu/extension/intergenerational/articles/intergenerational-contact-zones/introduction.

Miftah (2018). *The Palestinian initiative for the promotion of global dialogue and democracy*. Retrieved from http://www.miftah.org/Programmes/MIFTAHProfile2019.pdf.

Peretz, D. (1993). *Palestinians, refugees, and the Middle East Peace Process*. Washington, DC: United States Institute of Peace.

Swedenburg, T. (1990). The Palestinian peasant as national signifier. *Anthropological Quarterly*, *63*(1), Jan., 18–30.

Vanderbeck, R., & Worth, N. (Eds). (2015). *Intergenerational spaces*. London: Routledge.

PART VI
Methods

23

A TOOLKIT FOR INTERGENERATIONAL CONTACT ZONES APPLICATION

Mariano Sánchez and Philip B. Stafford

Why a Toolkit?

Intergenerational Contact Zones (ICZ) are about producing new spaces and transforming some already-existing ones. Currently, in our communities effective ICZ are scarce – while spaces may be inhabited by people of all ages, they may not be effective in creating or supporting interactions among people of different generations, and intergenerational environments in public spaces are still a little-explored option (Thang, 2015). Our toolkit aims to propose concrete ways to move purposefully towards new and effective ICZ.

The point of this chapter is not to simply present generic participation tools. Tools must be employed with reference to goals, such as:

• To put emphasis on the spatial dimension of social processes.
• To foster intergenerational relationships.
• To counter age and generational segregation.

With regard to the first goal, we understand space as "a relational arrangement of social goods and living beings at places" (Löw, 2016, p. xiv). The production of a space results from combining the *materiality of objects and bodies*, on the one hand, and *its appropriation and meaning*, on the other: "Space, in other words, is shaped and shapes action" (Fuller & Löw, 2017, p. 476). Then, we might say that the constitution of an ICZ needs (i) the presence of different generations in a specific place, (ii) subjective processes of appropriation through intergenerational interaction, and (iii) environmental affordance criteria (Layne, 2009) inviting positive meaning-making from that interaction.

It is through actions that bodily positioning, perceptions, and performances of subjects may be linked to material artifacts and institutional frameworks

(Schreiber-Barsch, 2017, p. 73) towards the generation of ICZ. Tools supporting ICZ should facilitate such actions for the emergence of concrete and lived-
in intergenerational non-ageist relationships.

Participatory Tools

Participation is at the basis of any effective ICZ. "Participation … provides
a collaborative process by which community inhabitants reach common goals,
engage in collective decisions, and create places, and these places, in turn,
serve as material expressions of their collective efforts" (Feldman & Westphal,
2000, p. 106). Regarding ICZ we'd need to combine participation and co-
design with involvement of different generational groups.

Whenever a group is planning an ICZ, there are multiple tools for citizens to participate in the process. These tools can, in fact, be utilized for a range of purposes:

- For conducting qualitative research into the daily (place-based) experiences of specific generational groups.
- For understanding the potential impact of ICZ on the daily lives of their
  intended users.
- For discovering and revealing the needs, skills, talents, and assets of individuals and groups from different generations, especially from those who
  might otherwise be invisible.
- For gathering and organizing diverse generations into processes designed
  to create a shared vision of a better future together at a given place.

The range of participation methods is enormous and growing constantly through the
creative efforts of community development activists worldwide (see Figure 23.1).

However, these techniques should not be considered as void instruments allowing any type of use. We contend that unless the theoretical and philosophical
underpinnings of citizen-as-generational-member participation are the background, these tools might be limited in their capacity to generate intergenerational
engagement that is "authentic" in the sense of being aligned with participants'
needs, interests, and experience. The essence of these participatory tools is that
they can help individual members of generational groups build their own capacity
to understand and get involved in the production of effective ICZ.

Participation itself has become widely respected as an essential process
underlying the co-design of spaces, technologies, products, and services
(Manzini, 2015). Here, we argue for the adaptation of methods that lend
themselves to intergenerational use, the creation of intergenerational learning, and the emergence of effective intergenerational contact zones.

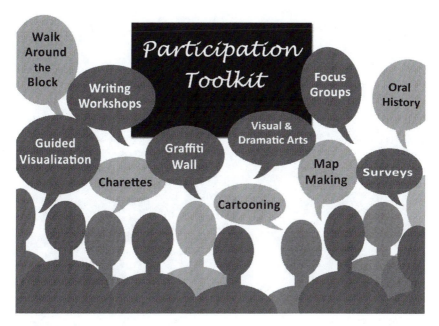

FIGURE 23.1 Participation methods

Becoming Generationally Aware

"Planning is simultaneously about people and place" (Ramasubramanian & Albrecht, 2018, p. 96). Planning ICZ is about generations and place. Hence, before beginning to plan an ICZ attention should be paid to raising generational awareness, i.e. augmenting the degree to which people involved in the planning are aware of both their generational position and that of others. We are talking about carrying out a previous mapping of generational environments (Biggs, n. d.). This exercise may look at which generational constituencies are in a given place, what are the generational priorities at a particular place, and what do place-based issues look like through an intergenerational lens.

This initial mapping may be carried out through *timelines* (see Figure 23.2). They are certainly a good tool to learn and build generational consciousness and have the nice benefit of enabling seniors and youth to feel validated regarding their position in life. Magic Me (MM), a leading intergenerational arts organization based in London, has put into practice timelines to visualize connectivity (McAvinchey, 2016). We have adapted MM's four steps to create a timeline so that they may fit better in the context of ICZ: (1) invitation to think of three significant dates and places that relate participants to the issue at stake; (2) contributions are arranged chronologically along a line; (3) facilitators add new historical and place-linked events to punctuate the decades; (4) participants are invited to examine the collaborative timeline and discuss what they observe in terms of time and space.

FIGURE 23.2 Timeline in progress. Source: McAvinchey (2016, p. 41)

A Range of Tools

Charrettes

"It is a participatory technique for approaching a design problem focused on a particular facility, community, or city. Through intense and possibly multi-day meetings, it involves consulting with and obtaining feedback from a group of stakeholders" (Kaplan, 2009, p. 117). In Bloomington, Indiana survey research for downtown senior housing affirmed that seniors wanted, by far, to be around people of all ages. This led to a charrette designed to bring such housing to the edge of a park heavily utilized by children of the Boys and Girls Club and discussions as to how the two generations could interact in this shared space (Stafford, 1997, pp. 309–311). The charrette was followed by a "Park Rangers" project in which teens interviewed elders about their history with the park, creating a public skit illustrating the stories.

Charrettes, as it is the case with all tools, may be used with other techniques. In Bloomington, a youth charrette combined oral history interviews by children of neighborhood elders with a walkabout and photovoice activity designed to illuminate built and natural features of a neighborhood. This was followed by a debriefing activity in which the youth identified "3 big and cool ideas" (Race & Torma, 1998) that would make the neighborhood a good place for both kids and elders. Debriefing sessions could also be formulated to obtain community planning recommendations that incorporate input from engaged older participants and other community stakeholders.

City as Play

James Rojas has developed this method "to unleash creativity through the use of common objects" (Derr & Tarantini, 2016). For instance, it was used when the City of Boulder, Colorado, was exploring options to upgrade a multigenerational mobile home park (Derr, Chawla, & Mintzer, 2018, pp. 104–105).

Rojas' main idea is encouraging the use of toys and all kinds of gizmos in a playful way to make serious models of how community spaces should be. Haas (2010) has laid out six steps for how *The-City-as-Play* approach works: (1) organize your materials, space, time, and attitude; (2) ask a great question to spark imagination; (3) provide some general instructions and loose criteria for people to build (rather than draw); (4) give participants (either individuals or groups) time to build their own models; (5) give every participant a minute to share with the group what was built; (6) synthesize all models into one combined model.

Drawings, Murals, and Graffiti

Whether on a piece of paper or on a wall, the creation of a *drawing* can provide a compelling and cross-generational language to visualize spaces. Derr et al. (2018) provide a nice example of its use with children and older residents:

> One way to understand how children's use of local environments changes from generation to generation is to compare children's drawings and explanations about the places that they currently use with older generation's drawings of their childhood environmental memories. If older residents are comfortable drawing, this activity can be integrated into an oral history about their childhood engagement in their community. If people hesitate to draw, an artist can illustrate the environmental stories that they tell.
>
> *(p. 73)*

Typically, *murals* have the added value of both their physical materiality and their potential to become a public object that it is exposed for appropriation and meaning making. An example of how murals can serve as interesting tools for community intergenerational work follows:

> When the University of Colorado established a Children, Youth and Environments Center on its Boulder campus, the center director invited the Society for Creative Aging, a nonprofit organization formed by senior artists and volunteers, to work with children to make murals to decorate the center walls. Elder artists worked with students in two elementary schools to depict a "child friendly community".
>
> *(Derr et al., 2018, p. 75)*

A low cost tool is the *graffiti wall*. It can be as simple as posting large rolls of news-print on a wall in a public space and, on the top line, offering a question to be answered with words, drawings, or pictographs. A well-conceived graffiti wall can produce a rich source of data regarding current and/or future thoughts and ideas from people of all ages. In one example in Bloomington, Indiana the top line ques-tion was "What makes a healthy neighborhood?" (see Figure 23.3).

Future Scenarios and Festivals

Scenario planning and *future wheels*, particular forms of mind mapping (Ramasubrama-nian & Albrecht, 2018, p. 81), are tools to visualize potential avenues for transform-ation of spaces and places. For one example, Manchester and Facer (2017) describe an *imagining the future* exercise in Bristol designed to generate ideas for how this city might further embrace goals for intergenerational engagement in diverse settings.

Future festivals are special events in which "residents come together to share their concerns and hopes for their community" (Kaplan, Higdon, Crago, & Robbins, 2004, pp. 119–146). Futures festivals are multimedia in nature:

> Through murals, models, photographs, theatrical displays, and other commu-nications media, community residents and public officials share their ideas about community development. Festival participants get the chance to answer (and learn how others answer) the all-important question: "What would you like to see in the future of your community?"
>
> *(p. 124)*

FIGURE 23.3 Graffiti wall in Bloomington. Author: Phil Stafford

Generation-led Tours

Loebach and Gilliland (2010) tested a child-guided protocol based on children leading researchers and city planners on guided walks with interesting outcomes:

> Thematic and spatial analysis of narratives and photographs revealed significant but complex patterns of neighborhood perception and use, suggesting that this child-led protocol is an effective tool for engaging children in community assessment and for revealing their local lived experience.
>
> *(p. 52)*

Similarly, diverse generational groups may lead tours and walkabouts to document and discuss spaces and places of significance to them.

Mapping

Ramasubramanian and Albrecht (2018) talk about *behavior maps* and *perceptual mapping*. The former is mainly focused on observation. Norouzi (2016) used place-centered behavior mapping for observing behavior and social interaction at intergenerational shared sites.

In the case of *perceptual mapping* people are asked to create maps from scratch according to their perceptions (Ramasubramanian & Albrecht, 2018, p. 94). For instance, perceptual (or mental) maps can be used as a way of assessing program impact on participants' knowledge and understanding about their communities. In one such example noted in Kaplan (2009), participants of an intergenerational visioning project in Long Island City in Queens, New York mapped out and labelled as much of their neighborhoods, including the school and their homes, as possible using an 11 inch by 17 inch sheet of paper. To determine the physical boundaries of the students' knowledge of their communities, or the range covered in their maps, lines were drawn around the clusters of the labeled elements in each map. The three images in Figure 23.4 represent a student's hand-drawn map of the local community (left), transposition of the student's map onto a base map of the community (center), and transposition of this map into a computer program for analyzing aggregate spatial data (right).

There are many other types of mapping. Derr et al. (2018) refer to *play maps* as composite maps of play spaces that could be used for various purposes, including to raise awareness about how play experience and opportunity can change over time as a function of rapid community development, as noted in Kinoshita (2014).

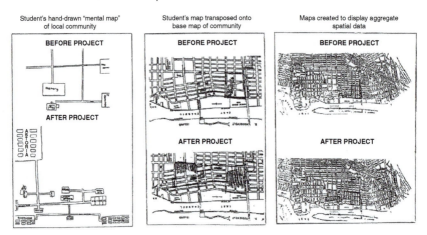

FIGURE 23.4 Mental maps in intergenerational visioning. Source: Kaplan (1991, pp. 344–346)

While more costly and time-consuming, participatory mapping enables citizens to exert power over their geography too often given over to expert cartographers.

Oral History

Oral histories are great tools for helping to better "understand people's relationships to a place in the past, or think about new possibilities for intergenerational design" (Derr et al., 2018, p. 53). A folklore field school in Bloomington engaged older students in an extended study of the town square and its specific uses by different age groups over time. While micro-environments shared by single generations described the current situation (teens hanging out at the library, seniors at Ladyman's Café), oral history work revealed that Saturday night on the square in the 1940s was similarly age-segregated, as adults met on sidewalks and teens cruised in their cars and hung on the limestone walls surrounding the courthouse (Stafford, Carpenter, & Taylor, 2004, pp. 14–34).

Photo Rating, Photogrid, Photovoice

Layne (2009) emphasized ways in which "the visual image can be used as an inroad into the way we think about a place, its given value" (pp. 188–9). For example, through a *photo rating* process he carried out a survey exercise to elicit features of desired urban public spaces for exchange between youth and older adults. Combining the use of photography with "visiting and documenting specific places that seem to exhibit the characteristics defined in this intergenerational space study" (Layne, 2009) – so called, *documentary photography* – may be a good complement to the rating of images.

In an account of a visioning and participatory design process of child friendly public spaces, Derr and Tarantini (2016) mention the application of a *photogrid* as a tool in a participatory research about child-friendly cities. Basically, "the students used flash cards to draw changes they would make to the Civic Area and located the flash cards on a site plan" (Whittier Students Share Ideas with City Council, n.d.).

McGovern, Schwittek, and Seepersaud (2018) describe an interdisciplinary student-led initiative in the Bronx, NY that adopted a *photovoice* approach to explore ageism across generations. Since this tool does not rely on elaborated cognitive skills, "it promotes inclusivity in knowledge production and serves as an advocacy platform for persons under-represented" (p. 3), as is often the case with "bookend generations." We might use a combination of photographs and oral accounts – presented as posters or slides, to explore beliefs about how places and spaces may become focal points for intergenerational relationships.

Make Tools

This section presents user-centered design approaches for people to express their ideas and feelings through making things with visual toolkits:

> Make Tools can vary from visual collages to three-dimensional artifacts, but the basic idea is the same: to allow people to construct design representations through visual elements as expression of need. [...] these toolkits work as scaffolds for experiences that support the creativity of everyday people.
>
> *(Vaajakallio & Mattelmäki, 2007)*

When Make Tools – in fact, an assembly of tools – are used on site to prompt thinking about how things might be with such a tool in place we talk of "situated Make Tools."

Prototypes are a case of "Make Tools." However, they can be considered as well at the design stage (along with scenarios and visioning). For instance, NESTA & Thinkpublic (n.d.) have developed a prototyping framework and guide which have been applied to intergenerational work in the UK and Portugal. The initiative supported 18 pilot projects whose aim was "to test and implement ideas for intergenerational activities and partnerships in which beneficiaries were involved in the co-design of people-centred schemes" (CGF, 2013).

Brandt, Binder, and Sanders (2013) explain that participatory prototyping may use probes such as immersion workbooks, diaries, the day-in-the-life exercise, send-a-camera home, image collaging, cognitive mapping, and Velcromodelling.

Conclusion

Facilitators and planning groups need to pay attention to the practical side of participation tools:

- Some tools work especially well with small groups but become hopelessly complex when applied to large groups.
- Some tools require real-time, *simultaneous* participation by all of the participants, others can serve a "drive-through" audience.
- Some tools are labor-intensive to develop, others extremely easy to implement even with limited human resources.

Since there are multiple factors to consider when selecting and adapting a tool for a particular purpose, we offer below a checklist of questions (see Table 23.1) to help lead you to the most appropriate tool. Following the precautions of the old adage "give a kid a hammer and everything becomes a nail," we encourage the prospective facilitator or planner to select and adapt tools in a deliberative fashion and not hammer everything in sight with one tool. The harder work of identifying the underlying goals and desired outcomes of a project should precede the selection of tools. Otherwise, they become empty, albeit enjoyable, and transitory.

It is necessary to make a final remark to draw attention to something specific about participatory processes in intergenerational practices. Working with diverse generations and ages can add another layer of complexity in terms of accommodating a broad range of options in terms of participants' physical and cognitive abilities, levels of experience, and life stage-related interests and pursuits. When selecting a tool, it is crucial to check its suitability for intergenerational interactions.

The strategic use of the participatory tools highlighted in this chapter will likely add to the likelihood that those who inhabit an ICZ site will find it relevant, meaningful, and compelling enough for them to spend time in that setting.

TABLE 23.1 Selecting and crafting the right tool. A checklist[1]

Selection Criteria for Tools	Charrettes	City as Play	Drawings	Murals	Graffiti	Future scenarios and festivals	Generation-led tours	Mapping	Oral history	Photography	Make tools
Desired outcomes											
Vision for the future	■		■	■	■	■	■				■
An understanding of the past								■	■		
An understanding of people's experiences			■	■	■					■	
An understanding of people's preferences		■				■				■	■
An understanding of the impact of a service, program, or policy			■		■		■	■		■	
Identification of a broad range of issues	■				■	■				■	
A deeper understanding of specific issues	■		■			■	■			■	
An advocacy position				■		■					
A proposal for funding	■					■					
A white paper or report	■					■			■		
A performance						■					
A media product	■								■	■	
A public exhibition	■		■							■	

(Continued)

TABLE 23.1 (Cont.)

Selection Criteria for Tools	Charrettes	City as Play	Drawings	Murals	Graffiti	Future scenarios and festivals	Generation-led tours	Mapping	Oral history	Photography	Make tools
Time requirements [low = 1 high = 5]											
To prep, deliver and report	5	4	2	3	1	5	5	4	5	4	5
Time required of participants	4	4	3	4	1	4	4	3	4	3	3
Costs to assume [low = 1 high = 5]											
Experts or paid facilitators	5	3	2	4	1	5	3	3	2	2	4
Facilities costs	4	3	2	2	1	5	1	2	1	1	3
Supplies costs	4	4	3	4	1	4	1	3	2	3	4
Food costs	4	3	2	3	1	4	2	2	1	1	2
Translation and/or interpretation	4	4	2	3	2	4	3	3	2	2	2
How important is diversity sought [1 = slight 5 = very] (to be completed by practitioner)											
Cultural background											
Age											
Education and literacy											
Race											
Tenure in the community											

Socio-economic status								
Political persuasion								
Degree of power and influence								
Physical and/or cognitive ability								
Numbeer of participants sought [low = 1 high = 5] (to be completed by practitioner)								
Absolute numbers non-random								
Absolute numbers random								
Expected form of engagement for participants [low = 1 high = 5] (to be completed by practitioner)								
Will talk in front of others								
May feel intimidated by requirements								
Assume risks to confidentiality								
Personal disclosure required								
Format is egalitarian								
Attendance at number of events								
Level of fun anticipated for participants								

(1) Empty rows in the checklist are questions to be answered by the user group.

References

Biggs, S. (n.d.). A generationally intelligent response to older abuse and ageism [Power-Point presentation]. Retrieved from www.combatingelderabuse.eu/wp-content/uploads/2016/06/okAgenerationally-intelligent-response-to-elder-abuse-and-ageism-4-short-version.pdf.

Brandt, E., Binder, T., & Sanders, E. B-N. (2013). Tools and techniques: Ways to engage telling, making and enacting. In J. Simonen & T. Robertson (Eds.), *Routledge International Handbook of Participatory Design* (pp. 117–144). London and New York: Routledge.

CGF. (2013, July 16). Designing all-age friendly approaches for communities: Launch of learning from the IntergenerationAll programme [Blog post]. Retrieved from https://gulbenkian.pt/uk-branch/designing-all-age-friendly-approaches-for-communities-launch-of-learning-from-the-intergenerationall-programme/.

Derr, V., Chawla, L., & Mintzer, M. (2018). *Placemaking with Children and Youth. Participatory Practices for Planning Sustainable Communities.* New York, NY: New Village Press.

Derr, V., & Tarantini, E. (2016). "Because we are all people": Outcomes and reflections from young people's participation in the planning and design of child friendly public spaces. *Local Environment: International Journal of Sustainability and Justice, 21*(12), 1534–1556. doi:https://doi.org/10.1080/13549839.2016.1145643.

Feldman, R. M., & Westphal, L. M. (2000). An agenda for community design and planning: Participation and empowerment in practice. In R. J. Lawrence (Ed.), *Sustaining Human Settlement: A Challenge for the New Millennium* (pp. 105–139). North Shields, UK: Urban International Press.

Fuller, M. G., & Löw, M. (2017). Introduction: An invitation to spatial sociology. *Current Sociology Monograph, 65*(4), 469–491. doi:10.1177/0011392117697461.

Haas, G. (2010, July 5). Jame Rojas: The city as play [Blog post]. Retrieved from https://drpop.org/james-rojas-the-city-as-play/.

Kaplan, M. (1991). *An intergenerational approach to community education and action* (Unpublished doctoral dissertation). CUNY Graduate Center, New York, NY.

Kaplan, M. (2009). Evaluating intergenerational programmes to improve community. In M. Sánchez (Dir.), *Intergenerational Programmes Evaluation* (pp. 103–121). Madrid: Spanish National Institute of Older Persons and Social Services, and Beth Johnson Foundation.

Kaplan, M., Higdon, F., Crago, N., & Robbins, L. (2004). Future festivals: An intergenerational strategy for promoting community participation. *Journal of Intergenerational Relationships, 2*(3-4), 119–146. doi:10.1300/J194v02n03_10.

Kinoshita, I. (2014). Play maps in Japan. In V. Johnson, R. Hart, & J. Colwell (Eds.), *Steps to Engaging Young Children in Research* (Vol. 2, pp. 111–114). Brighton, United Kingdom: University of Brighton.

Layne, M. R. (2009). *Supporting Intergenerational Interaction: Affordance of Urban Public Space* (Doctoral dissertation). Retrieved from NC State University Libraries (etd-07052009-221241).

Loebach, J., & Gilliland, J. (2010). Child-led tours to uncover children's perceptions and use of neighborhood environments. *Children, Youth and Environments, 20*(1), 52–90. Retrieved from: www.colorado.edu/journals/cye.

Löw, M. (2016). *The Sociology of Space: Materiality, Social Structures, and Action.* New York, NY: Palgrave Macmillan.

Manchester, H., & Facer, K. (2017). (Re)-learning the city for intergenerational exchange. In H. Sacré & S. De Visscher (Eds.), *Learning the City: Cultural Approaches to Civic Learning in Urban Spaces* (pp. 83–98). Cham, Switzerland: Springer International Publishing.

Manzini, E. (2015). *Design, When Everybody Designs: An Introduction to Design for Social Innovation.* Cambridge, MA: MIT Press.

McAvinchey, C. (2016). *Rooms with a View. Disrupting and Developing Narratives of Community through Intergenerational Arts Practice.* London, United Kingdom: Magic Me. Retrieved from https://magicme.co.uk/wp/wp-content/uploads/2018/03/Rooms-with-a-View-report-by-CMcAvinchey-2.pdf.

McGovern, J., Schwittek, D., & Seepersaud, D. (2018). Through the lens of age: Challenging ageism in the Bronx and beyond with community-based arts activism. *The International Journal of Social, Political and Community Agendas in the Arts, 13*(2), 1–8. doi:http://doi.org/10.18848/2326-9960/CGP/v13i02/1-8.

NESTA & Thinkpublic. (n.d.). *Prototyping Framework. A Guide to Prototyping New Ideas.* Retrieved from www.nesta.org.uk/documents/741/prototyping_framework.pdf.

Norouzi, N. (2016). *Intergenerational Facilities: Designing Intergenerational Space through a Human Development Lens* (Doctoral dissertation). Retrieved from http://hdl.handle.net/10919/79848.

Race, B., & Torma, C. (1998). *Youth Planning Charrettes.* Chicago, IL: Planners Press, American Planning Association.

Ramasubramanian, L., & Albrecht, J. (2018). *Essential Methods for Planning Practitioners. Skills and Techniques for Data Analysis, Visualization, and Communication.* Cham, Switzerland: Springer International Publishing.

Schreiber-Barsch, S. (2017). Space is more than place: The urban context as contested terrain of inclusive learning settings for adults and arena of political subjectivation. In H. Sacré & S. De Visscher (Eds.), *Learning the City: Cultural Approaches to Civic Learning in Urban Spaces* (pp. 67–82). Cham, Switzerland: Springer International Publishing.

Stafford, P. B. (1997). Collaborative design for healthy communities. In L. F. Heumann (Ed.), *Managing Care, Risk and Responsibility, Sixth International Conference on Systems Sciences in Health-Social Services for the Elderly and Disabled.* Chicago, IL: University of Illinois.

Stafford, P. B., Carpenter, I., & Taylor, D. (2004). Documenting local culture: An introductory field school. In M. Iris (Ed.), *Passages: The Ethnographic Field School and First Fieldwork Experiences* (pp. 14–34). Washington. D.C.: American Anthropological Association.

Thang, L. (2015). Creating an intergenerational contact zone: Encounters in public spaces within Singapore's public housing neighbourhoods. In R. Vanderbeck & N. Worth (Eds.), *Intergenerational Space* (pp. 33–49). New York: Routledge.

Vaajakallio, K., & Mattelmäki, T. (2007, August 25–27). *Collaborative Design Exploration: Envisioning Future Practices with Make Tools.* Paper presented at the International Conference on Designing Pleasurable Products and Interfaces, Helsinki, Finland. Retrieved from http://citeseerx.ist.psu.edu/viewdoc/download?doi=10.1.1.585.3633&rep=rep1&type=pdf.

Whittier Students Share Ideas with City Council. (n.d.). Retrieved from www.growingupboulder.org/civic-area-2014.html.

24

INTERGENERATIONAL PROGRAMS AND INTERGENERATIONAL CONTACT ZONES

Aligning Notions of "Good Quality"

Mariano Sánchez, María Pilar Díaz, Andrés Rodríguez, and Rosa Bonachela Pallarés

Introduction

In this chapter we are dealing with a methodological question: how may we enhance good quality in Intergenerational Programs (IP) through the application of Intergenerational Contact Zones (ICZ) as programming tool? ICZ is a framework that can serve as *conceptual tool*, *programming tool*, and *design tool* (Kaplan, Thang, Sánchez, & Hoffman, 2016). However, we'll be just looking into the practical potential of ICZ as *programming tool*. Our initial question might be formulated more precisely as follows: Which quality indicators should ICZ present to be able to enhance the quality of Intergenerational Programs (IP)?

In this volume's Introduction it has been noted that the ICZ concept "represents an endeavor to integrate what is often portrayed as separate spheres of transient intergenerational programs" (see p. 3). Obviously, ICZ and IP are connected since all IP need a space.

> Consequently with the programmatic nature of ICZ, we contend that it makes sense to align the introduction of good quality planning and implementation of programs aimed at purposefully bringing different generations together for individual, group, community and societal good – IP's ultimate mission – with efforts to set up spatial focal points for intergenerational meeting, interaction and engagement – as ICZ intend to do.

Since to the best of our knowledge there is no available list of quality indicators for ICZ, in this chapter we initiate the process to develop such a list in accordance with the suggested ICZ-IP alignment. How? By paying attention, first, to quality guidelines for intergenerational programs. Why? Because we understand that these guidelines may serve as conditional principles to establish indicators of quality for ICZ as programming tool. Otherwise said, if ICZ are approached as programming instruments contributing to the planning and implementation of high-quality IP, it makes a lot of sense carrying out the suggested exercise of mutual alignment between programs and settings. In fact, when developing their standards and guidelines to ensure effective intergenerational professional practices, Rosebrook and Larkin (2003) already noted the need for "thinking about the importance of the environment" (p. 142).

Quality Standards and Guidelines for Intergenerational Programs

Lists including features and components of successful intergenerational programs abound (Bressler, Henkin, & Adler, 2005; Epstein & Boisvert, 2006; MacCallum et al., 2006). We have as well examples of standards and guidelines of intergenerational practice (Larkin & Rosebrook, 2002; Rosebrook & Larkin, 2003; Sánchez, Díaz, Sáez, & Pinazo, 2014). What is more recent is the emergence of systematic efforts to create singular instruments that incorporate a range of quality features for IP derived from diverse streams of intergenerational theory and practice. In what follows, we'll focus on two such models.

TOY (Together Old and Young) for Quality Program

What is a good quality intergenerational program and how do we recognize it and promote it? This question has triggered partners in the Together Old and Young (TOY) consortium to develop the *TOY for Quality Program*, "a participatory process of reflection, discussion and action ... that can be used by practitioners and organizations engaged in any stage of planning or implementation of intergenerational learning initiatives" (TOY-PLUS Consortium, 2018, p. 9). The TOY approach to quality and evaluation of intergenerational learning, including an explanation of TOY for Quality Program, is one of the units in the TOY Online Course.

TOY approaches intergenerational programs as initiatives involving older adults and young children, therefore its quality dimensions focus specifically on the interaction of these two particular generational groups.

At the core of the TOY for Quality Program are six dimensions of quality:

- Dimension 1. Building relationships and wellbeing.
- Dimension 2. Respect for diversity.
- Dimension 3. Interaction with and within the community.
- Dimension 4. Learning with and from each other.
- Dimension 5. Professional development and teamwork.
- Dimension 6. Monitoring, evaluation, and sustainability.

The TOY for Quality Program's six dimensions of quality are described in Appendix 24.1.

ICIL Quality Standards

The International Certificate in Intergenerational Learning (ICIL) is an online course established as a partnership between the University of Granada, in Spain, and Generations Working Together, in Scotland. ICIL presents its students a set of nine quality standards in intergenerational work.

These standards were initially informed by The Beth Johnson Foundation's Approved Provider Standard framework (The Centre for Intergenerational Practice, 2008); Rosebrook & Larkin (2003)'s standards and guidelines; Kaplan, Larkin, and Hatton-Yeo (2009)'s list of personal dispositions for professional intergenerational practice; Sánchez et al., (2014)'s research about the professional profile of intergenerational program managers; the MATES Guide of Ideas for Planning and Implementing Intergenerational Projects (Pinto, 2009); and guidelines developed by ECIL (European Certificate in Intergenerational Learning) on intergenerational learning best practices. They represent proven principles and approaches that, over the years, have been shown to be present in good intergenerational programs. Not in order of importance, these nine standards are as follows:

- Standard 1. Intergenerational work encourages reciprocal intergenerational learning.
- Standard 2. Intergenerational work values generational diversity.
- Standard 3. Intergenerational work confronts age discrimination and stereotypes.
- Standard 4. Intergenerational work adopts a life-course perspective.
- Standard 5. Intergenerational work fosters intergenerational relationships and bonding.
- Standard 6. Intergenerational work relies on a cross-disciplinary knowledge base.
- Standard 7. Intergenerational work meets principles of good program management.
- Standard 8. Intergenerational work has to be evaluated.
- Standard 9. Intergenerational practitioners involved in intergenerational work demonstrate certain values, attitudes, and beliefs that influence their behaviors.

A description of each standard is available in Appendix 24.2.

TOY and ICIL Combined

There is much overlap between the TOY Quality dimensions and the ICIL standards. TOY's dimensions #1, #2, #4, and #6 clearly overlap with ICIL standards #1, #2, #3, #5, #7, and #8. There are also some distinctions between these systems; ICIL's list emphasizes the cross-disciplinary knowledge base required for good IP and the need to adopt a life-course perspective, whereas the TOY framework places greater emphasis on interaction within diverse community contexts. However, we argue that both proposals may be combined into four Quality Domains (QD) of IP quality:

- ○ QD1. Intergenerational relationships and wellbeing across generations.
- ○ QD2. Generational diversity.
- ○ QD3. Intergenerational program planning, implementation, and sustainability.
- ○ QD4. Intergenerational practitioners' know-how.

Quality Guidelines for IP

Now, taking into account all standards and dimensions introduced above, the TOY for Quality indicators, and other significant findings from research (Drury, Abrams, & Swift, 2017; Jarrott & DeBord, Naar, 2014; Weaver, Naar, & Jarrott, 2017), these four quality domains may be organized into nine guidelines (S) and 25 indicators (I) as follows (Table 24.1).

Aligning Quality in IP and ICZ

Finally, we get to the core step and most valuable contribution in the process that we are carrying out. We are at last in a position to wonder how conditions for quality ICZ may be aligned with the quality domains, guidelines, and indicators for intergenerational programs just presented (Table 24.1). For each of the four quality domains and nine guidelines outlined above we suggest some indicators that ICZ should integrate for such alignment. As it has been the case with Table 24.1, in the process of elaborating Table 24.2 we have incorporated some relevant research findings from a diversity of disciplinary fields (Jarrott et al., 2014; Kaplan, Haider, Cohen, & Turner, 2007; Kaplan, Thang, Sánchez, & Hoffman, 2016).

Limitations

We acknowledge that the process carried out to align notions of "good quality" faces several limitations. Firstly, the selection of TOY's and ICIL's models as primary cornerstones of this review and integration of ideal quality tools for IP reflect the authors' experience and perceptions of the intergenerational field. Considering the rapid expansion of the intergenerational field in recent years, it is difficult to maintain awareness of the full range of quality assessment tools that exist at any one time.

TABLE 24.1 Quality domains (QD), guidelines (G) and indicators (I) for intergenerational programs

---

QD1. Relationships and wellbeing across generations
G1. The program fosters intergenerational relationships and bonding (e.g. friendship)

I1 The program enhances cooperation (e.g., through sharing goals) and reduces competition
I2 The program makes possible the sharing of personal information across generations
I3 All generations involved think positively about intergenerational relationships formed in the program

G2. The program promotes reciprocal intergenerational learning

I4 All generational groups are given the opportunity to teach and learn from one another
I5 Exchange of resources (e.g., knowledge, skills) is at the matrix of the program

G3. The program increases the wellbeing of all generations involved

I6 Program participants enjoy engaging in the program and consequently are improving their sense of wellbeing (e.g., psychosocial and physical wellbeing)
I7 The program benefits all stakeholders, not just children, youth, and elder participants

QD2. Generational diversity
G4. The program values generational diversity

I8 The program gives opportunities for generations from diverse backgrounds to share their knowledge, culture, and experiences
I9 All generations feel acknowledged, accepted, and welcomed

G5. The program confronts age discrimination and stereotypes

I10 Pre-intervention tools are used to identify and confront potential age discrimination and stereotypes
I11 Program participants have developed more positive views of generations involved

QD3. Intergenerational program planning, implementation, and sustainability
G6. Program planning, implementation, evaluation, and sustainability pay attention to specificities required by intergenerational approaches

I12 There is evidence of attempts to identify and meet the needs of all generations involved, and of the wider community
I13 Program environment is accessible to and adaptable for people of all generations
I14 All activities in the program are age- and role-appropriate
I15 The program carries out continuing evaluation with participation of all generations involved

---

(Continued)

TABLE 24.1 (Cont.)

QD3. Intergenerational program planning, implementation, and sustainability

I16 The quality of engagement in the program is strong and makes likely the continuity of intergenerational relationships formed

G7. *The program facilitates interaction with generations with and within the community*

I17 The program welcomes collaboration with generations in the community
I18 The program is contributing to the development of new connections between disconnected generations in the community

QD4. Intergenerational practitioners' know-how
G8. *Practitioners rely on a cross-disciplinary knowledge base*

I19 Intergenerational practitioners have been trained to know the intergenerational field (theory, research, and practice)
I20 Intergenerational practitioners understand the distinctive features of intergenerational programs
I21 Intergenerational practitioners are skilled at promoting contacts, social relationships, interactions, and bonds between different generational groups
I22 Intergenerational practitioners are skilled at establishing and strengthening social networks and partnerships between services working with different generations
I23 Intergenerational practitioners approach aging as a lifelong, dynamic, and contextualized process of human development

G9. *Practitioners involved in the program demonstrate certain values, attitudes, and beliefs that influence their behaviors*

I24 Intergenerational practitioners are reflective and caring professionals, with vision and passion to facilitate intergenerational encounters
I25 Practitioners demonstrate a commitment to collaboration and partnership through effective networks

---

Secondly, we are aware of the non-systematic review of ancillary sources that we have introduced to enrich TOY's and ICIL's models at the time of listing guidelines and indicators. However, it has not been our intention to produce a definitive set of indicators but to show how the process may be methodologically carried out to connect quality requirements for IP with quality features for ICZ. If ICZ is a good programming tool and therefore may help to settle better IP, ICZ will have somehow to be connected to IP's quality indicators.

Finally, the applicability level of indicators in Table 24.2 varies. For one example, I2 ("The ICZ counts on structured space that fosters both structured and unstructured intergenerational interactions") and I19 ("Intergenerational practitioners understand the distinctive features of ICZ") require a different type of translational effort to put them into practice.

TABLE 24.2 Quality domains (QD), guidelines (G), and indicators (I) for ICZ as programming tool

---

QD1. Relationships and wellbeing across generations
G1. The ICZ fosters intergenerational relationships and bonding (e.g., friendship)

I1 The ICZ's physical and built environment has been staged to promote interaction and relationships

I2 The ICZ counts on structured space that fosters both structured and unstructured intergenerational interactions

G2. The ICZ promotes reciprocal intergenerational learning

I3 The ICZ's learning environment (built and natural) is equipped with various accessible and appropriate materials that stimulate the agency of participating generations to explore, learn, and interact

I4 The ICZ's learning environment (built and natural) is one that is experienced as physically safe and accessible for people of all ages and easily supervised

G3. The ICZ increases the wellbeing of all generations involved

I5 The ICZ allows participants to explore choice, autonomy, and agency in pursuing their needs and interests for personal growth and development as well as social engagement

I6 The ICZ strives to contribute to an intergenerational environment encouraging positive feelings of social engagement, value, self-esteem, self-confidence, and/or purpose (e.g., through visual cues reminding the benefits of being together)

I7 The ICZ increases the level of emotional comfort for generational groups through providing opportunities for safe access into and withdrawal from spaces where intergenerational interaction is taking place

QD2. Generational diversity
G4. The ICZ values generational diversity

I8 The built environment is flexible to accommodate generations from diverse backgrounds

I9 The ICZ facilitates for the different age groups appropriate access and amounts of cognitive, social, and physical stimulation and activity layering according to their capacities and degree of commitment

I10 The ICZ is able to hybridize conventional and modern elements to make the space meaningful to all generational groups involved

G5. The ICZ confronts age discrimination and stereotypes

I11 The ICZ contributes to locate the intergenerational program in a neutral environment where all participants feel welcome and the equality of status between generational groups may be achieved

I12 The ICZ gives visibility to positive images of different generations (e.g., using artwork, photos) both at the space where interactions take place and at adjoining spaces

---

(Continued)

TABLE 24.2 (Cont.)

QD3. Intergenerational program planning, implementation, and sustainability

G6. The ICZ's planning, implementation, evaluation, and sustainability pay attention to specificities required by intergenerational approaches

I13 The ICZ's design, management, and evaluation practices are participatory and empower all generations involved

I14 The ICZ affords opportunities for program participants to engage at different levels of involvement, including with mere observation, and to disengage

I15 The ICZ has been planned and organized in such a way as to facilitate interaction without violating people's need for privacy

G7. The ICZ facilitates interaction with generations with and within the community

I16 The ICZ takes advantage of proximity of mono-generational spaces in the community to connect them while respecting the necessary level of personal and program autonomy

I17 The ICZ facilitates the sharing of premises or outdoor spaces among different organizations representing different generational groups

QD4. Intergenerational practitioners' know-how on ICZ

G8. Practitioners rely on a cross-disciplinary knowledge base

I18 Intergenerational practitioners have been exposed to comprehensive knowledge (tying into areas of theory, research, and practice from different fields such as environment behavior studies, environmental psychology, and related sub-disciplines) to become aware of the importance of space and place in intergenerational endeavors

I19 Intergenerational practitioners understand the distinctive features of ICZ

I20 Intergenerational practitioners are skilled at using ICZ to promote contacts, social relationships, interactions, and bonds between different generational groups

G9. Practitioners involved in ICZ demonstrate certain values, attitudes and beliefs that influence their behaviors

I21 Intergenerational practitioners are able to include elements to do with spaces in their vision and passion to facilitate intergenerational encounters

I22 Practitioners include spaces and places as significant elements whenever entertaining efforts to make collaboration and partnership through effective networks possible

I23 Practitioners understand the need to incorporate flexibility into environmental designs so that ICZ spaces can evolve to accommodate changes in program priorities, local demographic and social dynamics, and participants' social, emotional, and intellectual capabilities

However, it is our hope that the many tips and examples included in this book may be helpful in further developing and refining the 23 quality indicators for ICZ outlined above.

Acknowledgments

We express our gratitude to Dr. Margaret Kernan for her comments on an earlier version of this chapter.

References

Bressler, J., Henkin, N., & Adler, M. (2005). *Connecting generations, strengthening communities. A toolkit for intergenerational program planners*. Philadelphia, PA: Center for Intergenerational Learning.

The Centre for Intergenerational Practice (2008). *Approved provider standard guidance notes*. Stoke-on-Trent, UK: The Beth Johnson Foundation. Retrieved from https://generationsworkingtogether.org/downloads/592ff7e581c34-BJF%20Approved%20Provider%20Standard%20Guidance.pdf.

Drury, L., Abrams, D., & Swift, H. (2017). *Making intergenerational connections – An evidence review*. London: Age UK. Retrieved from www.ageuk.org.uk/globalassets/age-uk/documents/reports-and-publications/reports-and-briefings/active-communities/rb_2017_making_intergenerational_connections.pdf.

Epstein, A. S., & Boisvert, C. (2006). Let's do something together. *Journal of Intergenerational Relationships, 4*(3), 87–109. doi:10.1300/J194v04n03_07.

Jarrott, S. E., DeBord, K. B., & Naar, J. J. (2014). *Project TRIP: Transforming relationships through intergenerational programs*. Best Practices Modules 1–12. Retrieved from http://campus.extension.org/course/search.php?search=intergenerational.

Kaplan, M., Haider, J., Cohen, U., & Turner, D. (2007). Environmental design perspectives on intergenerational programs and practices: An emergent conceptual framework. *Journal of Intergenerational Relationships, 5*(2), 81–110. doi:10.1300/J194v05n02_06.

Kaplan, M., Larkin, E., & Hatton-Yeo, A. (2009). Leadership in intergenerational practice: In search of the elusive "P" factor – Passion. *Journal of Leadership Education, 7*(3), Winter, 59–72.

Kaplan, M., Thang, L. L., Sánchez, M., & Hoffman, J. (Eds.). (2016). *Intergenerational contact zones – A compendium of applications. online publication*. University Park, PA: Penn State Extension. Retrieved from http://aese.psu.edu/extension/intergenerational/articles/intergenerational-contact-zones.

Kernan, M., & Cortellesi, G. (Eds.). (2019). *Intergenerational learning in practice. Together old and young*. London, UK: Routledge.

Larkin, E., & Rosebrook, V. (2002). Standards for intergenerational practice: A proposal. *Journal of Early Childhood Teacher Education, 23*(2), 137–142. doi:10.1080/1090102020230205.

MacCallum, J., Palmer, D., Wright, P., Cumming-Potvin, W., Northcote, J., Booker, M. … Tero, C. (2006). *Community building through intergenerational exchange programs*. Australia: National Youth affairs Research Scheme. Retrieved from https://

docs.education.gov.au/system/files/doc/other/community_building_through_inter generational_exchange_programs.pdf.

Pinto, T. A. (Ed.). (2009). *Guide of ideas for planning and implementing intergenerational projects. Together: Yesterday, today and tomorrow.* Portugal and Estonia: Association VIDA & Rääma Young People Union Youth.

Rosebrook, V., & Larkin, E. (2003). Introducing standards and guidelines. *Journal of Intergenerational Relationships, 1*(1), 133–144.

Sánchez, M., Clyde, A., & Brown, S. (n.d.). *Intergenerational certificate in intergenerational learning. Course contents.* Retrieved from https://ecampus.ugr.es/moodle/course/index.php?categoryid=40.

Sánchez, M., Díaz, P., Sáez, J., & Pinazo, S. (2014). The professional profile of intergenerational program managers: General and specific characteristics. *Educational Gerontology, 40*(6), 427–441. doi:1080/03601277.2013.844037.

The TOY-PLUS Consortium (2018). *TOY for quality programme guidelines, Project.* Retrieved from www.toyproject.net/publication/latest-publications/toy-quality-programme-guidelines/.

Weaver, R. H., Naar, J. J., & Jarrott, S. (2017). Using contact theory to assess staff perspectives on training initiatives of an intergenerational programming intervention. *The Gerontologist, 54*(4), 770–779. doi:10.1093/geront/gnx194.

Appendix 24.1 TOY for Quality Program's Six Dimensions with Summary Description (Kernan & Cortellesi, 2019)

- **DIMENSION 1. Building relationships and wellbeing.**
  Intergenerational learning initiatives build relationships between older adults and young children and reduce the separation between generations. This is an enriching experience for all generations, counteracting isolation and bringing disparate age groups together.

- **DIMENSION 2. Respect for diversity.**
  Intergenerational initiatives facilitate connection and understanding between citizens of diverse communities, providing a space for collaboration, connection, and acceptance between different age groups and people with different backgrounds, in this way contributing to social inclusion. Through interaction with each other, stereotypes about age, gender, and culture are challenged, fostering values of solidarity, respect, and acceptance of the "other."

- **DIMENSION 3. Interaction with and within the community.**
  Intergenerational learning initiatives take shape within a community and contribute to create different levels of interaction among citizens of often disparate age groups as well as among various community services, initiatives, and groups. These interactions can originate at an institutional level (e.g. cooperation between early childhood education and care services and centers for older adults), among different agencies (intra-agencies) or as informal cooperation.

- **DIMENSION 4. Learning with and from each other.**
  Intergenerational initiatives offer more active learning opportunities, where old and young can experience fun and enjoyment when engaging in both teaching and learning roles. Young children are creative in their learning and can be active agents in areas such as technology, creativity, and innovative thought. Older adults, on the other hand, can be teachers in crafts, folklore, and behavior modelling, and can pass down important life experiences to younger generations. Each age group has a unique outlook that can be of value to the other. It is important that the design and layout of the physical intergenerational environment (outdoors as well as indoors) is supportive of the physical and emotional wellbeing of all age groups, to allow for these rich learning relationships to form.
- **DIMENSION 5. Professional development and teamwork.**
  The composition, qualities, skills, knowledge, values, and attitudes of the people who facilitate intergenerational initiatives (paid staff, volunteers, community leaders, etc.) are essential to ensure quality intergenerational practice. Quality intergenerational initiatives are implemented by people who are engaged in professional and personal development, reflect on their practice and work cooperatively with others.
- **DIMENSION 6. Monitoring, evaluation, and sustainability.**
  The sustainability of intergenerational initiatives refers to their durability and the chances of maintaining and continuing them in the short and long term. Participatory monitoring and evaluation of the service is the best way to ensure the quality and sustainability of the intergenerational initiative, taking into consideration the views and experiences of staff, children, older adults, and their families.

Appendix 24.2: The Nine ICIL's Standards in Intergenerational Work (Sánchez, Clyde, & Brown, n.d.)

- **STANDARD 1. Intergenerational work encourages reciprocal intergenerational learning.**
  Good intergenerational work emphasizes and fosters reciprocal learning – i.e. learning through an exchange of resources between different generations.
- **STANDARD 2. Intergenerational work values generational diversity.**
  Intergenerational work works across generations, valuing diversity and inclusion throughout the life cycle, and promotes social cohesion through intergenerational justice and equity.
- **STANDARD 3. Intergenerational work confronts age discrimination and stereotypes.**
  Preventing and challenging age discrimination and stereotyping is a key component of all good intergenerational work.

- **STANDARD 4. Intergenerational work adopts a life-course perspective.**
  On the one hand, this standard means that intergenerational work approaches ageing as a lifelong, dynamic and contextualized process of human development. On the other hand, intergenerational work does not focus just on age groups but on generational groups living in particular social structures, at a particular time and with particular life trajectories.

- **STANDARD 5. Intergenerational work fosters intergenerational relationships and bonding.**
  Intergenerational work not only focuses on facilitating intergenerational interactions: their real aim goes further and is to build mutually beneficial, interdependent, ongoing relationships between participant generations. Hence, intergenerational work is able to enhance social capital through social connectedness and trust. Therefore, intergenerational practitioners must support the development of intergenerational relationships and employ effective communication in doing so.

- **STANDARD 6. Intergenerational work relies on a cross-disciplinary knowledge base.**
  Intergenerational work integrates knowledge from a variety of relevant fields of theory, research, and practice (from social sciences, humanities, the arts, and so on). For instance, such practices draw upon what psychology teaches us about human development across the lifespan.

- **STANDARD 7. Intergenerational work meets principles of good program management.**
  Good intergenerational work needs thoughtful and purposeful program planning, development, and implementation. It must be able to address real needs which are identified by participants and/or residents in the community. Despite the diversity of participants involved, intergenerational work has to be made meaningful to all participants and should likewise recognize the importance of all of them.

- **STANDARD 8. Intergenerational work has to be evaluated.**
  Evaluation both of program processes and outcomes must be carried out, i.e. practitioners must employ appropriate evaluation techniques to inform program development for diverse generational groups and settings.

- **STANDARD 9. Intergenerational practitioners involved in intergenerational work demonstrate certain values, attitudes, and beliefs that influence their behaviors.**
  For instance, intergenerational practitioners are reflective, ethical, and caring professionals, with vision and passion to facilitate intergenerational encounters. They understand and demonstrate a commitment to collaboration and partnership through effective networks.

25

EVERYONE CAN MAKE A MAP

Multigenerational and Intergenerational Explorations of Community

Philip B. Stafford

Introduction

Mapmaking and maps seem to have a wide appeal across the generations. Perhaps it's our fascination with our personal place in the universe – "this is my home" – that motivates this interest. Perhaps it's the visual, non-linear nature of maps that draws upon our right-brain, creative side, and connects with bodily experience. Whatever the reason, maps and mapmaking can provide fertile material for discussions of community life and neighborhood improvement. As Doug Aberley argues (1994:13), maps should not be merely the product of experts since every one of us inhabits a place and can create its map.

As for participatory mapmaking, there is the process and the product. The process enables the direct engagement of citizens (and residents) of all ages in a collaborative exploration of the meaning of a (local) place. Participation can occur early on in the planning of an event, in the recruitment of a targeted group, in a physical survey (walkabout) of a targeted space, in the actual production of maps, and in the presentation of maps to targeted audiences such as policy and decision makers. As Aberley asserts, (homemade) maps have "teeth;" they can serve as powerful testimony to the impact on individuals and communities of past or present conditions, and proposed changes to the natural and built environment.

One could imagine that the most powerful maps would reflect the interior and experiential worlds of people of all characteristics and situations. In this volume, of course, age is of predominant concern. The example provided below foregrounds the experience and perspectives of young people, while positioning elders as "subjects" within a range of topics to be explored. Lessons were certainly learned, and important recommendations emerged regarding environments for aging. However, older adults did not plan or "do" the project in partnership with the youth. This multigenerational approach, while involving older people, was designed to improve environments for children. See Kinoshita (2009) for a similar model.

Whereas participatory mapmaking by and for children (and other populations) has become widely accepted in geography curricula (Bednarz, Acheson, & Bednarz, 2006), true intergenerational mapmaking, involving the joint planning, participation, and activism of children and older adults is rare. A brief review of the literature on participatory mapmaking provided no examples of fully intergenerational approaches – approaches that brought ages into direct collaboration with common purpose. As Biggs (2016) points out, creating "generationally intelligent environments" can emerge through a deeper understanding of the spatial experiences of both children and older adults. Participatory mapmaking with both groups can be a tool for that purpose. However, he suggests that "environments should be designed so that they enhance the cooperative and emotionally empathic capacity to *share* space (my emphasis). This will include recognition of the need for generational privacy as well as of interaction and solidarity" (2016, p. 272). Such an outcome is more likely to occur when multigenerational mapmaking becomes *intergenerational*. Older adults can learn about the world of children from their maps. Children can learn about the way older people experience the world from their maps. Actually, making maps *together* challenges two generations to represent their common worlds to a larger audience.

Perhaps the example offered below, while not fully intergenerational (in the sense of joint planning, participation, and activism), can serve as a platform for such an effort.

Crestmont Discovery Project: Bloomington, Indiana, 2004

Goals

- Assist young members of the Crestmont Boys and Girls Club to explore and learn about the physical, natural, and social environment of the club and the surrounding neighborhood.
- Connect Boys and Girls Club members with neighborhood elders.
- Empower youth to identify and act upon their ideas for neighborhood improvement.

Activities

Day One: Mapping your Neighborhood
Day Two: A Walk Around the Block: Neighborhood Exploration and Documentation
Day Three: Debriefing and Social Action Discussion

Resources Needed

- Responsible chaperones for the "walk around the block" phase.
- Volunteers or older students to assist with preparation of materials and group process.
- Neighborhood GIS base map(s).
- Disposable cameras.
- Prepared neighborhood checklist booklet.
- Digital camera or video camera (optional).
- 11 x 17 paper sheets for individual children's personal maps.
- Art supplies: newsprint, markers, colored pencils, matte paper, tracing paper.
- Community volunteers on the receiving end of visitations.

Preparation

Going into somebody else's neighborhood "to help them" is risky business, however benevolent your motivation. Hence, building a linkage with an authentic neighborhood institution is the critical first step in a project like this. It might be a church or synagogue. It might be a community-based organization. Whatever the partner might be, its legitimacy within the eyes of the neighborhood residents is important to your success. Government institutions and universities might look like good partners from the outside but the object of suspicion from within.

In Bloomington, this project was organized around an Indiana University service-learning class entitled Field Seminar in Cultural Documentation, offered by the author, a cultural anthropologist and his colleague Dr. Inta Carpenter, of the IU Folklore Institute. Crestmont is a public housing community that has been subject to stigmatizing attitudes within the larger community over its 50-year history. Our approach to the neighborhood was through the Resident Council. Through the council, we were directed to the Crestmont Boys and Girls Club, a satellite of the downtown club, and housed in a converted duplex within the public housing stock of homes and apartments. The director of the Boys and Girls Club was thrilled with the idea of the project and offered staff assistance with gaining access to and support of the children.

One month prior to the event, the instructors secured a GIS (Geographic Information System) base map of the target neighborhood from the City of Bloomington Utilities Dept. The map was intentionally plotted to include the fringe areas beyond the public housing community itself, in order to explore and challenge the children's notions of their neighborhood boundaries. Data layered onto the GIS map included streets, street names, house footprints, and numbers, railroads, and other structures/features of significance. Utilities and other layers of data are not needed for this project.

We secured a roll of newsprint (obtain "ends" from your local newspaper) and, with masking tape, erected a paper wall approximately 8' x 4'. This mural remained in place for the time needed to transfer the GIS map to the blank mural.

The standard GIS map (approx. 24" x 36") needs to be cut into sections that are sized 8 1/2" x 11" in order to create transparencies that can next be projected onto the large blank mural. Using Sharpie pens, our college students created a giant map of the neighborhood on the blank mural. Different colors were used for streets, house footprints, and other structures of significance (swimming pools, parks, etc.). Each house included its corresponding house number. This project required several person/hours of labor but was very enjoyable for the students. (The college students were introduced to the neighborhood in prior "walk-throughs" and were required to write about their impressions in field notes and haiku poetry.)

In addition to the "big map," we prepared and duplicated for each prospective youth participant a checklist to be employed on a chaperoned exploratory walk through the neighborhood. The booklet provided each child with a set of questions to be answered as they walked through the neighborhood, not unlike a scavenger hunt. In the spring of 2004, the theme for our project was Alice's Adventure through Wonderland. (A digital copy of the booklet is available from the author.)

Day One: Kids Draw Their Personal Maps

Following the creation of a flyer/permission slip to be sent home with the children, the Boys and Girls Club staff helped recruit and gather children for Day One of the exercise (an afterschool project, needless to say). Before breaking into smaller groups, we facilitated a general discussion in front of the large GIS map with the children. Then we asked our college students to work with small groups of kids, each child being provided with markers, colored pencils, and a large blank sheet of drawing paper. The following script was provided to small group leaders:

"After you get the kids' attention, and before passing out materials, you can start with some trigger questions."

How many here live in this neighborhood?
Was anyone born in this neighborhood?
If not, when did you move here?
Find out who has lived here the longest?
Find out who is the newest resident …
How did you learn about your new neighborhood?

Explore with your bike?
Ask questions?
Find a friend?
What's the best thing about this neighborhood?
What would you change if you were in charge?
So just what is this neighborhood?
   What is its name?
   Does anyone know other names for this place?
   Does anyone know how it got these names?
   What is your favorite name?
What would you say are the boundaries of this neighborhood?
Where does it end?
Which direction is north, and so on for the other three boundaries?
OK – now we're going to have you put your ideas on paper so you can tell people
   about your neighborhood.
Tomorrow, we're going on an adventure walk to see things first hand, but today,
   we're walking through the neighborhood with our imaginations.

Pass out the materials that each child can use to draw a map of their neighborhood as they see it. Ask them to wait for further directions.

You have the entire piece of paper to work on. You have lots of different colors to work with. Before you start, close your eyes and picture your house or apartment. You can be a bird flying above it and looking down. Or you can imagine walking out the front door. Think about where your neighborhood begins and ends. It might be at a street or at a building. When you are ready, open your eyes and draw a map of your neighborhood. You can put anything you want in the map. There's plenty of time.

When you think you are done ... put some notes on the map that show things that are important to you: your favorite place, your scariest place, where your best friend lives, where you spend a lot of time, those kinds of things. If time allows, ask the kids to share their maps with each other, discussing some of the questions asked previously.

When everyone is done ... don't forget tomorrow we will be meeting at 4 pm for the walk. Don't be late since we have people waiting for us at different places to help us in the adventure.

It was revealing to observe a shift in the orientation of the students towards space over the course of the project. Personal maps were typically drawn as elevations – their home as seen from the sidewalk. Following the walkabout, they were more capable in seeing their neighborhood from above, as represented in the "official" maps. This level of awareness can perhaps reveal an increase in their sense of power as they begin to generalize about their environment (Figure 25.1).

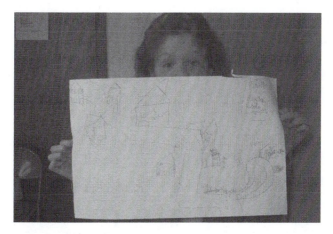

FIGURE 25.1 Personal maps were typically elevations

After the children completed the exercise, we posted the maps and/or pictures of the exercise around the club. We used a digital camera profusely to document the process for and with the kids.

Day two: A walk around the block[1]

In preparation for this exercise, the planning team discussed and decided upon a small number of destinations and themes to be explored by small student groups in a chaperoned walk around the block. In the 2004 exercise, the following challenges were identified:

- One group would identify water features in the neighborhood. (This involved pre-arranged meetings with city officials from utilities and parks/recreation to meet the students and help them learn about a water supply tower, street drains and a community swimming pool.)
- One group would visit a straw bale house being constructed in the neighborhood by Habitat for Humanity and visit to interview Mrs Harris, one of the oldest residents of the neighborhood (Figure 25.2).
- One group would receive a "behind the scenes" tour of the Opportunity House thrift shop.
- One group would visit the community kitchen and a one-stop convenience grocery to do research on price comparisons retrieved ahead for other major groceries outside of the neighborhood by the college students. We priced standard staples (bread, sugar, rice, as well as fresh fruits and vegetables).

FIGURE 25.2 Mrs Harris tells the kids about her history in the neighborhood

Before the walk, we gathered around the big map to discuss boundaries and landmarks, distributed the Alice's Adventure booklet and disposable flash cameras (Figure 25.3).

Following the organized chaos of gathering the kids and constituting the groups, the discovery walk was begun. A ratio of two adults to four children was maintained. Adults in each group were provided, in advance, with directions for their specific destination.

The groups returned to the Club after approximately 45 minutes to work with the giant map, using markers and colored pencils to embellish the map, label destinations, and record observations. Several located and labeled their own homes on the map as well as the homes of their friends.

Day Three: Debriefing and Social Action

On Day Three of the project, the kids re-convened around the giant map and continued, initially, to add notations and labels. A general discussion was facilitated to draw reactions from the kids regarding things they learned about the neighborhood from their walk. Once again, they discussed favorite places, places that need to be cleaned up, places to play, places to shop, places to meet their friends, etc. With encouragement, these solicited comments were transferred to the map (Figure 25.4).

In a final component of the discussion, the kids were asked to think carefully about four "big and cool" ideas for neighborhood improvement.[2] The question "what would make this a good neighborhood to live in?" generated four core responses:

FIGURE 25.3 Kids love the photovoice method of documentation

FIGURE 25.4 Recording observations of the neighborhood for everyone

- "More gardens like Mrs Harris's."

  ○ Mrs Harris, the elder interviewed by one group, maintains a lush and attractive flower garden outside of her apartment.

- "The trash dumpster should be moved from the circle."

  ○ Near the playground sits a large dumpster subject to use by people who have no connection with the neighborhood.

- "People should be nicer to each other."
- "More park benches for old people are needed."

Digital photos drawn from the previous two days, downloaded, and matted for the students, were distributed and provided some immediate feedback and reinforcement of the enthusiasm for the project. The kids felt rewarded and acknowledged in a very direct way through this little gift.

Follow-up and Social Action

Two subsequent events at the main Boys and Girls Club provided an opportunity to showcase the work of the kids: the annual awards banquet and fair. The university students assembled project artifacts into a display to be erected and our videographer created a 15" video with titles that could be shown on a laptop.

Another public event in the neighborhood – National Night Out – provided an opportunity to share the project results with a broader audience beyond Club kids and their parents (see https://natw.org information about this national initiative). At this display, a voting table was set up highlighting the four big and cool ideas and residents voted with beans for their top choices.

At a subsequent meeting of the Residents' Council for the public housing community, two of the project participants were assisted to give a presentation, with the video, on the project and reveal the results of the informal street fair poll. When informed about the problems associated with the dumpster the housing authority director installed video surveillance and created a campaign for residents to track license plates of illegal dumpster users. Eventually, the dumpster was simply relocated.

Lastly, a local artist who specializes in public and collaborative art projects agreed to help follow up with this project and during the period 2005–2006, in a discussion at the club, the kids expressed a desire to make the club a more welcoming and better known place. The artist suggested an archway leading to the club and a collaborative sculpture project emerged. The authors created a successful proposal for National Endowment for the Arts funding and, with other local funds and donations, a "bike archway" was created from designs of bicycles produced by children, then fabricated from recycled materials with the assistance of a neighborhood welding business. In the summer of 2006, children cleaned and painted the fabricated bikes and the welcoming arch was completed, installed, and named with a festive celebration (Figure 25.5). See a video of the project here: www.youtube.com/watch?v=tQx0corvX0Y&t=12s

Summary

Multiple learning goals can be met through a project of this nature in terms of the potential of mapmaking as a tool to enhance the ICZ (Intergenerational Contact Zone) properties of spaces. It generated age and youth encounters and it would have been only a short step to bring the young and older participants together to critically evaluate place and envision ICZ opportunities. Young people are introduced to elders in the neighborhood and these elders have their own knowledge and experience affirmed and validated. The children are enabled to work with older students as well as adults in an egalitarian way. Through their research, they identify both community problems and community assets and, with follow up, build trust with adults to help them work through neighborhood problems. Follow up is essential, as ordinary contacts with charitable adults coming through the Club are fleeting.

FIGURE 25.5 The Crestmont Bicycle Arch

Two years later, with an additional grant, the artist worked with the Housing Authority and children to create whimsical stabiles covering protruding water drains in the neighborhood toddler park.

Future Directions

It should be noted that this mapmaking project was youth-centric in character. While older adults were involved with the project and meaningful interactions emerged, older adults themselves were not equally involved with either the design of the project nor the process of mapmaking itself. Doing so would have added an essentially historical lens to the meaning of place (over time) and an opportunity to negotiate and create an intergenerational common voice to address programs and policies affecting the quality of public places. For example, an intergenerational photovoice walkabout could document spatial "zero signs" (Sebeok, 1974), drawing on elders' historical knowledge of "what used to be here." Mapmakers could together share their physical experiences of the quality of sidewalks, the acoustic environment, where to sit or rest and reflect, the presence or absence of shade, feelings of safety or risk, seeing the world from different heights, the effort required to reach a destination, etc. All of these stories weave a collective narrative of place that lends itself to sketch mapping by all participants. Sketch maps can then become the focus for extending the narrative to a wider audience through presentations, exhibitions, and workshops with a social action purpose. Discussions informed by joint, consensus recommendations formulated by children and older adults *together* (an intergenerational lens) would be that much more powerful.

Notes

1 This project takes inspiration from four sources in particular: Graves (1997), Morrish and Brown (1994), Race and Thorma (1998), and *Maps with Teeth* (MacAndrew, Springbett, & Campbell, 1997).
2 The phrase "big and cool ideas" comes from Race & Thorma (1998).

References

Aberley, D. (1994). *Futures by design: The practice of ecological planning*. Gabriola Island, B. C., Canada: New Society Publishers.

Bednarz, S. W., Acheson, G., & Bednarz, R. S. (2006). Maps and map learning in the social studies. *Social Education, 70*(7), 398–404, 432.

Biggs, S., & Carr, A. (2016). Age-friendliness, childhood and dementia: Toward generationally intelligent environments. In T. Mouleart & S. Garron (Eds.), *Age-friendly cities and communities in International comparison* (pp. 259–276). New York: Springer.

Graves, G. (1997). *Walk around the block*. Prairie Village, KS: The Center for Understanding of the Built Environment.

Kinoshita, I. (2009). Charting generational differences in conceptions and opportunities for play in a Japanese neighborhood. *Journal of Intergenerational Relationships*, 7(1), 53–77. doi:doi.org/10.1080/15350770802629024.

MacAndrew, H., Springbett, D., Producers, & Campbell, P., Director (1997). *Maps with Teeth* [Educational video]. Oley, PA: Bullfrog Films and Asterisk Productions.

Morrish, W. R., & Brown, C. R. (1994). *Planning to stay*. Minneapolis, MN: Design Center for the American Urban Landscape/Milkweed Publications.

Race, B., & Thorma, C. (1998). *Youth planning charrettes*. Chicago, IL: American Planning Association.

Sebeok, T. A. (1974). Semiotics: A survey of the state of the art. In T. Sebeok (Ed.), *Current trends in linguistics, vol. 12, linguistics and adjacent arts and sciences* (pp. 210–264). The Hague: Mouton.

CONCLUSIONS

Some Lessons Learned about the Design and Functioning of Intergenerational Contact Zones

Matthew Kaplan, Mariano Sánchez, Leng Leng Thang, and Jaco Hoffman

Intergenerational Contact Zones (ICZ) as a Sensitizing Tool

In the Introduction to this book we stated that its uniqueness resides in its specific focus on the new concept of *Intergenerational Contact Zones* (ICZ) and its potential for stimulating new ways of thinking, planning, and practice regarding the design, sustainability, and evolution of intergenerationally enriched environments.

The ICZ conceptual framework is intended to function as a "sensitizing tool." For those who plan and operate intergenerational programs, the topic of *Intergenerational Contact Zones* provides a reminder to pay attention to the role of the environment (natural, built, and virtual) in influencing how participants across generations meet, feel about, and find opportunity to get to know one another. It is a conceptual vehicle for thinking spatially about intergenerational engagement. For those who operate in the arenas of environmental design, community planning and development, an incisive look into how ICZ spaces function provides a reminder as well as a trigger to consider psychological, social, institutional, and other factors that affect what takes place in intergenerational settings.

In this conclusion, we highlight some of the main principles and lessons learned regarding developing effective and innovative ICZ spaces. These preliminary principles are presented not as a rigid set of rules or guidelines, but rather as part of a broader effort to crystallize our understanding of the overall ICZ concept and lay the foundations for exploring new applications for intergenerational living and learning.

The contributors to the 25 chapters in this volume demonstrate their capacity to conceptualize, and in some cases actualize, ways to transform familiar community settings – such as parks, libraries, museums, pools, gardens, community centers, and university classrooms – into vibrant hubs of intergenerational activity.

We draw from the chapter authors to coalesce some themes central to the ICZ framework and how it can be used to:

- aid in the study of complex, multigenerational community settings,
- broaden the range of intergenerational activity possibilities in diverse community settings, and
- generate innovative ideas for developing intergenerational meeting "spaces" which may be converted into socially meaningful "places."

Proximity and the Quest for Meaning, Purpose, and Human Connection

Physical proximity, as found in age-integrated facilities, can certainly increase the odds of bringing people together across the generational divide, however, is it enough to generate authentic intergenerational engagement? The consensus response of chapter authors would be "no."

Whereas "smart design" could reduce physical distance, the alignment with intergenerational programs and activities (through supportive organizational policies and practices) helps to reduce the psychological and social distance between generations. The perspective we advocate expands beyond enabling a generational-diverse group of participants to "be together" (i.e., in physical co-location); also encompassed is the goal of enabling them to "interact together" (i.e., in relationships).

Henkin and Patterson (Chapter 17), in their examination of senior housing facilities in the U.S. that serve as community hubs for intergenerational interaction, emphasize the role of both, environmental design measures – such as sharing space with schools, childcare facilities, and universities – as well as intergenerational programs and activities for sowing the seeds for intergenerational relationships to emerge.

It is also important to consider qualities of community settings that affect their capacity to function as invigorating intergenerational gathering places. McNulty (Chapter 1) has provided several examples of arts and cultural institutions – such as the Queens Museum (New York City) and the Dance Exchange (Takoma Park, Maryland) – that preserve local character and serve as anchoring institutions for reinforcing a sense of place and belonging for residents of all ages and backgrounds. He notes that their capacity to "animate" diverse gatherings of young and old to associate and mingle depends not only on their specific design, but also on a deeper philosophy of "creative placemaking."

These and other examples in the volume illustrate how connecting emotionally with a compelling ICZ *physical space* could touch and push the boundaries of one's *psychological and social space* (in this context, their psychological sense of community).

Promoting Social Inclusion and Age Integration

There is a growing body of literature aimed at studying and developing intervention strategies to counter the social exclusion and sense of loneliness experienced by many individuals across the lifespan (HM Government, 2018). *Loneliness* is not just an older person's issue. In Chapter 16 *Cocktails in Care Homes*, young adults in the UK indicated that they come to *Cocktails* because having moved to London for education or employment, they find themselves living and working amongst their own generation, missing intergenerational contact with older relatives. The time they spend with care home residents, as the program name suggests, implies more than just superficial contact; they "party" together.

At a time when social isolation and *loneliness* are a public health concern for older and younger individuals alike (Cacioppo & Hawkley, 2003; Chatters, Taylor, Nicklett, & Taylor, 2018), intergenerational shared sites such as University-Based Retirement Communities (UBRCs) can be a naturally occurring intervention to enhance social connectedness by providing space and time for intergenerational interaction (see Montepare & Sciegaj, Chapter 13). Our attention here is on considering this issue not on a personal level, such as focusing on strategies for modifying individuals' attitudes and behaviors (e.g., as found in handouts such as one recently distributed by the (U.S.) National Institute on Aging, 2019), but rather a community challenge. More specifically, we aim to highlight promising place-based strategies for promoting social inclusion and age integration.

The essence of the ICZ framework is to not only consider the perspective of the individual (or one's own generational position) but to also zero in on *the relational*. The shift goes from *my sense of place* (and the personal meanings I derive from a particular ICZ space) to *our shared sense of place* (the overlap between our respective meanings of this ICZ space). The ICZ perspective expands one's attention to the capacity of places to exude a broader sense of community, one which welcomes and affords a sense of belonging to an age-diverse populace. In this vein, in Chapter 21, Tam, Jones, and Quinlan have made a sound statement: "ICZ need to transcend the abstraction of space as a functional setting to that of a physical place that is embodied with meaning, belonging and emotional bond for all ages." (p. 230).

We find additional insights from chapter contributors who have developed or reported on community interventions with clear implications for promoting social inclusion and age integration.

For example, Kuraoka (Chapter 20) describes a multifaceted community-based pilot project designed to strengthen social networks and support systems in several Tokyo communities. The model involved opening some older adult oriented "*Saron*" (salon) or "*kafe*" (café) community spaces to younger adults and children and youth. On pages 222–223, Kuraoka notes:

> Through various public venues, it was made clear that these spaces had been reconceptualized as intergenerational rather than just monogenerational settings. Clarification of this reconceptualization and its implications for project planning and site management were key themes in how volunteers for the intergenerational space are trained and supported over time.

Other examples of transformed community facilities originally designed with an orientation of "serving older adults" to one of "connecting them" (to the community) could be found in Henkin and Patterson's (Chapter 17) review of senior housing facilities that have partnered with schools and childcare facilities to establish "intergenerational shared sites."

Such initiatives place an intergenerational twist on the "aging in place" mantra which is prevalent in literature and practice tied to the age-friendly cities and communities movement (Neal & De la Torre, 2016), the "Villages" movement,[1] and other such endeavors. Our preferred refrain to "aging in place" is "aging in place *without isolation.*"

The examples in this section frame socially inclusive environments from within, or beginning with, an elder-centric context. Our orientation, however, is to consider inclusion across the age continuum in intergenerational terms, as was done by the UN's *Towards a society for all ages* campaign launched in 2002.

When addressing issues of inclusion and integration, we also subscribe to the point of view that considers the "environment" as consisting of virtual as well as physical space. Hence, we see value in exploring the potential of anchoring ICZ in virtual space. We are reminded by Eyu Zang (Chapter 19) that even digital gaming systems designed for audiences across ages can be quite effective in strengthening intergenerational connections. As is the case for the physical environment, there are design principles and recommendations to keep in mind when designing digital platforms for strengthening intergenerational contact and relationship building. In this regard, Zang highlights the importance of features that stimulate inter-player sharing of gameplay knowledge, skills, and perspectives.

In an original approach, Winkels, Artrip, Tupinio, and George (Chapter 11) suggest that ICZ may be prescribed as post-treatment intervention to overcome disconnection: "a physician formally 'prescribes' a gardening intervention as a means of pursuing better health, may be worthwhile to pursue." (p. 123). In this way, the therapeutic nature of ICZ comes into play, whether it is for reasons of health or social rehabilitation.

Participation, Choice, and Flexibility in an Intergenerational Community Design and Planning Context

In drawing from the literature on participatory approaches to community development, Sánchez and Stafford (Chapter 23) remind us that participation is understood as a way of providing "a collaborative process by which community inhabitants reach common goals, engage in collective decisions, and create places, and these places, in turn, serve as material expressions of their collective efforts" (from Feldman & Westphal, 2000, p. 106).

Certainly, participatory frameworks are prevalent and play a significant role in how many of the ICZ spaces highlighted in this volume are conceived, planned, developed, and run. Chapter contributors make ample use of phrases such as "participatory design," "bottom-up" planning, "joint planning," "co-design," "participatory site redevelopment," (citizen) "empowerment," and "participatory philosophy."

Chigeza, Claasen, and Roos (Chapter 2) use the term "ethical community engagement" to refer to their participatory way of studying and working in rural areas of South Africa to regenerate traditional practices for intergenerational transmission of indigenous knowledge about traditional foods. They frame their concept of "ethical community engagement" with indigenous communities with the following four principles:

1) "Communities are functioning social units with a lifespan that extends beyond the often-momentary involvement of researchers and programmers; their autonomy and independence should be recognized and respected.

2) A bottom-up approach should be adopted, and community stakeholders and an advisory board should be involved to decide if, how, and what interventions are necessary and appropriate to the cultural context.

3) Indigenous knowledge and traditional practices are the community's to use; and

4) Social structures inform and guide intergenerational relations – what may be acceptable in one context may not be relevant in the next." (p. 35).

This "ethical community engagement" orientation is quite consistent with the "ethical dimension" woven into the ICZ framework, as laid out in Table I.1 in the Introduction chapter. Emphasis is placed on providing all individuals who inhabit ICZ spaces with opportunities to impart meaningful input into site design, development, and evaluation.

Across the board, in practice, we see how inhabitants of vibrant and effective ICZ spaces are active in constructing and refining meanings associated with these spaces and in determining which intergenerational engagement possibilities to pursue. They also (pro)actively influence how these settings function. At times they even create new, previously unthought of opportunities for intergenerational learning, living, recreating, and taking civic action.

The process is not simple nor readily predictable. In fact, weaving in an intergenerational dimension to the planning process can add time and complexity. This is specifically the case when additional steps are needed to facilitate or navigate dialogue and debate within the age-diverse group of participants, even before engaging in a collaborative planning process with design professionals. In this context, it has been instructive to read the chapters on mapmaking (Chapter 25, by Stafford) and other participatory tools and techniques (Chapter 23, by Sánchez and Stafford) that can help foreground the participation of youth and elders in community planning and assist them in concretizing their intergenerationally negotiated recommendations for improving intergenerational spaces.

Some other examples of chapters that embrace participatory ideology and strategies for engaging laypersons in the (design) process could be noted.

Azevedo (Chapter 8) describes how public interest, commitment, and community organization and volunteer group involvement were key elements in stimulating government agency action in revitalizing three urban parks in Portugal, including the restoration of open spaces that historically worked well as multigenerational gathering spots for friends and family.

Zheng (Chapter 15) emphasizes how in most cohousing communities, participatory planning as well as community-oriented designs contribute to a vigorous commitment to intergenerational living. On page 167 she writes:

> The experience of discussing, debating, negotiating and finally deciding together the features and layout of their future community not only makes for a better, more suitably customized design but also build relationships and communications skills that will figure critically in community life after move-in. This process also creates communities that better serve the needs of all their residents, both young and old.

Zheng also cautions when planning intergenerational engagements in cohousing communities to ensure not to violate people's need for privacy or inhibit their access to retreat routes from forced social interaction. "Choice" is a keyword in the ICZ glossary.

Avoiding over-programming public gathering places is furthermore conveyed in O'Neill's (Chapter 7) description of the social ecology of effective ICZ spaces in heavily utilized parks in China such as West Lake (in Hangzhou) and Lake Dian (in Kunming City in Yunnan province). She identifies several factors that contribute to the sites' success and popularity, such as the inclusion of great amenities that are "age neutral" and then leaving it to park visitors to "follow their own interests" in exercising choices about which activities to engage in and with whom.

Authors' emphasis on providing inhabitants of ICZ spaces with choice regarding the nature of their engagements with others within these settings is consistent with lessons learned from other studies of community settings designed to welcome and engage age-diverse populations. For example, research supported by the Joseph Rowntree Foundation and Carnegie UK Trust conclude that one of the key principles for creating "welcoming" civic spaces that counter social isolation and loneliness is to include opportunities for people to gather "free from [an] agenda" (Ferguson, 2017, p. 5). That is, they provide at least some non-scripted opportunities for interaction. Ferguson (n.d.) further expands on this theme:

> We found that often the places we might first think of as places to come together are not always the most welcoming to all. Many public and voluntary sector provided spaces are connected with an agenda (directing people towards "improving activities") and we found people choosing the supermarket as an easier place just to be with others.

"Caring spaces" (Ferguson, 2017) as well as ICZ spaces are likely to receive more support and attention from the intended users when they themselves are involved in *setting the agenda* for what facilities will be built, what activities will be planned, and how the sites will be managed over time.

Providing users with "choice" and "flexibility" – to accommodate various needs, interests, and types of use – are positive components of the planning process. For a good example see Lai's contribution (Chapter 14) where he suggests that in creating an ICZ atmosphere in a language center, "various alternatives are explored for providing 'choice' in the content and format of student exposure to the English language." (p. 150).

This is also a prompt to approach the design of ICZ spaces with an open mindset. At a minimum, members of the environmental design and development team should consider the question in developing new ideas for ICZ space design and utilization: Does the ICZ design scheme provide "opportunities" and prompts for spontaneous (unplanned) meetings, informal interaction, and user participation.

The Role of Creativity and Imagination in Setting up Lively ICZ Spaces

The challenge of "animating" an intergenerational space is difficult to operationalize, particularly since it is not always known when, where, or from whom the creative "spark" will materialize.

How about from a seven-year-old boy's imagination? Jason Danely (Chapter 6) writes about tapping his seven-year-old son's imagination for converting a sterile bus stop – in terms of generational interaction – into a vital ICZ. One of his son's provocative, "out of the box" ideas for spicing up the experience of waiting at bus stops involves building giant electronic chess sets into the physical infrastructure of bus stop stands. These sets would have the capacity to generate holograms and audio announcements of the moves.

Danely's chapter has introduced two key themes about ICZ creation that are worth keeping in mind:

(1) The value of employing creative methods for eliciting input from participants, from all who use or inhabit sites, regardless of age or position (including seven-year-olds).
(2) The value of infusing a sense of "play" as a way of enlivening "intergenerational placemaking." In Danely's words (p. 73):

> Is it too much to aspire to make places not only "age-friendly" but "age-fun"? But having fun comes natural to experts in play, both young and old. What these interlocutors remind us is the fun of becoming unstuck from socially determined categories of age, place, and well-being.

And he concludes, "ICZ can teach us that taking perspective also means playing with perspective."

Yvonne Ng (Chapter 3) also draws on the theme of collective play in her description of the catalytic effect that youth have on older adults during their Toronto library-based intergenerational dance activities (p. 43):

> The youth, with their boundless energy and exuberance, allowed the older adults to be lured into play.

Thus, creativity and play combined together take the "creative placemaking" concept raised by McNulty (Chapter 1) one step forward into creative and playful placemaking as a basic ingredient when planning ICZ spaces. Conceptually this draws on Turner's (1957) idea that the most creative human spaces are those on the margins; sites of frolic, play, and joking, as opposed to those of earnest workaday routine. Significant human contact and creativity flow from the margins to the centers more often than the reverse.

With an ICZ lens, one starts to see and appreciate the rich abundance of locally created, highly inventive examples of ICZ spaces designed with the intent to counter the loneliness that so many people experience on a daily basis. Examples include a Dutch supermarket that created a "chat checkout" line (De Gooijer, 2018) and "happy to chat benches" in a town in England; the benches are identified by a sign saying, "Sit here if you don't mind someone stopping to say hello" (Solomon, June 20, 2019).

Paying Attention to Routines, Rituals, History, and Sociocultural Norms

Socially (and culturally) defined norms, traditions, and values (especially those concerning the understanding and use of public places) affect how inhabitants view and behave within any given ICZ setting.

O'Neill (Chapter 7) notes how large natural parks in China function as epicenters of local music, dance, tai chi, Chinese chess, and other activities that reflect the shared cultural heritage and sense of cultural identity that attract people of all generations, and that invite them to interact.

Tham, Jones, and Quinlan (Chapter 21) emphasize how the widespread social, civic, and cultural significance of pools and beaches in Australian society contributes to their acceptance, across generations, as compelling intergenerational gathering sites. The authors note that these culturally specific and treasured settings "embody the values of Australian identity" and are popular places where people "socialize, picnic, play and exercise."

Kaplan, Windon, and Zavada (Chapter 4) describe how the selection of a 150-year-old barn for the site of a daylong intergenerational programming retreat in Central Pennsylvania was an ideal choice of location. The deep historic and cultural meaning associated with the barn was emblematic of intergenerational thinking and values of community collaboration that helped generate an atmosphere of openness and inclusivity throughout the collaborative planning process.

Material Culture and Social Practices Can Serve as Mediators for ICZ Spaces

The recognition of ICZ-generating properties in objects from different cultures and of different kinds adds to a material dimension of the ICZ concept. Drawing on the work of Appadurai (1986), it is evident that these objects potentially represent a valuable point of entry to revive interest in intergenerational bonding, because they induce such behaviors. This explains why going to the museum to view historical objects and relics could be a good intergenerational activity, where objects can generate conversations and interaction. Appadurai (1986) suggests that "even though from a theoretical point of view human actors encode items/objects with significance, from a methodological point of view it is the things-in-motion that illuminate their human and social context" (p. 5). Through the biographical aspects of and the socio-historical symbolism that some objects exude, they might possess more explicitly ICZ generating properties – depending on how they are valued and utilized.

Yamamoto and Thang (Chapter 18) write an account of how the Japanese teapot, as a symbol of efforts to restore cultural traditions of tea brewing, can also promote values and behaviors related to intergenerational interaction at home. The making of the tea in the teapot; the sharing of the tea; the waiting time; drinking time - they give space and time for conversations and connections.

Several other chapters note other objects that have elements that are authentic and culturally and intergenerationally meaningful for participants. For example, Whitehouse, Whitehouse and Sánchez (Chapter 12) reflect on how the shared experiences around books have become the glue that connects generations in schools that work as ICZ settings.

Hammad (Chapter 22) describes the importance of the olive tree and how it functions as an ICZ entity and symbol in the Palestinian cultural context. This is also an example of how broader forces, in this case of a geopolitical nature, can endanger ICZ spaces. At the same time, it also shows how certain objects in those spaces, in this case the olive tree, can serve as symbol of resistance and epicenter of certain place-protecting measures. Hammad's words serve as a reminder that political activism is an important part of the political dimension of ICZ. She refers to how olive trees have been transformed into "a locus for cross-generational resistant acts." (p. 251).

Jointly Promoting a Green Infrastructure

As Ingman, Benjamin, & Lusky (1998/99) assert, the environment is the quintessential intergenerational issue of our time; we all breathe the same air and appreciate drinking clean water.

To promote a sense of "ecological caring," which McNamee (1997) notes develops gradually over time and through caring interpersonal relationships, people need to be exposed to nature in ways that raise awareness and understanding about natural ecosystems and the relationship between human health and environmental health.

Several chapters in this volume highlight intergenerational approaches to environmental education that introduce children and youth to older adult educators, role models, mentors, and co-learners. Such relationships, whether rooted in family or community contexts, can serve as powerful motivators and anchors for creating and sustaining a highly engaged, environmentally aware, and active populace.

• Nature has great potential to connect children and adults as "companions in wonder" (Dunlap & Keller, 2012):

Sobko and Chawla (Chapter 9) note how green spaces, even when found in unlikely places such as rooftop gardens erected in heavily urbanized cities such as Hong Kong, could function as effective ICZ spaces. They have also noted how evidence-based intergenerational environmental education programs, such as "Play&Grow," can boost the ICZ potential of such green spaces (p. 99):

The program encourages caregivers, who are often grandparents, to create hubs of nature on the closest available rooftops, where their children and grandchildren come to play, grow and learn. The gardens serve as intergenerational contact zones (ICZ) as well as places for environmental appreciation and learning. They provide easy access to nature for both young and old, in a city that is often named as a true example of a concrete habitat, and they provide time and space for families to experience and enjoy nature together.

Smith and Kaplan (Chapter 10) introduce a distinct intergenerational "living history" model that has the capacity to convert forest landscapes into ICZ spaces. Forest stewards, educators, and volunteers – often older adults – create on-site scenes and vignettes drawn from examples of real historical figures. As part of their portrayal of common folk who once lived and worked in the woods, they share stories about past conditions, forestry practices, and people's lives that help young visitors see forests, not as a separate domain from their lives, but as an important part of history and their lives today. The authors further note how locating ICZ spaces in settings that are rich in history (such as longstanding forests) can be an effective way to encourage "youth and older generations [to] reflect together on the impacts of time." (p. 111).

- Nature and its capacity to generate healing relationships and healthy lifestyles across generations:

Winkels, Artrip, Tupinio, and George (Chapter 11) focus on an intergenerational health promotion intervention that is rooted in both a community garden on the grounds of the Penn State Hershey Medical Center in Hershey, PA (US), and in the relationships that form between young adult cancer survivors and older adult "master gardener" mentors who engage them in activities designed to improve their diet and physical activity. Project benefits for both the mentees and mentors were grounded in the intergenerational relationships that developed among participants.

One young adult participant stated (p. 121):

> I think it's been really helpful, just very reassuring, very supportive – definitely she challenged me to plant things that I didn't necessarily want to plant, and she was just like "plant it and try one thing with it". If you don't like it then you never have to plant it again. What is the harm? I think that is really cool that she gave me the challenge to plant outside my comfort zone.

As one mentor reflected (p. 122)

> I think anytime you teach someone, you get out of it more than what you put into it. Like for me, what was the most fun in the world, I never planted a garden to nourish someone's soul before. I loved working with her, and finding out what are her favorite colors, what are her favorite things to eat. That felt so satisfying, that satisfied me as a person.

In an earlier publication by Kaplan & Liu (2004), and complementing the perspectives offered in this volume, a broader framework is put forward on what is compelling about such an intergenerational approach to environmental education and action:

- Learning how environments change over time.
- Learning is experience- and reflection-rich.
- Learning about environmental issues that transcend age.
- Engaging and empowering multiple generations.
- Creating new allies for environmental education and action.
- Providing additional focal points for strengthening intergenerational relationships.

Recognizing and Transcending the Obstacles

In their *Next Avenue* article, "Intergenerational places help young and old thrive," Donna Butts and Trent Stamp make a strong case for intergenerational shared sites (Butts & Stamp, 2018, November 8). They note numerous ways in which participants of all ages benefit, provide some inspiring examples of such sites, and share survey results indicating broad public interest and support for such facilities. However, they also provide a reality check in noting some challenges. They ask the question that many in the intergenerational studies field have asked:

> Given the efficiency and benefits to old and young alike, why haven't shared sites flourished?

Their response:

> The unfortunate answer is that we haven't made it easy. Obstacles include multiple accrediting bodies with different standards, narrowly-focused funding streams and the boutique nature of the programs that inhibits many well-intended developers.

Several chapter contributors in this volume zeroed in on additional obstacles to effective ICZ planning and development and shared some strategies for transcending them.

Sobko and Chawla (Chapter 9), who report on intergenerational initiatives rooted in Hong Kong rooftop gardens, note that in "densely populated cities where there is intense competition for space, integrating nature into people's daily lives can be a great challenge." (pp. 98–99).

Danely (Chapter 6) alluded to the challenges that ICZ developers face in trying to follow cultural norms and conventions while at the same time aspiring to develop vibrant and exciting spaces. He wrote (p. 70):

> ICZ must also supply a set of norms and conventions that utilize and enhance shared experiences while minimizing the disruptive effects of cultural barriers. But how does one do this without creating something so constrictive that it is only engaging for a select few, or so boring that it fails to enhance life?

Montepare and Sciegaj (Chapter 13) emphasize how ageism can be a formidable barrier in educational settings. They wrote (p. 142):

> Ageism is a "two-way street" and negative stereotypes about youth abound. Both are barriers to teaching and learning. Beliefs that older adults are "set in their ways" are just as detrimental as expectations that young adults are "constantly connected yet unengaged." Moreover, given that manifestations of ageism may be socially tolerated (consider humorous birthday cards), students of all ages may be quick to assert ageist assumptions or use age-stereotypic language in classroom exchanges.

As a way of offsetting such stereotypic references, Montepare and Sciegaj recommend to "situate age discussions around 'us, as we age' rather than around younger versus older age comparisons." (p. 143).

Changing social norms in support of healthier lifestyles can be a slow process. Modifying transportation systems that have a bearing on health-related lifestyle behaviors can be far slower, more arduous, and more tenuous. Jones and Spencer (Chapter 5) note that in the UK, although there is "a general consensus that cycling should be promoted as healthy and sustainable mobility," "... the majority of the UK population seldom engages with cycling in any form – around two-thirds of the population use cycles less than once a year or never (UK Department for Transport, 2018)" (p. 60). The main culprit is "UK mobility culture ... shaped by mass car ownership which in turn has shaped how the transport system has evolved under a paradigm that has fueled faster and longer distance travel" (p. 61). To help change the narrative, and demonstrate to the public (and public officials!) that change is possible, they describe in detail a host of measures taken in some "cycle-friendly" cities and neighborhoods, where road space is reallocated and redesigned, from solely motor vehicle use to a more diverse landscape that allows residents to use streets as social spaces, including for side-by-side cycling which helps foster cycling as a family oriented recreational activity.

Institutional barriers – in the form of policies, permits, and regulations – make it hard as well to develop innovative intergenerational spaces in highly regulated settings, such as schools, retirement communities, and health care settings. Nevertheless, as demonstrated by several of the chapter contributors, it is possible to break down institutional barriers with sensible, evidence-informed ideas and strong leadership. It begs for a balanced approach to creating intergenerational places, recognizing the potential for intergenerational misunderstanding and tension. At the same time it is also imperative to work proactively to establish programs, policies, and environmental design strategies that encourage people to challenge negative age-related stereotypes, learn about one another, communicate in open relationship-enhancing ways, and act together for the common good.

For example, Whitehouse, Whitehouse and Sánchez (Chapter 12) describe the rationale, supporting evidence, and history behind the "Intergenerational School" model that first took root in Cleveland, OH. This model entails a reconceptualizing of the school as a "shared (intergenerational) space" that functions as a bridge to the community that welcomes older adults as volunteers, co-learners, and conduits for enriching student learning experiences.

Lai (Chapter 14) presents an intergenerational ESL (IG-ESL) program model that in effect upended policies and procedures for how English Language Centers (ELC) in Hong Kong secondary schools, function. Beyond some relatively minor strategic modifications to the classroom environment, older adult volunteers with excellent English language skills and students with intermediate level skills worked closely together to create new activities, some outside of the ELC setting, breaking the tradition of having students learn through asocial, routinized and somewhat repetitive exercises. Students and adult volunteers engaged one another in ways that stimulated unscripted conversation about shared interests. They co-constructed games they wanted to play together (such as "finger soccer") and created or accessed websites with content likely to ignite new lines of conversation. Post-intervention, students alluded to positive intergenerational exchanges in the language learning process, such as sharing stories about each other's childhoods, visions for the future, and favorite jokes. This is a far cry from the pre-intervention comments such as the ELC setting as "a space of loneliness" and "it is so hard to find anyone to speak to."

Appraisal of a Testing Exercise

The editors approached this volume as an opportunity to appraise, refine, and explore new applications of this distinct framework for understanding intergenerational settings. Book contributors were thus provided with the concept and dimensions of ICZ as presented in the Introduction chapter but were given the flexibility to consider and explore new interpretations as well as applications. It is contended that such an open approach has allowed for new and unexpected turns in the initial formulation of ICZ spaces that make this publication more alive and interesting.

For instance, some of the authors were able to connect intergenerational programs (IP) and ICZ further. This is especially evident in Chapter 24, where Sánchez, Díaz, Rodríguez, and Bonachela make an attempt to align quality in IP and ICZ (p. 274):

> it makes sense to align the introduction of good quality planning and implementation of programs aimed at purposefully bringing different generations together for individual, group, community and societal good – IP's ultimate mission – with efforts to set up spatial focal points for intergenerational meeting, interaction and engagement – as ICZ intend to do.

In accepting the challenge to use, test, and develop the original concept of ICZ further, new language has been generated in the way of connected terms with different semantic stakes that intersect with the ICZ concept: "intergenerational contact (and dance) zones" (Chapter 3); "spatial justice" (Chapter 5); "zone for mutual development" (Chapter 14); "intergenerational living zones" (Chapter 15); "organic ICZ" (Chapter 21); "naturally occurring ICZ" (Chapter 22); "intergenerational engagement hubs" (Chapter 8); and "generationally intelligent environments" (Chapter 25).

It is indeed "intergenerationally intelligent" and prudent for generations to relationally face the big challenges of the 21st century as it relates to particular contexts/places. As an African (Madagascar) proverb advises: "Cross the river in a crowd and the crocodile won't eat you."

To this end, we focus on the challenge of creating community spaces that engender an important dimension of social connectedness, i.e., intergenerational engagement. We posit that *Intergenerational Contact Zones*, if designed in ways that are consistent with people's interests and needs for strengthening their connections with family, friends, and neighbors, can have a profound impact on the quality of life of all community residents as well as on the sustainability of their environments.

Note

1 The Villages [movement] in the U.S. involves establishing neighborhood-based nonprofit organizations working to keep people aging in their homes and communities. Volunteer and vetted or discounted vendor services are provided for "Village" members. Research has proven that Villages do help to "age in place" particularly for older adults not yet at risk of institutionalization (Graham, Scharlach, & Kurtovich, 2018).

References

Appadurai, A. (Ed.). (1986). *The social life of things: Commodities in cultural perspective.* Cambridge: Cambridge University Press.

Butts, D., & Stamp, T. (2018, November 8) Intergenerational places help young and old thrive. *Next Avenue*, November. Retrieved from Link is correct but leads to a different web page: https://www.nextavenue.org/intergenerational-challenge-reinvent-work place/.

Cacioppo, J. T., & Hawkley, L. C. (2003). Social isolation and health, with an emphasis on underlying mechanisms. *Perspectives in Biology and Medicine, 46*(3), 39–52. doi: https://doi:10.1353/pbm.2003.0063.

Chatters, L. M., Taylor, H. O., Nicklett, N. J., & Taylor, R. J. (2018). Correlates of objective social isolation from family and friends among older adults. *Healthcare, 6*(1), 24. doi:10.3390/healthcare6010024.

De Gooijer, M. (2018). Dutch supermarket introduces a unique "chat checkout" to help fight loneliness. Brightvibes. Retrieved from https://www.brightvibes.com/1367/en/dutch-supermarket-introduces-a-unique-chat-checkout-to-help-fight-loneliness? fbclid=I.

Dunlap, J., & Kellert, S. R. (Eds.). (2012). *Companions in wonder: Children and adults exploring nature together*. Cambridge, MA: The MIT Press.

Feldman, R. M., & Westphal, L. M. (2000). An agenda for community design and planning: Participation and empowerment in practice. In R. J. Lawrence (Ed.), *Sustaining human settlement: A challenge for the new millennium* (pp. 105–139). North Shields: Great Britain; Urban International Press.

Ferguson, Z. (2017). *The place of kindness: Combating loneliness and building stronger communities*. Dunfermline, Fife (UK): Carnegie UK Trust. Retrieved from https://d1ssu070pg2v9i.cloudfront.net/pex/carnegie_uk_trust/2017/07/LOW-RES-3110-Kindness-Overcoming-Risk-Report.pdf.

Ferguson, Z. (n.d.). A caring place – designing in kindness. Blog published by Architecture & Design Scotland. Retrieved from www.ads.org.uk/kindness_acaringplace_zoeferguson.

Government, H. M. (2018). *A connected society: A strategy for tackling loneliness. UK Government report. Department for Digital, Culture, Media and Sport*. London. Retrieved from https://assets.publishing.service.gov.uk/government/uploads/system/uploads/attach ment_data/file/750909/6.4882_DCMS_Loneliness_Strategy_web_Update.pdf.

Graham, C., Scharlach, A. E., & Kurtovich, E. (2018). Do villages promote aging in place? Results of a longitudinal study. *Journal of Applied Gerontology, 37*(3), 310–331. doi:10.1177/0733464816672046.

Ingman, S. R., Benjamin, T., & Lusky, R. (1998/99). The environment: The quintessential intergenerational challenge. *Generations, 22*(4), 68–71.

Kaplan, M., & Liu, S.-T. (2004). *Generations united for environmental awareness and action*. Washington, DC: Generations United. Retrieved from http://aese.psu.edu/exten sion/intergenerational/program-areas/environmental-education/generations-united/generations-united-for-environmental-awareness-and-action.

McNamee, A. S. (1997). Ecological caring: A psychological perspective on the person environment relationship. In P. J. Thomson (Ed.), *Environmental education for the 21st century* (pp. 259–267). NY: Peter Lang.

National Institute on Aging (2019). Expand your circles: Prevent isolation and loneliness as you age. Retrieved from https://eldercare.acl.gov/Public/Resources/Brochures/docs/Expanding-Circles.pdf.

Neal, M. B., & De la Torre, A. (2016). The case for age-friendly communities. Grant-makers in aging. Retrieved from https://pdxscholar.library.pdx.edu/aging_pub/20/.

Solomon, K. (June 20, 2019). Police create "chat benches" to combat loneliness, "help make life a little better". Yahoo! Lifestyle. Retrieved from www.yahoo.com/lifestyle/police-create-chat-benches-to-combat-loneliness-help-make-life-a-little-better-210135136.html.

Turner, V. (1957). *Schism and continuity in an African society: A study of Ndembu village life.* [Republished by Berg Publishers (Oxford; Washington, DC)]. Manchester, UK: Originally published by Manchester University Press.

UK Department for Transport. (2018). *Transport Statistics Great Britain.* London: DfT.

INDEX